Hokan

thanks for you
support and assistance
in making this
book a reality.

Murray Warmath

Hokan ————————
Many Thanks to you and The
M Club.

Mike Wright Jr

# THE AUTUMN WARRIOR

## MURRAY WARMATH'S
## 65 YEARS IN AMERICAN FOOTBALL
### BY MIKE WILKINSON

BURGESS INTERNATIONAL GROUP INC

7110 Ohms Lane, Edina, MN 55439

Copyright © 1992 by Mike Wilkinson and the Murray Warmath Book Committee
ISBN 0-8087-5262-6

Printed in the United States of America.
J  I  H  G  F  E  D  C  B  A

Address orders to:

BURGESS INTERNATIONAL GROUP, Inc.
7110 Ohms Lane
Edina, Minnesota 55439-2143
Telephone 612/831-1344
EasyLink 629-106-44
Fax 612/831-3167

*To Susan*

# Foreword

Thanks, coach!

I have said many times that I am what I am today primarily because of the many lessons I learned through my athletic and social experiences at the University of Minnesota.

In order to properly characterize my relationship with Coach Warmath, I need to share a brief history with you. I was recruited by Coach Warmath from segregated North Carolina in 1963. This was a time when southern white colleges were not recruiting or playing black athletes.

My recruiting by Coach Warmath was made easy because of former North Carolinans who were having, or had, successful experiences at the University of Minnesota—players such as Bobby Bell, Carl Eller, Bill Crockett, Jay Sharp, Randy Staten and Hall of Fame basketball player, Lou Hudson. The one common theme I constantly heard was Minnesotans were fair and supportive and Coach Warmath would use the best players. So it was easy to understand that coming from segregated North Carolina, the theme of "fair" was important to me. Especially with a white coach whose southern drawl was heavier than mine.

My decision to trust Coach Warmath was one that turned out for the best. It was interesting in that I narrowed my two choices of universities between Minnesota and Michigan State. It was a decision based on built-in North Carolina support and trust of a southern white man with whom I never had any formal contact in my life, versus that of Duffy Daugherty, then the head coach at Michigan State. I guess southern roots are southern roots.

Murray's success as a coach at the University has been well-documented, including his two Rose Bowl appearances, national championship and Big Ten championships. I am proud to say I was part of his last championship team in 1967. Unfortunately, we didn't go to the Rose Bowl and with an 8-2 record, we simply packed away our uniforms.

Why was Coach Warmath successful? I guess the simple reason is like all successful coaches, he had a good staff and he recruited good players. Obviously, there are always intangibles and as I look back at Coach Warmath, I see the intangibles to his success as fairness, communication and aura. All any football player wants is the opportunity to compete for a job or playing time and to know that if he is the best, he will play. In my four years, I constantly saw that.

Coach Warmath's communications skills could be described as succinct and to the point. Like most people I know from the South, he said what was on his mind. I appreciated that style and never did like having to read between the lines. That was one of the great things about living in the South—you always knew where you stood.

I think his aura is probably the most difficult to describe, but there was something about him that made me feel good. I don't know any other way of saying it.

In closing, the legacy of Murray Warmath at the University of Minnesota is clearly one that is outstanding and representative of the success on the playing field and in the classroom. Murray's successful athletes range from being the first black athletic director in the Big Ten, to lawyers, to doctors, to president of a professional basketball franchise, to CEO of one of the largest and most successful companies in Minnesota. Also included are many successful professional athletes, including several wearing Super Bowl rings.

Murray was ahead of the times. As I have stated since my arrival at the University, our motto will be that academics and successful athletics need not be mutually exclusive of each other. He lived that motto at the University of Minnesota since 1954. Thanks, coach.

—*McKinley Boston, men's intercollegete athletic director, University of Minnesota*

# Author's Notes

I first met Murray Warmath in January of 1990. It was at his home in Edina, Minn. It was to be the first of many meetings I held with him that year as part of the interview process for this book. I learned many things about him in those meetings, both from an historical perspective as well as about his personality. As is the case with any biographical work, I also spent hundreds of hours interviewing his many former players, assistant coaches and friends, as well as going through newspaper archives and related information on this man who has spent over eighty percent of his life in the game of football.

What I learned was there are five very unique things about Coach Warmath:

First, there is probably no one alive today, with the exception of Sid Gillman, who has been so directly involved in the game of football for so many years. Beginning as a high school player in the late 1920s in Humboldt, Tenn. until today, he has followed a unique path for six decades in the game he so dearly loves.

Second, there is no one who saved his job in such dramatic fashion as he did in 1960 when he won the national championship and took the University of Minnesota Golden Gophers to the first of two consecutive Rose Bowls. From late 1957 through the end of the 1959 season, the Monday Morning Quarterbacks were asking for his hide. What they didn't know was he knew more about football than all of them combined and he knew better days were just ahead. He was certainly right.

Third, he was a major force, if not the major force in the advent of the black athlete in collegiate football in the late 1950s and early 1960s. As a white southerner in a time when segregation ruled the South, it was both noticeable and unusual for something of that magnitude to happen. However, for those who know Murray Warmath, they know that he judges people on things far more important than their race, religion or creed.

Fourth, he coached an incredible number of young men who went on to be very successful in later life. In a time when college sports is often criticized for churning out athletes who are ill-equipped to deal with demands away from the playing fields, courts or rinks, Warmath has had the satisfaction of seeing so many of his players become leaders in medicine, law, business, education and coaching. While their successes are mainly of their own doing, to a man they will tell you that Warmath was a major figure in their lives and a role model who set wonderful examples of how character, integrity and dedication pay off in all aspects of life.

Finally, Warmath is a man of the highest principles. He is a devoted family man, much in love with, and deeply appreciative of, his wonderful wife of over 50 years, Mary Louise, his children and his grandchildren. He is a classic no-nonsense guy. He expects nothing more from others than he asks of himself. He is extraordinarily fair and honest. A tireless worker and detail-oriented, it is clear that he would have been successful in any endeavor. Fortunately for those who love football, he chose coaching.

It is my fondest hope that this book will not only give its readers a history of this man, but also make them fully aware of what a wonderful person he is and appreciative of all he has given of himself.

# Acknowledgements

The undertaking of this book was the idea of an old, dear friend, Dave Shama. For years, Dave felt, and rightfully so, that a book needed to be written on Murray Warmath. I was honored he asked me to write it and deeply appreciative of his ongoing support and constructive help during the writing process. Dave's contacts into the world of Coach Warmath, especially former players, coaches and friends, were instrumental in making the book happen.

I also want to thank the steering committee who oversaw the fundraising for the book and for the Murray Warmath Scholarship Fund at the University of Minnesota. The members of the committee and the major contributors to the book are listed. However, several of them were directly involved with me and deserve my thanks for their specific help. They include Dick Larson, who did such a masterful job of coordinating the overall project. Bobby Cox was always encouraging and genuinely enthusiastic about the book. Bob McNamara did a terrific job of orchestrating efforts on the book to coincide with Murray's 80th birthday party in the fall of 1992. Finally, a special thanks to Dana Marshall who was my point person on the project, ongoing confidant, strong editor, avid supporter and is the best living source of both critically important historical facts and disregardable trivia.

Mike Lamey of the St. Paul Pioneer Press did a superb job of editing the manuscript and offering good, constructive suggestions. His contributions were most helpful.

Jan Westberg designed the book and her work was as professional and skillful as always. Her cover design was especially well-done. A life-long friend, Jim Boylan, contributed his graphic skills in the design of the ads and order forms for the book. He did 11th hour work for us and I am deeply appreciative.

John Snyder and his staff at Burgess International (Janet Neilson, Cheryl Silseth, Morris Lundin and Michelle Batt) were terrific to work with on the production and printing of the book.

Obviously, this book wouldn't have happened were it not for the dozens of players, former assistants, friends and media people who took time to meet with me, and in the case of the media, write wonderful accounts of Coach Warmath and the Warmath years which gave me the important details and insight into this special man. I trust I have cited each of them at the appropriate points in the book. Especially helpful was coach Billy Jack Murphy who steered me toward some good sources for further information on the Warmath years at Mississippi State and Minnesota.

The efforts of Mark Davy and the M Club were crucial to this effort and deeply appreciated, especially in the early days when the first efforts were underway to get this book done.

McKinley Boston, the Gopher men's athletic director and former Warmath player, gave strong support and enthusiasm for the book.

Several sports information departments were invaluable. At the University of Minnesota, Bob Peterson and Mark Ryan were very helpful on the promotion of the book. Wendell Vandersluis, Hank Liu, and Karen Zwach arranged for photographs from Warmath's Minnesota years. In addition, Bob Jansen and Laura Scher of the Star Tribune did a great job in securing for us several much-needed photos from their files on the Warmath years.

Bud Ford, sports information director at the University of Tennessee and Joe Dier, sports information director at Mississippi State University and their staffs, were invaluable in getting me information from their schools. Bob Hartley, the assistant athletic director for communications at Mississippi State and a long-time Warmath friend, was a wonderful source on MSU gridiron history.

Two special people deserve my thanks. First, Jerome Fine, a long-time Gopher fan and dear friend who was always encouraging, and second, my wonderful wife, Susan, who believed in the book and supported me throughout the project.

Finally, to Coach Warmath himself. He was a pleasure to work with and get to know. I am honored to have authored his biography and trust I have done the best job possible of telling the readers about this great coach and wonderful man.

*Mike Wilkinson*
*September, 1992.*

# Preface

On a muggy, hazy August afternoon in Minneapolis, nearly 100 collegiate football players are beginning fall practice a few weeks prior to the start of yet another season.

The coaching staff, trainers, equipment men and student managers intermingle with the University of Minnesota players.

Along both sidelines, a handful of parents, team boosters and fans watch as the players execute individual and team drills.

At one end of the field where a group of offensive lineman are involved in blocking practice, a man in his late seventies watches intently. He is about six feet tall and has a slightly stooped, but blocky, muscular frame. He is flat-faced with a firm jaw and a small nose. His thick, wavy hair, though gray, still is liberally sprinkled with the dark brown of his youth. He is wearing a short-sleeved pink and white searsucker shirt, khaki slacks and a pair of white athletic shoes.

After several minutes, he sits down on a nearby blocking dummy, resting his legs which for the vast majority of his life have treked across hundreds of football fields from coast-to-coast in his role as a player, coach and, now, professional scout.

His look is intense. He knows football and he knows what he is looking for as he scrutinizes the young men who may someday play in the National Football League.

One of the Minnesota assistant coaches strolls by.

"How ya' doing', Murray?" he asks.

"Well, pretty good, pretty good," he answers in his gravely Southern drawl. His face breaks into a broad grin.

As the dinner hour approaches, the Minnesota squad congregates around the coaches for a few parting comments. The trainers and managers begin gathering equipment and loose footballs. The handful of parents and interested observers start out the exit gates.

The old scout puts his pen in his shirt pocket and sticks his notes into the back pocket of his slacks. He turns and slowly walks back toward the buildings of the football complex.

He does not share his thoughts with anyone. Yet, there is little question that he is thinking of football. It is the season.

Perhaps he is remembering his 18 years at this same institution when he was once its head football coach. He has been gone from that position more than 20 years. When he headed the program there were Rose Bowl trips, national prominence and producing some of the game's finest players.

But, that was some time ago and this is a new season. When the year is over, he will be nearly 80 years old. As he has nearly every Fall since the mid-1920s, he is getting ready for his game. When it comes to the game of football, time for him never seems to stand very still.

The rising pitch of autumn is near. It is another in a never-ending string of seasons and Murray Warmath is as ready as ever as he enters his eighth decade in football.

# One

The State of Tennessee is geographically divided into three major sections resulting from the flow of the Tennessee River.

The eastern portion consists of rolling foothills and the Great Smoky Mountains, famed for their majestic beauty. The central portion of the state is called the Nashville Basin and is noted for its cattle and horse farms as well as having some of the nation's richest phosphate deposits.

The western third of Tennessee is part of the multi-state area called the Gulf Coastal Plain, a stretch of fertile farming country originating at the Gulf of Mexico and continuing north to the southern tip of Illinois. This rich agricultural area is one-fourth of the area of the state and is flanked by the Mississippi and Tennessee rivers.

Nestled in the Gulf Coastal Plain is the city of Humboldt, which has a population of approximately 10,000. Humboldt is an hour's drive northeast of Memphis en route to Nashville. The community's well-being always has been tied to the agricultural economy. The area is an extension of the Mississippi Delta and truck farming was prominent in the late 19th and early 20th Centuries. Virtually everyone in those days was either a Southern Baptist or a Methodist and toiled from dawn to dusk. Most of the people of the area worked the land. Their struggles were constant and they eked out a living producing crops for the market. Those not working the land directly were usually involved in providing the goods and services for those who did.

It was in this hard-working, yet friendly, city that Murray Warmath was born on Dec. 26, 1912.

1

Warmath was the only child of Carl and Imogene Warmath. His father grew up just outside Humboldt, his mother in Milan, a similar-sized farming community 12 miles northeast of Humboldt.

Warmaths had been part of northwest Tennessee, and in particular, Gibson County since the 1830s. Murray's great-grandparents came to the area from Nashville in 1832. Henry Warmath was a farmer and a member of the Whig Party. The next couple of Warmath generations had occupations ranging from farmers to Methodist ministers and several of Henry's sons served with Confederate militia units in the area which fought invading Union troops during the Civil War.

Murray Warmath's early childhood was typical and without any unusual events. He attended grammar school in Humboldt. Like many young boys, he was involved in sports, especially football which by the end of World War I was growing in popularity throughout the South.

"Historically, football in the South, and in particular high school and college football, has been an integral part of the social fabric of the community," Warmath said. "Towns like Humboldt were, and continue to be, caught up in the fortunes of their local high school teams."

Warmath took to football because of his natural ruggedness and a willingness to mix it up. Unlike today, football in the 1920s required players to play both offense and defense.

Warmath's life, in an active and relatively carefree childhood, was tragically changed at age 10.

"My mother died and within a few months of her death, my father, seeking to fulfill a business opportunity, left to work in Jackson, a larger city to the south of Humboldt. He went into business with another guy there and they opened up what today we would call a sports bar...a place catering to men where they could get a meal, a drink and talk sports and place a bet or two.

"My father was somewhat of a free-spirit. I loved him and felt he loved me, yet, he went his own way and I was sort of forced to go mine."

From the time he left Humboldt and until his death in 1960, Carl Warmath saw his son only two to three times a year.

Because it was decided young Murray would be better off staying in Humboldt, he was sent to live with his mother's sister, Maggie Barksdale, and her husband, Tom. The Barkdales had a farm outside of Humboldt, but decided to rent it out and moved into the Warmath's house in town with their 10-year-old nephew.

Tragedy struck again when Maggie died of cancer when Murray was 13.

"My Uncle Tom decided to go back to the farm and in order to stay in town and close to school, I went to live with my father's sister, Mary Shane Foltz and her husband, Howard. Howard, whom everyone called H.J., was the mayor of Humboldt for many years, a prominent business leader, and, naturally, a popular figure in town."

C.T. Shane, another uncle, was a produce broker and bought and sold fruits and vegetables from the local truck farmers which he in turn marketed to wholesalers who shipped them to Memphis, St. Louis, Chicago and New York. Warmath worked for him the summers of his junior high school years. It was long, tedious work in which he made 25 to 50 cents an hour for working from sunrise to nearly midnight with very few days off.

"To give some perspective as to the amount of produce sent out of Humboldt, an average summer season would see over 500 refrigerated box cars full of fruit and vegetables shipped to distant markets," Warmath said. "Strawberries were very popular and were the first of the items harvested, usually in early May."

Beans, tomatoes and cabbage were among the other commodities harvested and Warmath performed nearly every kind of laborious task possible in getting those goods to market in the summers of the mid-1920s.

3

Whatever personal misfortunes had befallen him, young Murray Warmath had shown he possessed a strong work ethic and a strong constitution. These attributes would bode well later in his life when he faced major challenges as an athlete and coach. The absence of his parents in his teen years, especially his father, he observed, "deprived me of the chance to have someone close to me during adolescence, namely a male, whom I could confide in."

He nevertheless has "the fondest memories of growing up in Humboldt and even to this day, whenever possible, I will make a point of returning there to visit friends."

"Though I was without my parents, I was treated with the utmost kindness by my aunt and uncle and their friends and family. I was never wanting for basic personal comfort or attention."

Murray was popular with his classmates and was maturing into a handsome young man with a thick crop of dark wavy hair, a muscular frame and a wide, beaming smile. His social life was full and he and his friends were active in not just sports, but in their leisure time activities as well.

"I learned to dance when I was about 14," he recalled. "Some of the girls from school took a few of my buddies and me over to one of the girl's houses, rolled back the rug and cranked up an old Victrola. Pretty soon, we could dance with the best of 'em."

Warmath attended Humboldt High School from eighth through 11th grade. In small cities such as Humboldt, boys involved in athletics usually played more than one sport. In Warmath's case, it was football, basketball and baseball.

"While football was my primary sport, I was pretty good at baseball," he said. "I was a pitcher on both the high school team and on the summer ball team. The University of Tennessee didn't have varsity baseball when I attended. Had they, I would have gone out for the team.

"We were eligible for high school varsity football as 9th graders and I was on the squad. However, I managed to break my collarbone at the start of the season and had to sit out the year. My sophomore year I was a sub and saw little action. We had an older and winning team, which was the case the entire time I attended Humboldt. By my junior year, I started at end offensively and played as an interior lineman defensively."

In 1928, Warmath's junior season, the local newspaper, the Humboldt Courier-Chronicle, called his play in one game, "sensational." "Warmath caught several beautiful passes and his punting was as fine as ever."

Along with his athletic talents, Warmath also was a good student. Since his abilities both in athletics and in the classroom were evident, Warmath realized that a college education was within his grasp. While Humboldt High School had provided him with some of the basics, he needed to hone his educational skills and was accepted at Branham-Hughes Military Academy in Spring Hill, 30 miles south of Nashville.

"Branham-Hughes was a West Point/Annapolis and Vanderbilt prep school and had a number of graduates of Vanderbilt University on its faculty," Warmath said. "It was a boarding school and operated as a typical military prep school with heavy emphasis on discipline and academics."

Warmath improved his academic skills and his skills as a football player caught the attention of some Southern colleges. His coach at Branham-Hughes was Fred McKibben, a Vanderbilt alum. Yet, it was the new coach at Humboldt High School who pointed Warmath in the direction of the University of Tennessee.

"Houston Herndon came to Humboldt the summer after I was through high school," Warmath recalled. "He knew about me as a player both at Humboldt and at Branham-Hughes. Since he always was on the look-out for players for his alma mater, he approached me about enrolling at UT.

"Naturally, as a native of the state, I was interested in attending my state's major university. However, in those days, Vanderbilt had a big following and so the two schools often fought over the same good high school players. On the whole, Tennessee had a somewhat stronger following because they were a public institution whereas Vanderbilt was private and its alumni and general association with the state at large was not as great. Tennessee historically was somewhat ahead when it came to landing in-state players."

Herndon's recommendation of Warmath to the Tennessee staff was the deciding factor in Warmath's decision to enroll at Knoxville. In August of 1930, he enrolled in school and tried out for freshmen football.

There were no scholarships in those days, so his father paid for his freshman year at school.

Awaiting him and nearly 150 other players was a man who not only shaped the course of Tennessee and American collegiate football, but also was to have a major influence on Warmath's life.

# Two

 University of Tennessee immortal Robert R. "Bob" Neyland ranks as one of college football's all-time great coaches. A graduate of West Point, he was an outstanding athlete excelling as a football and baseball player and was the Corps of Cadets' heavyweight boxing champion. He played football with Dwight D. Eisenhower and Omar Bradley on some of Army's greatest teams.

Following his graduation in 1916, he was assigned to the Army Corps of Engineers. He returned to West Point after his initial four year tour of duty and became a teacher and an assistant football coach under John McEwan. McEwan was a former teammate and still is regarded as one of football's great centers.

Neyland came to Tennessee in 1926 at a time when the program needed a boost. By the time he was done 26 years later, he brought Tennessee and to a large extent, Southern football, national recognition. Prior to his arrival, the Volunteers had been playing slightly better than .500 and played in a stadium consisting of bleachers for 3,000 people. That is in sharp contrast to the nearly 97,000 who attend Tennessee home games today.

The official reason for Neyland coming to Tennessee was to head the R.O.T.C. program. But the school was in need of a football coach since M.B. Banks had resigned due to poor health. Neyland took over the program and wasted little time in establishing a winner.

"Neyland was a perfectionist whose practices and game plans never missed a detail," Warmath recalled. "His main emphasis was on defense and the kicking game."

Few teams in the history of college football were as able to utilize defense, ball control and a disciplined kicking game as well as the Volunteers. Former UT sports information director Charles "Gus" Manning once wrote that, "Neyland is a living legend in college football. His defensive record is truly phenomenal. In 188 regular season games played over 21 seasons, his Tennessee teams held the opposition to an average of only five points a game."

Including regular and post-season games, Neyland's squads scored 4,917 points to the opposition's 1,215.

Herman Hickman, one of the great collegiate interior lineman of the first half century and one of many outstanding linemen produced by Neyland, commented that if a Neyland team scored a touchdown against an opponent, he had them beat. If he scored two it was a rout.

"We spent an unusually large portion of practice on defense and kicking," Warmath said. "Neyland believed that ball position, as opposed to possession, was the critical factor. A well-honed kicking game that kept the opponent backed up deep in its end of the field and a defense that forced him to punt the ball back to us on fourth down, was Neyland's approach."

Neyland's stint at Tennessee, particularly from 1926 to the beginning of World War II, is clearly one of football's greatest. His 1926 team lost only to Vanderbilt. A year later, the Volunteers tied them, the only blemish on the season's record. In 1928, 1929, 1930, 1931 and 1932, they lost only once and were tied a total of four times. In 1933, they lost three times and in 1934, they lost twice. In his first nine seasons at Knoxville, Neyland was 75-7-5 in regular season games and beat New York University in a post-season charity game in 1931.

Warmath believes "Neyland's ability to get other teams to err or make mistakes, often deep in their own territory, was masterful. His disciplined football centered around gang tackling, pressuring the other kicker, forcing fumbles and

8

interceptions...those very critical things that resulted in our getting the ball in good field position."

The list of players coached by Neyland included Bobby Dodd, Beattie Feathers, Hickman, Bob Suffridge, Bowden Wyatt, Ed Molinski, Paul Hug, Gene McEver, Buddy Hackman, Doug Atkins, Hank Lauricella, Ted Daffer and Bert Rechichar.

It was Dodd, later to gain greater fame as Georgia Tech's outstanding coach in the Forties, Fifties and Sixties, who was the first "name" player for Neyland.

When Warmath enrolled in 1930 as a freshman, Dodd, Hug, McEver and Hackman were in their final seasons.

"Dodd was from Kingsport, Tenn. and actually was somewhat less heralded that Hug, his high school classmate," Warmath said. "Tennessee and Vanderbilt fought tooth n' nail to recruit Hug and Dodd, but it was Hug everyone really wanted. Both of them showed up at Vanderbilt for the start of freshman ball in the fall of 1927, but a Tennessee alum got to them and they left after two days and immediately went to Knoxville."

While Hug was a fine player (all Southern Conference), it was Dodd who was the heart of Neyland's early teams. He was the classic, triple-threat back operating out of the single wing formation.

Hickman later reflected that, "Bobby Dodd was the brains and the tailback on the 1929 and 1930 teams. He was a coach's player: cool, calm and a masterful punter without the power of Beattie Feather's leg, but more accurate. He was such a pin-point passer that the conservative Neyland allowed him to pass from behind our own goal line. Over a period of two years, he did not have a pass intercepted."

As was the case with Warmath several years later, Dodd went directly from being a college player to being a collegiate assistant coach. Sixty years later, Warmath laughed when recalling how that transition came about for Dodd.

"It was right after Thanksgiving in 1930 and our coaches were out of town recruiting," Warmath said. "Dodd happened to be in the football office when a call came in from Bill Alexander, the head coach at Georgia Tech. Tech was playing in an upcoming Bowl game against a team we had played earlier in the season...I don't remember who that was...and 'Coach Alex' as he was known, wanted to get some information on them from our coaches.

"The secretary informed him they were all gone, but said Dodd was standing there and did Alexander want to talk to him. Well, ol' Coach Alex said sure and got Dodd on the line. They talked at some length and Dodd offered to write a report.

"Since he also was planning to come to Atlanta anyway within a few days, he promised to deliver the report to Alexander.

"Bobby wrote the report, headed for Atlanta and delivered it. Alexander was so impressed he hired Dodd on the spot to become one of his assistants. Well, Bobby never came back. He just up and left and stayed there for 35 years."

To compound the problems for the Volunteer opposition, Tennessee also had McEver (no relation to the West Point coach) and who led the nation in scoring in 1929, and Hackman, a wingback who was a brilliant runner, outstanding pass receiver and, according to Hickman, "the best man on pass defense I have ever seen."

Most college teams throughout America played an eight game schedule in the Twenties and Thirties. However, Tennessee and most Southern schools got in an extra game or two because of the good late season weather in the South.

Virtually every team opened its season in late September, meaning practice began about Labor Day. Freshmen usually reported with the varsity to commence fall practice. In Warmath's freshman year at Tennessee, however, Neyland decided to get a head start.

"Neyland had the frosh report in late August. As I recall, it was at least five days prior to when we were allowed to report "The practice field at Tennessee then was located next to some railroad tracks. One day that first week, a passenger train came by and aboard was a Georgia Tech alum heading to Atlanta. He saw the practice and was knowledgeable enough to see we were practicing ahead of the official collegiate start-up date. As soon as he got to Atlanta, he called the conference office (then the Southern Conference) and reported us."

Neyland was notified that Tennessee was under investigation, but by the time he had to answer to conference officials, he had fully prepared (in true Neyland fashion) a sound defense.

"Hell, all he did was document a bunch of other schools in the conference guilty of the same thing and the matter was quickly dropped," Warmath explained with a laugh.

Freshmen and members of the junior varsity played any number of games against other schools. In 1930, the Vols, under freshman coach William Harkness, were undefeated in five games. The only blemish was a 7-7 tie with Sewanee. The freshmen defeated Tennessee Wesleyan and Centre in their first two games, tied Sewanee, then closed the year by trouncing Vanderbilt, 53-0, and Kentucky, 37-0. Warmath saw plenty of action both ways at end.

Meanwhile, the varsity went 9-1, losing only to Alabama, 18-6, in Tuscaloosa.

From the time Warmath enrolled at Tennessee until he finished, he rarely returned to Humboldt. Economics was the reason. When not in school or playing ball, he worked.

"By the time I arrived as a freshman, the Depression was in full swing," Warmath said. "Practically every student, even athletes, were working part-time jobs during the year and full-time jobs when school wasn't in session."

Warmath, who had pledged Sigma Alpha Epsilon fraternity, worked during the school year busing and cleaning dishes in

11

dorms or at the frat house. In the summer, he and several players had jobs on the Tennessee River working for the Army Corps of Engineers.

"Neyland was still a commissioned officer and chief district engineer," Murray related. "His connections resulted in several players getting summer jobs. We would go up and down the river all summer long on barges and do such things as paint and repair navigational markers in the channel and do general cleanup work which was part of the Corps' overall requirements. We made just enough money to get by."

They earned $90 a month, paid $30 of that for room and board (often staying with local farm families) and kept $60. Annual tuition at UT was $105.

Athletic scholarships, at least the early versions of such, didn't come into existence until the 1935 season, the year after Warmath's playing days were over.

"We scrapped for everything we could and when it came to money, you were thankful for anything you got," Warmath said.

The 1931 season was to have been Warmath's first as a varsity player. But like the early days of his high school career, injuries prevented him from playing. This time, a knee injury in fall practice resulted in his being red-shirted for the entire year.

It was a good season that Warmath watched from the sidelines. That was because on the heels of Bobby Dodd and company came another fine player who helped continue Neyland's winning ways.

William Beattie Feathers was in Warmath's opinion, "the best all-around runner I was ever associated with as a player or a coach. He was not only fast and quick, but a punishing runner who loved to bowl over tacklers. He went on to average nearly 10 yards a carry with the Chicago Bears as a pro and was in the same backfield as Bronko Nagurski. With the Bears, he became pro football's first back to rush for more than 1,000 yards in a season. He was also a terrific punter.

12

"In 1932, my third season at Knoxville, we played Alabama at Birmingham," Warmath recalled. "A torrential rain storm had come through the area the previous day and continued throughout the game turning the field into a quagmire. Probably the greatest punting duel in the history of football ensued. Feathers and Alabama's Johnny Cain each punted the ball 20 times with Beattie averaging 48 yards and Cain 45 yards a kick. That's over a mile in total combined kicking yardage for one game."

Tennessee eked out a 7-3 victory with Feathers scoring the game's only touchdown.

The Vols got out of the blocks in great shape in 1931 by shutting out Maryville, Clemson, Mississippi, Alabama and North Carolina. They then beat Duke, 25-2, shut out Carson-Newman and beat Vanderbilt, 21-6. The season finale against Kentucky proved to be the only blight on their record when the game ended in a 6-6 tie in Lexington.

The team got some redemption when it beat New York University, 13-0, in the charity game in New York City the week after Thanksgiving.

The 1932 season saw the Volunteers, behind the spectacular play of Feathers, equal their previous season's record when they again went 9-0-1, this time the tie being with Vanderbilt, a scoreless contest played late in the season in Nashville.

The Vandy game was marked by 5,000 gate crashers who stormed the field in Nashville. Police couldn't control them and both schools threatened to call off the game. Order was restored, however, and the 5,000 were allowed to stay and watch from the sidelines.

Warmath started at end in '32 which was his sophomore season in football even though he was a junior academically. Playing at between 190 and 200 pounds, he was in his own words "an above average college player and just a fair pass catcher." His description was most modest, however, for he was named third team All-America at end that year. One of his better games was against Kentucky in which he recovered a fumble and caught an important pass in the third quarter which set up a Volunteer touchdown.

Following the 1932 season, the new Southeastern Conference became home for 12 schools, including Tennessee. Colleges in the Carolinas and Maryland formed the Atlantic Coast Conference. Georgia Tech was an original SEC member, but later became an independent in the mid-1960s.

Graduation hurt the 1933 team. Even though Feathers was back as a senior and would be again named All-America and the year's SEC Most Valuable Player, Tennessee stumbled to a 7-3 record, losing to Duke, Alabama and Louisiana State by a total of 21 points. Following the season finale against LSU, the Tennessee coaches approached Warmath about switching positions as the team returned by train from Baton Rouge.

"Looking ahead, they saw they were going to need help in the interior line and wanted me to shift from end to guard," Warmath said. "I had played in the interior line in high school, so I was somewhat familiar with that type of position. Besides, in the days of the old single wing and Neyland-style football, that sort of change was not difficult. Those who played end were expected to be as adept at basic blocking and tackling as were guards or tackles."

While Warmath prepared himself for the change during the off-season in 1933-34, he also had another new responsibility. He was elected the student body president.

"Realize that in the South in the Thirties, such positions were really the result of winning what would best be called a popularity contest," he pointed out. "In those days, there was no storming of the administration building or riots on campus. People nominated for student body officers were done so by a group or organization to which they belonged. In my case, it was my fraternity.

"There was little in the way of controversial issues for us to grapple with. We became involved in such matters as improved student parking."

The student newspaper, the Orange and White, reported the election was suffering from the lowest student interest since the early 1920s. Warmath's opponent was football teammate, Lou Pounders.

Warmath won a clear 444-259 victory.

Warmath's natural charm, good looks and popularity as an athlete and a student leader didn't hurt his chances when it came to meeting and winning the heart of the woman he calls, "clearly the most beautiful girl on campus."

Mary Louise Clapp of Knoxville was three years younger than Warmath. They met on a blind date Warmath's senior year.

"Some well-to-do alum had a very nice home outside of Knoxville and held an annual hayride and poolside party for my fraternity. She and I were fixed up on a blind date. It was a nice evening, but it was nearly a year before we dated again. She had a wonderful personality on top of being so good-looking. She won several beauty contests back in those days including being the school's homecoming queen and was elected Miss Tennessee."

Mary Louise graduated in 1938, taught school for two years in Jacksboro, Tenn. and married Warmath in 1939.

Warmath, an education major with an emphasis in the history of Tennessee, completed his undergraduate work in the spring.

"Logically, with such a degree, I should have gone into teaching," he recalled. "However, I had known for some time that I wanted to coach football. Plus, I had one more year of eligibility left which I obviously wanted to complete."

Warmath enrolled in graduate school during his senior year of football. The 1934 season got off to a good start for the Volunteers as they won their first three games, but then lost again to Alabama.

Warmath vividly recalls that game with the Tide.

"It was in Birmingham and that's when Bear Bryant (a redshirted junior) and the great Don Hutson were Alabama's two ends. The game was a bloodbath.

"Phil Dickens, who later coached against me when he was at Indiana, was our sophomore halfback and was clobbered on a play resulting in a badly broken nose."

"I remember the trainer using a device that looked like a pencil with gauze on the end and sticking it up both nostrils to clear out the air passages. Dickens was in a lot of pain, but continued to play. Then, unbelievably, he broke his nose again. At the hotel that night he was delirious and thought he was still in the game. He had to be physically restrained for fear he'd hurt himself. His staying in the game was one of the most incredible acts of courage I ever saw in football."

The game also was marked by Bryant being tossed out for committing an unsportsmanlike foul.

"Bryant was a rough and tough son-of-a-bitch who gave no quarter. He didn't have the talent of Hutson (later one of the National Football League's great pass receivers with the Green Bay Packers), but Bear really smacked people."

Bryant actually was the victim of a bad call, Warmath contends. He was thrown out for supposedly punching Dickens. The culprit was really fellow Tide player, Bill Lee, who punched Dickens after the whistle.

"That was one tough game," Warmath recounted. "In those days, the officials were pretty lenient when it came to the rough stuff. Injuries were more prevalent back then because they were slow with the whistle. If you hadn't grown up before the start of one of those games, you sure had by the time it was over.

"Alabama had to work awfully hard that day to beat us. On three separate series, we made goal line stands in which we took our defensive stances with our feet in the end zone. They only scored once on those three efforts, however."

The Vols other loss in 1934 was 13-12 to Fordham at the Polo Grounds in New York City, the first Saturday in November. Fordham was coached by Jim Crowley, one of the famed Four Horsemen of Notre Dame in the 1920s. A member of the Fordham team was a sophomore lineman named Vince Lombardi.

Renowned sports writer, Arthur J. Daley covered the game for the New York Times and wrote that Fordham's Tony Sarausky "stumbled as he sped off tackle early in the fourth quarter, teetered uncertainly under the grasp of restraining Tennessee hands and then shook loose for 60 yards and the touchdown that gave Fordham a 13-12 upset victory over the Volunteers."

Daley called the Vols the better team, one which uncharac-teristically had relied on the pass (17 attempts with 7 comple-tions, including a touchdown) to move the ball against the tenacious Fordham defense. Daley cited Warmath as one of several Tennessee players who performed well that afternoon.

Not only did Warmath and Lombardi collide that day, the two met 15 years later when they were assistants together at Army.

Tennessee closed out the season with consecutive wins over Mississippi State, Vanderbilt, Kentucky and LSU.

For Warmath it had to be a satisfying year. At the conclusion of his first and only season at guard, he was named to the All-Southeast Conference team and was the only member of the 1934 team to receive post-season honors.

Warmath was further honored when he was approached at season's end about becoming an assistant on the Tennessee staff for the 1935 season. Neyland, still commissioned in the Army, was being reassigned to the Canal Zone. That pending reassign-ment was common knowledge even before the '34 season. Bill Britton, who had been a Neyland assistant since 1926 and coached Warmath as an end, was promoted to head coach. When spring practice rolled around, Warmath, only 22 years old, reported as the Volunteers new end coach.

It was the first of what would be 36 years as an assistant and head coach.

# Three

 With Neyland gone for an unknown period and Britton now the head coach, Tennessee's staff headed into the new year facing unique challenges. Aside from no longer having the services of the man who led them to nine great seasons, the 1935 squad lost several quality players through graduation, Warmath among them. Rebuilding was the main task ahead.

Warmath began recruiting as soon as the '34 season ended. While the Vols always had done well in getting Tennessee and Virginia prepsters, they began to expand their horizons in the mid Thirties and set their sights on West Virginia, Pennsylvania and Ohio.

"One of my first assignments was to make a recruiting trip into Ohio," Warmath said. "I stopped in Massillon which, even to this day, has one of the finest high school football programs in the country."

The Massillon coach at the time was the late Paul Brown who gained far greater fame at Ohio State and then with the Cleveland Browns and the Cincinnati Bengals.

"Brown was, in my estimation, one of the geniuses in the game," Warmath said. "He was the first coach I know to begin using aptitude tests. He gave his players written exams to judge a player's intelligence. He was a strict disciplinarian who got the most out of his talent."

The 1935 freshmen class was the nucleus of some of the great pre-World War II teams. A Massillon player of Brown's with whom Warmath made contact and who later came to Tennessee was Ed Molinski, a stalwart guard on some of the Vols' great teams of the late 1930s.

19

"Back home, we grabbed Bowden Wyatt, a fine high school player from Kingston, Tenn." Warmath recalled. "In his senior year, (1938), he was All-America at end and team captain."

Wyatt went into coaching in 1939 when he and Warmath became assistants for Allyn McKeen at Mississippi State. He later was head coach at Wyoming and Arkansas and returned to Tennessee and coached the Vols from 1955 through 1962. His 1956 squad, headed by present Tennessee coach Johnny Majors, went 10-1 and Wyatt was named national Coach of the Year.

While the 1935 freshmen recruits had an abundance of talent which paid off later, the '35 varsity didn't have a great season by Tennessee standards (or anyone else's, for that matter), going 4-5. The team opened the season by hosting Southwestern and won 20-0. The next week, North Carolina came to town and trounced Tennessee, 38-13. The Vols rebounded the next week in Birmingham and defeated Auburn, 13-6. Their record fell to .500 again the next Saturday when Alabama won 25-0 in Knoxville.

The balance of the season was not much different. Tennessee beat Centre and Mississippi, victories sandwiched around a loss to Duke. The last two games were losses to Vanderbilt and Kentucky. The dropoff in performance by the 1935 team is interesting when one notes they gave up 155 points in the nine games. The 1931, '32, '33 and '34 teams gave up only 156 points over four seasons!

Neyland's one year stint in Panama for the Army ended when he resigned his active commission with the rank of major, and returned to Knoxville and resumed his duties as the head football coach. Britton went back to coaching the ends and Warmath was named assistant line coach as the staff prepared to regroup and get ready for the 1936 season.

While the '35 season had been disappointing, the staff was able to continue recruiting good high school players. Noteworthy among the 1936 freshmen class were backs George "Bad

News" Cafego and Sam Bartholomew. Cafego was from Scarboro, W. Va. and was an outstanding runner and passer who operated the single wing for Neyland as the tailback. He made All-America in 1938 and 1939 and was later named to the National Football Foundation College Hall of Fame.

The 1936 team rebounded to post a 6-2-2 record.

"We didn't open the season well, though," Warmath remembered. "We had a shutout (13-0) win at home over Chattanooga, lost our next two games on the road to North Carolina and Auburn which was followed by a scoreless tie against Alabama in Birmingham."

The Vols got things turned around the fifth week when they edged Duke, 15-13, then a shut out Georgia, 46-0, in Athens. Three at-home victories followed over Maryville, Vanderbilt and Kentucky. The season ended with a scoreless tie against Mississippi in Memphis.

The return of Neyland was evident not only in the 6-2-2 record, but also in the improvement of the defense. When compared to 1935, the 1936 team reduced by two-thirds the number of points allowed for the season.

The Neyland years entered the second of three phases. The level of intensity increased and those associated with the team realized they were on their way back to the glory days of the late 1920s and early 1930s. Following the '36 season, the coaching staff started out on one of the best recruiting trips in the history of Tennessee football.

In the fall of 1937, the freshmen recruited were to lead Neyland's teams through the first of three of the finest seasons ever witnessed in the history of college football. The cream of the incoming frosh was guard Bob Suffridge and it was Warmath's privilege to be his position coach.

"Suffridge was the equal of any lineman with whom I was ever associated," Warmath said. "The two others would be Tom Brown and Bobby Bell at Minnesota.

"Suffridge was a Knoxville boy and he had it all. He was tough as nails and quick as a beam of light. He had no flaws as a lineman, either on offense or defense. He was a three-time All American."

Sports Illustrated's 1969 annual college preview, which honored the 100th anniversary of American college football, picked their all-time greatest 11 players in the history of college football. One of the two guards named was Bob Suffridge. Equal accolades came later when the Football Writers Association of America selected him to their All-Time All America Team.

"Bob was a devastating blocker and a vicious tackler and it was extremely rare when he made a noticeable mistake or was out of position," Warmath said.

Other players who made major contributions in 1938, '39 and '40 were Abe Shires, an outstanding tackle, Hodges "Burr" West, another tackle, and backs Bob Foxx, Breezer Andridge, Fred Newman, Van Thompson and Buist Warren.

Ed Molinski was the other guard and although he was a year older than Suffridge, he had been redshirted after his freshman year, so they played three years together.

While the 1937 freshmen squad went 2-1 (beating Chattanooga and Kentucky, and losing to Vanderbilt) the varsity continued to rebuild the Tennessee gridiron program under Neyland, albeit with a record nearly identical to the 1936 season. They finished 6-3-1. They opened with shutout victories at home over Wake Forest and Virginia Tech, then traveled to Durham, N.C. where they wound up in a scoreless tie with Duke. They suffered their first loss of the season when Alabama beat them for the fifth year in a row, 14-7 at Knoxville.

They got back on the winning track by shutting out Georgia and Sewanee by the identical scores of 32-0. A trip to Birmingham the following week saw Auburn beat them, 20-7. They returned home to another loss, 13-7 to Vanderbilt. The Vols wrapped up the season with back-to-back shutouts of Kentucky and Mississippi, 13-0 and 32-0.

While the overall record from the year before had not changed appreciably, the defense was showing signs of those old Neyland ways. They had allowed only 47 points in 10 games.

Warmath also was active in other duties while at Tennessee. He served as the varsity boxing coach.

"Several of the boys on the football team had experience as Golden Glove fighters before they enrolled at Tennessee," Warmath said. "Suffridge, Molinski, Shirers, Joe Perry Little and Bob Woodruff were the five down lineman on the 1939 team that went to the Rose Bowl and all five were boxers.

"Molinski probably was the best of the five. I was not what you would call well-versed in boxing, but I knew enough about it to at least organize the team and give them a few pointers and lots of encouragement. We competed about six times a year against other schools in the area like Kentucky, Mississippi State, The Citadel and Appalachian State."

When the 1938 spring practice rolled around, the Vols had the right mix of players from the varsity—veterans such as Cafego and Wyatt—and an infusion of talented underclassmen such as Suffridge and Shires.

"Spring football was a critical stage in the development of Southern football," Warmath contends. "Up until the mid-1930s, the best football teams had come from the East and Midwest. Certainly the South and other parts of the country had their share of fine teams. Generally, however, Eastern and Midwestern ball was considered by the experts to be slightly better.

"But the advent of spring football changed that. Simply, the fact that springtime in the South came earlier and allowed teams to get a head start on the schools in other parts of the country paid off. It didn't take long before football south of the Mason-Dixon line was the equal to any in the country."

Spring football and good weather aside, the 1938 Tennessee team began an unbelievable three year assault on their opponents as well as several collegiate records. Led by six players who would earn All-American honors during those years, the Vols destroyed their opposition.

They opened with two victories marked by something that turned out to be uncharacteristic: allowing points by the other team. They beat Sewanee, 26-3, and Clemson, 20-7. Then, over the next nine games, they achieved a remarkable feat: they allowed only one score. In the sixth game of the year, LSU scored a touchdown (it missed the PAT). Previous to that, they shut out Auburn, 7-0 and Alabama 13-0. After LSU, they blanked (in succession), Chattanooga, Vanderbilt, Kentucky, Mississippi and Oklahoma, the last triumph coming in the Orange Bowl on Jan. 1, 1939 when they beat the Sooners 17-0. The Vols were 11-0 and finished second to Texas Christian in both the AP and UPI polls. TCU was led that year by the legendary Davey O'Brien, winner of the '38 Heisman Trophy.

"There is no question that the '38 team was not only perhaps the greatest in Tennessee's history, but one of the best in the history of college football," Warmath said. "It was a team that had abundant talent and did everything right."

At the conclusion of the 1938 season and the Orange Bowl victory, Warmath fully expected to be coaching another season at Tennessee. However, a series of events followed which would see him make the first of two eventual coaching moves that landed him at Mississippi State.

"Allyn McKeen had been the coach at West Tennessee State Teacher's College (now Memphis State) and was hired after the 1938 season to head the football program at Mississippi State," Warmath recounted. "He hired me and asked if I would hire one other assistant. I selected Bowden Wyatt who had completed his eligibility at Tennessee."

The three joined forces for the 1939 season, the start of some of the finest years in Mississippi State gridiron history.

# Four

The new Mississippi State coaching staff had a Tennessee flavor to it. McKeen, Wyatt and Warmath were all graduates of UT. It is hard to believe in today's era where college staffs consist of anywhere from 10 to 15 coaches, that a major college team had only three coaches. But small staffs of five or less were the norm at most schools in the pre-World War II days.

When the new staff came to Starkville in the spring of '39, they inherited a program which had played about .500 for most of the 1930s. McKeen would quickly turn things around and by the time he retired after the 1948 season, Mississippi State was among the South's better programs.

When McKeen coached at West Tennessee State Teacher's College, he led the team to an undefeated and untied season in 1938, winning the Southern Intercollegiate Athletic Association championship. A Tennessee player in 1925, '26 and '27, he came highly-recommended by Neyland for the State job. At West Tennessee State, he was a part-time assistant coach and part-time attorney until 1937 when he was named head coach. He had two fine seasons before Mississippi State called.

In Starkville, State athletic director Dudy Noble said, "we are interested in installing a permanent system here and we believe the Tennessee system is what we want."

The announcement of the appointment of McKeen drew disgruntled remarks by some State fans who believed hiring a teacher's college coach was not the way to improve the program. Soon, they were biting their tongues.

Initially, State was at a numbers disadvantage. Only 24 players lettered that year. However, there was some talent led by

Erwin "Buddy" Elrod, an All-American end. Other quality players included backs Harvey Johnson and Jack Nix, end Arnold "Bear" Moore and linemen Hunter Cohorn, John Tripson and Guy McDowell.

In his book, *The Maroon Bulldogs*, William Sorrels, a Mississippi State alum and former managing editor of the Memphis Commercial Appeal, quoted fellow journalist Walter Stewart, a famed Memphis and New York sportswriter. "Allyn McKeen has the personality which makes for a successful career in coaching or selling mousetraps. He drives men hard, but the iron hand is always buried in the velvet glove."

The '39 squad had an 8-2 record, a marked improvement from the previous year's 4-6 record. Both the '39 losses were identical scores of 7-0 to Auburn and Alabama. The Auburn loss was the result of an untimely fumble of the second half kickoff which gave Auburn possession at the Bulldog 20. A fourth-down pass was good for the game's only touchdown. Earlier, the officials blundered when they turned the ball over to Auburn deep in its territory after only three downs by Mississippi State.

At Alabama, the Tide scored early, held on and had luck go their way when Elrod was tossed out for unsportsmanlike conduct. The game was played on Elrod's birthday and was the only time in his collegiate career he was ejected from a game. He came to the bench with tears in his eyes and told McKeen, "coach, I lost the game for us."

Of the eight wins, six were shutouts. Mississippi State beat Howard College of Birmingham, Arkansas, Florida, Southwestern, Birmingham Southern, LSU, Millsaps and Mississippi.

The previous season, State had given up 131 points. The first year under McKeen, they allowed only 32. Noble had indeed gotten his "Tennessee system."

Warmath maintained his contacts in Knoxville and when the regular season ended in '39, Neyland asked him to help assist the Tennessee staff in getting ready for the 1940 Rose Bowl.

If the 1938 Tennessee team had made the football world sit up and take notice, then the '39 squad received even more attention. It did not allow a point in 10 games. That's a record that still stands today. The Vols scored an average of 21.1 points per game and after they stopped Auburn, 7-0, in the season finale in Knoxville, they were invited to the Rose Bowl.

"Following our final game at Mississippi State, an 18-6 victory over Mississippi, Neyland contacted me and asked if I would go with one of Tennessee's assistant coaches to Los Angeles and scout Southern Cal which would be the Tennessee Rose Bowl opponent," Warmath said.

The two went to L.A. and watched the Trojans take on UCLA, which had a young, talented running back named Jackie Robinson.

"Robinson was one of the finest athletes I have ever seen and although his legend was as a baseball player, had he stayed with football, he would have been equally as successful because he was that good a natural athlete," Warmath said.

"The USC squad had more talent than UCLA and it was a virtual certainty that they would be Tennessee's opponent on New Year's Day. UCLA, however, made a hell of a game of it and Robinson was having a terrific day against USC in a game which went down to the wire. Southern Cal tied it on a field goal. We were so enthralled with Robinson we almost forgot at times to pay attention to USC."

Southern Cal was coached by the legendary Howard Jones, who had taken the Trojans through an undefeated season in 1939 with ties against Oregon and UCLA. Jones had two full teams and would play one in the first and third quarters and the other in the second and fourth quarters. There was an abundance of talented tailbacks, including Doyle Nave, an excellent passer.

Jones pulled off an upset in Pasadena on Jan. 1st. When the gun sounded, it was his Trojans who played the great defensive game, upsetting Tennessee 14-0, which was without Cafego who didn't dress for the game because of injuries, and Suffridge who was lost early in the game due to an injury.

Warmath returned to Starkville and in 1940, the Bulldogs (or Maroons as they were also called in those days with both nicknames being used equally) continued where they had left off in 1939. The 1940 team showed even greater improvement. Buddy Elrod was again one of the mainstays.

Elrod vowed after the previous season's loss to Alabama, the game from which he was ejected, that he would lead the Maroon to victory over the Tide. The lighter, quicker State line ripped up Alabama's forward wall on offense and was unmovable on defense. The level of line play was reflected in the fact that not one opponent scored on the ground against State's starting defensive line in 1939 or '40, a line coached by Warmath.

Mississippi State went 10-0-1, the tie coming in the third game, 7-7 against Auburn. They shut out four teams, including Alabama and Mississippi, and went to the Orange Bowl to meet Georgetown.

The Hoyas had fielded one of the East's better teams. Under coach Jack Hagerty they were undefeated and untied in 1938, tied by Syracuse in 1939 for the only non-win of the season and lost 19-18 to Boston College in 1940. When they arrived in Miami to meet Mississippi State, they were led by All American guard Augie Lio, fullback Jim Castiglia and tackle Al Blozis.

Warmath was assigned to scout the Hoyas.

"Nobody scouted a game any better than Murray," recalled Billy Jack Murphy, a State halfback. "His attention to detail and the tendencies of opposition players was legendary among his teams and fellow coaches. We went into the Orange Bowl totally prepared."

The Maroon won, 14-7.

The Associated Press ranked Mississippi State ninth in the country in its final poll. That year, Minnesota was national champion and, ironically, a previous Mississippi State coach was heading the Gopher program in 1940. Bernie Bierman had been the State coach in 1925 and 1926.

That year was also significant in that Murray and Mary Louise had their first of three children. Murray, Jr. was born in Starkville. Today, he is a physician in San Diego.

Several players who were instrumental in the success of 1939 and 1940, graduated. They included Elrod, Cohern, McDowell and Moore. However, McKeen, Warmath and Wyatt had recruited well and the young player who stepped right up was running back J.T. "Blondy" Black. McKeen called him the best runner Mississippi State had up until that point. He was a 195 pounder with 9.6 speed in the 100 yard dash. Beginning in 1940, he was instrumental in leading the Bulldogs to three excellent seasons.

Also recruited by Warmath was Murphy, a very versatile player from Siloam Springs, Ark. who not only played for Warmath, but later served as his assistant at State and Minnesota. Murphy eventually went on to have 14 very successful years as the head coach at Memphis State.

"Murray sent penny postcards to myself and a fellow high school player, Paul Davis, inviting us to come to Starkville and join the team," Murphy said. "To show how much things have changed in 50 years, we hitchhiked to Starkville."

As a freshman in 1939 and a redshirt the next year, Murphy got a close look at the staff in practice. "They were very disciplined," he recalled. "They were totally versed in the game. McKeen remarked years later that Warmath knew more about the game of football than he did and I believe it."

The 1941 team had another fine year with an 8-1-1 record. They opened the season with victories over Florida and Alabama then traveled to Baton Rouge where they were tied by LSU, 0-0. Three more victories followed (over Union, Southwestern and Auburn) before they suffered their first, and only, loss of the year, 16-0 to Duquesne in Pittsburgh. A 6-0 win over Mississippi and a season-ending 26-13 win over San Francisco in San Francisco,

29

capped another great year. Little did Warmath or anyone else realize on the day of the victory over the Dons, events within 24 hours would drastically change everyone's life. That game was played on Dec. 6, 1941.

"We took the train back from San Francisco and went through Los Angeles. While there, McKeen called the team together in the club car to tell us about the attack on Pearl Harbor," Murphy remembered. "He said not to worry, we'd have the Japanese beat in three months."

Murphy, who was later awarded the bronze star for heroism in the Pacific while serving with the Marines in World War II, remembered sending a letter to McKeen from Okinawa in 1945 in which he told his coach he was "worrying".

Within 18 months of the start of the war, Warmath too would join millions in the Armed Forces. However, his position in football still had some time to go before he was to join the Navy. In the summer of 1942, Neyland was named the coach of a group of All-Star collegians who had just been inducted into the Armed Forces, but had yet to be assigned permanent duty. Neyland himself was back in the Army, called into full-time service before the start of the 1941 season and America's entrance into World War II.

John Barnhill, the former Vol player and Neyland assistant, took over the UT program during the war years. Barnhill had been the best man at the Warmath wedding.

"Neyland asked me to be an assistant coach for his All-Star team," Warmath said. "The other coaches were Bob Woodruff and Herman Hickman. There were three games scheduled in eight days against the Brooklyn Dodgers, the Giants and the Bears."

The All-Stars practiced at Yale and the proceeds from the games were for the War Widows Fund. The man behind the idea was Stanley Woodward, sports columnist for the New York Herald Tribune.

"I remember Hickman was available because he was leaving Davidson as an assistant coach and heading to West Point to take an assistant's position for the 1942 season," Warmath said.

"I had known Herman when I first arrived as a freshman at Tennessee and we kept a close friendship after we both got into coaching. After he was graduated from Tennessee, he played pro ball for the old Brooklyn Dodgers and also did some professional wrestling."

Warmath traveled with Hickman for about a week one winter when Hickman was on the pro wrestling tour. He recalled with a laugh one of Herman's more memorable bouts.

"He was wrestling in New York at Madison Square Garden and the 'script' called for him to be tossed out onto the ring apron. A guy about Herman's size (around 300 pounds) was sitting in the front row smoking this big cigar when Hickman comes flying through the air at him. The guy panicked and jumped out of his seat, dropping the cigar on the floor. Herman landed right on top of that burning cigar. The routine called for him to lie there for a while as if he were hurt. Well, he did and the whole time that cigar is burning right into his belly. He was yowling and screaming like he was in pain. He was 'cause his stomach was on fire."

Hickman, despite his size and liking of rough and tumble sports, was anything but a dumb jock. He was the state declamation champion in high school when he was 16, enjoyed literature and poetry and once was called "the poet laureate of the Great Smokies" by Grantland Rice. He often would go camping in the mountains with a backpack full of books.

When the 1942 All Star team was practicing at Yale, Hickman won prize money for correctly answering questions on literature and poetry on a radio quiz show.

"Herman also had an insatiable appetite and liked a good drink now and then," Warmath said. "Once on the wrestling tour, we were in a hotel and he called room service before breakfast and ordered a dozen fried eggs, a couple of pots of coffee, two quarts of orange juice, a half dozen slices of toast and a pound of bacon. He then turned and asked what he should order for me!"

The All Stars went to Brooklyn and New York and beat both the Dodgers and the Giants. The Bears came to Boston and won the third game from the collegians.

"It was my first contact with players from the University of Minnesota," Warmath said. "Harold VanEvery and Vic Spadaccini, two former Bierman players, were on the team."

After completing his duty for the War Widows Fund, Warmath returned to Starkville. He believed Mississippi State would remain as one of the South's best teams in 1942.

The '42 team was led by "Blondy" Black who had support in the backfield from Lamar Blount and Billy Jack Murphy. It was a sound backfield with Murphy excelling as a kicker and passer. The line consisted of veterans such as Hillery Horne, Mike Mihalic, Curtis Patterson, R.V. Ray and Andy Kowalski.

State went 8-2, the two losses coming in the second and third games when they were beaten by Alabama 21-6 and LSU 16-6. The eight victories were over Union, Vanderbilt, Florida, Auburn, Tulane, Duquesne, Mississippi and San Francisco. A record of 8-2, however, was not good enough for a bowl invitation.

The season was Warmath's last under McKeen. Like many schools, varsity sports were dropped during the war. There was no football at Mississippi State in 1943. It was reinstated in 1944 under McKeen who would continue as the State head coach through the 1948 season. He retired after that with a 65-19-3 record. He had given the school its only Southeastern Conference championship. He has the finest coaching record in the school's history and is enshrined in the National Football Foundation College Hall of Fame.

It is interesting to note that in the four seasons Warmath served as an assistant, State played only 14 of their 41 games at home, due in large part to the small 10,000-seat capacity of the home stadium. Mississippi State won all of those home games. From 1939 through 1942, 27 games were on the road. If one doesn't count the 1941 Orange Bowl victory over Georgetown played at a neutral site along with four other neutral site games played in Memphis, State had to venture into enemy territory 22 times. As visitors, they were a remarkable 15-5-2 and won all four of the games in Memphis.

McKeen was praiseworthy of his players and his assistant coaches alike. Of Warmath, he said he was the greatest line coach he had ever had.

"He was tremendous in working with individuals. When he came to Starkville in 1939, Warmath knew more about football than I did," added McKeen, reflecting an opinion of Warmath expressed later by Neyland.

# Five

It was 1943, America was involved in a full-blown two theater war and like the majority of able-bodied young American men, Murray Warmath was in uniform. Like most other young men, he knew military service was inevitable so he enlisted in the Navy.

"While many of the larger universities continued with some form of varsity football that fall, many others, like Mississippi State, temporarily dropped the program," Warmath recounts. "There weren't enough kids to field a team. I was technically out of a job, so going in the service was the logical option."

A "90 Day Wonder" in Officer Candidate School, Warmath was commissioned an ensign in gunnery school. He had gone through officer's training at the University of Arizona where Mary Louise and Murray, Jr. joined him. Then he went to gunnery school at Gulfport, Miss. and his wife and son went to live in Knoxville.

"I met Wally Johnson in Gulfport. He later would become the University of Minnesota's wrestling coach, the freshman football coach and an assistant on my staff when I came to Minneapolis in the 1950s."

Warmath later was assigned to communications and then sent to Harvard University for additional training. By mid-1944, he was on permanent duty in Brazil as part of an air/sea rescue unit.

"Planes being shipped back from the European Theater, particularly older ones, often were sent from Europe to Africa to South America and then through Central America to the States," Warmath said. "The reason for this was they flew less miles non-stop over open water by coming across the South Atlantic rather than going directly from Europe to the U.S. over the North Atlantic. In case of an emergency landing, the availability of land was far greater on the southern route."

Warmath stayed in the Navy until January, 1946 and was among the last naval officers to leave Brazil when the war was over.

He returned to Knoxville with the idea of picking up his family which now included a one-year-old daughter, Carol, and going back to Starkville to rejoin McKeen and at Mississippi State.

In the meantime, moves were underway to reconstruct a coaching staff at Tennessee. Neyland was still on active duty with the Army Corps of Engineers (now a brigadier general) in India where he had worked on projects to build roadways supplying China. Neyland was to resume his coaching duties once the war ended. Interim coach, John Barnhill, had continued the excellent winning tradition leading Tennessee to a record of 32-5-2 in 1941, 42, 44 and 45 (there was no season in 1943). Included in those years were trips to the Sugar and Rose bowls. Barnhill left for Arkansas in 1946 to become the head coach and athletic director.

While Neyland sweated out the early months of 1946 in India, his wife, Peggy, began contacting men regarding positions on the coaching staff. She knew Warmath was in Knoxville and asked him to become the new line coach for the Vols. He accepted and returned to his alma mater.

Joining him on the staff were venerable Bill Britton, Harvey Robinson (who later succeeded Neyland as head coach), John Mauer and Ike Peel.

The spring practice of 1946 saw a blend of varsity players as well as returning war veterans who still had eligibility.

"One of the returning service veterans was Denver Crawford, a tackle from Kingsport, Tenn. He played varsity ball in 1942 prior to being inducted into the service and became our captain in 1947."

35

"The attitude by these fellows was that the war had interrupted their playing careers and they wanted to prove they still had what it took. That spring and fall, the service veterans teed off on the returning lettermen and the incoming freshmen in practice," Warmath recalled.

"I had played three years of service football during the war as had several of the other war vets who returned in 1946," Crawford said. "It wasn't as if we had been completely out of touch with the game."

The war years didn't change Neyland's approach to football. He still operated out of the single wing despite the trend toward the T-formation and his belief that games were won by forcing the opposition to stay deep in its own territory and to make mistakes was unwavering.

Warmath took charge of coaching the line and when the 1946 season opened, the Vols were in good shape.

They began the season with four impressive victories over name competition. The inaugural game saw the Vols defeat Bobby Dodd's Georgia Tech team 13-9 in Knoxville. The next weekend Tennessee traveled to Durham and edged the Duke Blue Devils 12-7 and followed with a 47-7 route of Chattanooga and a 12-0 shutout of Alabama, both back in Knoxville.

The next Saturday, an average Wake Forest team arrived in Knoxville with the Vols and their fans confident of a victory. But Tennessee played uninspired ball and the Deacon Demons left town with a 19-6 win.

Neyland rallied his troops, however, and the team went on to win the rest of its regular season games which were 20-14 over North Carolina, 18-14 over Ole' Miss, 33-13 over Boston College, 7-0 over Kentucky and 7-6 over Vanderbilt. The Orange Bowl liked the 9-1 Vols' record and they were invited to meet Rice in Miami on New Year's Day. The season closed on a sour note as the Owls shut them out, 8-0.

Graduation hit the 1947 team hard and the inexperience showed when the Volunteers posted their worst record since 1935. In uncharacteristic Neyland fashion, Tennessee opened with two losses—27-0 to Georgia Tech in Atlanta and a 19-7 homecoming loss to Duke. The team got its first victory the following week when they beat Chattanooga 26-7. The third loss in four games took place in Birmingham when the Crimson Tide shut out the Vols, 10-0.

A triumph over rival, Tennessee Tech 49-0 brought the Vols' record to 2-3, but things got worse with losses to North Carolina and Mississippi. The Vols were now 2-5, the worst start since Neyland came to Knoxville in 1926.

"We simply were outmanned and were facing more and more teams going to the new, more wide-open T-formation," Warmath recalled.

The Volunteers managed to salvage the season when they beat Boston College 38-13, Kentucky 13-6, and Vanderbilt 12-7 to finish up with a very mediocre 5-5 record.

The 1948 season proved to be as ho-hum as 1947. In fairness, Neyland was in a rebuilding period. His efforts wouldn't begin to show until 1949 and it culminated in 1951, his next to final season as coach, when Tennessee won the national championship.

However, 1948 was a transition year as the Volunteers went 4-4-2, 2-3-1 in SEC play. They hosted Mississippi State in the season opener and lost 21-6, then tied Duke 7-7 in Durham. Three victories followed, all in Knoxville. They beat Chattanooga, 26-0, had a homecoming win over Alabama 21-6, and routed Tennessee Tech 41-0. The next week, the Vols lost to North Carolina 14-7.

The balance of the season continued up and down. Tennessee beat Georgia Tech 13-6 in Atlanta and then got edged by Mississippi 16-13 in a game played in Memphis. The final home game was a 0-0 tie with Kentucky. Vanderbilt beat them 28-6 in

Nashville to close out the season. It was the first Vandy win over the Volunteers since 1937.

Warmath reassessed his situation at Tennessee and explored the possibility of a change.

"Neyland was obviously going to be sticking with the single wing," he said. "Clearly, the T-formation was where the game was headed and if I was to realize my dream of eventually getting a head coaching position, then I needed to know the particulars of the T and I needed to learn from someone who had mastered it."

Warmath's reputation as an outstanding assistant was well known among head coaches around the country. Immediately after the 1948 season ended, Warmath got an offer from a man who both knew the T-formation and ran one of America's great collegiate football programs. Warmath weighed the offer for three weeks, then decided to leave Knoxville for West Point, N.Y. and become defensive coach with the immortal Col. Earl "Red" Blaik.

Upon hearing Warmath's decision, Neyland told Crawford, "I just lost the best line coach in America."

# Six

 Warmath arrived at West Point in early 1949 to become part of the staff of a man whose reputation as a college football coach was the equal of Neyland's.

Earl "Red" Blaik is the finest football coach ever in the history of the United States Military Academy. During the 1940s and 1950s, his Army teams routinely ranked among the best in the country. Allison Danzig in his *History of American Football* refers to Blaik as "one of sports finest characters, a gentleman of the old school, mild, soft spoken, and almost shy, teaching the modern game at its best as an organizer and strategist of the first mark."

"This quiet man had a genius for fabricating sound, modern vehicles of attack, characterized by imagination, daring, and deception, and for taking opposing attacks apart, analyzing them and devising the appropriate defenses. Former Army coach Biff Jones, characterized him as a brilliant student of the game and a splendid teacher.

"Quiet, retiring and given to few words in a crowd, Earl Blaik, a favorite of General Douglas MacArthur, is one of the wisest and also one of the hardest-working coaches. He is equalled by few in his knowledge of the game and in the amount of time he devotes to charts and diagrams in plotting his attack and defense and in devising new plays. As an organizer, he has no superior and his success is owing no little to his shrewdness and sound judgment in selecting aides," Jones added.

With the selection of Warmath, Blaik continued a tradition of naming assistants who would go on to greater fame in American football. Those who served under Blaik included Vince Lombardi, Sid Gillman, Stu Holcomb, John Sauer, Herman Hickman, Paul Dietzel, Paul Amen, John Green and Andy Gustafson.

Blaik was born in Dayton, Ohio in 1897 and went to Miami of Ohio where he lettered in football, baseball and basketball. Upon graduation, he then went to West Point. In those days, men were permitted to continue their education at a service academy and to play varsity sports. Blaik played end on the football team for two years. He received his commission in the spring of 1920 and was assigned as a cavalry officer to Fort Riley, Kan., then transferred to Fort Bliss, Texas. He resigned his commission in 1922 to return to Dayton and assist in his father's business. However, he became an assistant football coach at Wisconsin in 1926 and then in 1927, went to West Point to become an aide to Biff Jones. For seven seasons, the Cadets were among the country's finest teams amassing a 58-12-1 record. Their best season was 1933 when they were 10-0. It is interesting to note that Army didn't play Navy in either 1928 or 1929.

Besides being a highly-valuable assistant to Jones for the 1927, '28 and '29 seasons, Blaik stayed on with head coaches Ralph Sasse (1930, '31 and '32) and Gar Davidson (1933).

Blaik became Dartmouth's head coach in 1934 and in seven seasons led the Indians to a 45-14-4 record. Dartmouth was the Ivy League champion in 1936 and 1937 and ranked seventh in the country in 1937 when they were 7-0-2.

Following the 1940 season, Army beckoned and Blaik returned to the Academy and remained its head coach through the 1958 season, the longest stint in the school's history. His record was exemplary. He was 121-32-4 for a winning percentage of .790. He won two national titles (1944 and 1945), was ranked second in the country twice and third, fourth, sixth and seventh once each. Four times his squads were chosen Eastern champions. When combined with his record at Dartmouth, Blaik was an amazing .779 with 166 wins, 46 losses and 8 ties. He coached 29 first-team All-America players including three Heisman Trophy winners (Glenn Davis, Felix "Doc" Blanchard and Pete Dawkins).

He was named Coach of the Year twice.

Of all Blaik's teams, none were more famous than the 1944, 45 and 46 teams. They were led by Davis and Blanchard and had only one blemish on a 28-game schedule, a 0-0 tie in '46 against Notre Dame.

"Blaik was the consummate gentleman," Warmath said. "In all the time I was with him, I never heard him swear, never saw him drink or smoke and knew him to be a totally dedicated and loving husband and father. He was completely dedicated to his family, his players, his assistants and to West Point and college football."

When Warmath arrived in the winter of 1949, Army was coming off an 8-0-1 year having been tied in the season finale with Navy 21-21. The 1949 squad was expected to be as good as the great 1948 team.

Besides Warmath, Blaik's staff consisted of Lombardi, Sauer, Green, Amen and Doug Kenna. Very few staffs in post-World War II history were as solid. The combination of great athletes and stellar teachers would result in further accomplishments for the Academy gridiron team.

"When I arrived and got together with Blaik and the rest of the coaches, I knew I was involved with a group of some of the greats," remembered Warmath. "For starters, I was replacing Sid Gilman, who had been at West Point for just one year before leaving to take the head coaching job at the University of Cincinnati. Lombardi also was new to Blaik's staff that year."

Warmath quickly became aware of Blaik's approach to the game.

"There wasn't anyone who was better organized, better prepared and put in more time getting ready for the season or a specific game than Col. Blaik," Warmath said. "The third game of the 1949 season was scheduled against Michigan, the defending national champions. When I arrived in January, Blaik was already immersed in his game plan for the Wolverines."

Blaik's idea of a fun time was to study game films ad infinitum. Exploit another team's weakness, kill their morale and use strategic innovation was the Blaik approach.

The 1949 squad was led by All-America quarterback Arnold Galiffa; end and team captain John Trent; linebackers Don Beck and Elmer Stout; fullbacks Gil Stephenson and Karl Kuckhahn; and halfback Jimmy Cain.

The team opened by routing Davidson 47–7 with Stephenson and Dan Foldberg each scoring two touchdowns. One touchdown was the result of a blocked punt by the Cadets' Harold Loehlein, a sophomore end from Kimball, Minn.

In the second game, Army whipped Penn State 42-7 led by Galiffa's great passing and two sneaks for touchdowns.

The first two games were just warmups for the showdown in Ann Arbor.

Michigan was ranked No. 1 in the country and had a number of players back from its 1948 national championship team. It was riding a 25-game winning streak, but that ended when Army won convincingly 21-7.

"The Cadets rattled Michigan at every turn and made the seasoned Wolverines as jittery as a freshman belle at her first college prom," reported Tommy Devine of the Detroit Free Press.

In fairness, the Wolverines, lost their excellent tailback, Chuck Ortmann, early in the game and completed only three of 23 passes for 16 yards. With no passing game, the Army defense (in a 6-2-2-1 alignment) beat up on the Michigan offense. Galiffa ran an offense that mixed up the plays and kept the Wolverines back on their heels all day. Army led 14-0 at half on a first quarter touchdown by Frank Fischl and a touchdown by Cain following a Michigan fumble at its own 10.

Michigan got back in the game early in the fourth quarter when fullback Don Dufek scored on a short plunge and made the score 14-7. But Army came back after stopping another Wolverine drive. Hal Schultz returned a punt 25 yards to the Michigan 30. Kuckhahn scored a few plays later on a seven-yard run.

The next week in Boston, Army scored 54 points against Harvard, the most ever scored up until then against the Crimson. Stephenson scored four touchdowns and Cain two. Army gave up 14 points in the second half after running up a 41-0 halftime lead.

The Cadets clobbered Columbia, 63-6, VMI, 40-14 and Fordham, 35-0, all in games at West Point.

Finally an opponent tested Army.

Penn hosted the Cadets on Nov. 12 in Philadelphia. Favored by three touchdowns, the Cadets ran into an inspired Quaker team which took Army down to the wire. Penn had more first downs (23-10) completed 16 of 26 passes for 202 yards and would have won or tied that game had it not been for a Harold Loehlein block of a 20-yard field goal attempt. Army escaped with a 14-13 victory.

Army was 8-0 and returned to Philadelphia's Municipal Stadium two weeks later for the clash with Navy. It was the Golden Jubilee game between the military academies and Army did all the celebrating with a 38-0 win over the Middies. The crowd that day was 101,000 and included President Harry Truman and Great Britain's World War II military leader, Field Marshal Bernard Montgomery.

It was Navy's worst defeat by Army and capped off the eighth unbeaten season in the Cadets' history. The Army win streak reached 20 games.

As a testimony as to how tough the collegiate season was in 1949, unbeaten Army finished fourth in the AP poll behind national champion Notre Dame, Oklahoma and California.

•    •    •

Recruiting at Army always was a chore because of the stringent academic standards. Nevertheless, Army football in the Forties and Fifties still attracted a large number of outstanding young men who were excellent students and fine athletes. So, in Warmath's years at West Point, the pool of talent continued to feed the West Point program.

"We were very optimistic about the 1950 season because we returned so many fine players," Warmath said. This was despite the loss of players like Galiffa and Trent (the latter was killed in action during the Korean War).

That optimism was well-founded for the Cadets went 8-1 with the only loss being a shocking upset 14-2 upset by Navy. It was the Middies first win over West Point since 1943.

Among those leading the Cadets was Bob Blaik, son of the coach, who took over for Galiffa at quarterback. While not the most naturally gifted athlete, he was nevertheless determined and spent much of the off-season perfecting his skills and, of course, learning the game from his father. He later went into coaching and served as an assistant to Warmath in 1956 at Minnesota. The '50 team returned Stephenson, Cain, Pollack, Schultz and Fischl and had another strong defense for Warmath to coach led by Ray Malavasi, who also served as a Warmath assistant at Minnesota and in the late 1970s coached the L.A. Rams to the Super Bowl.

The Cadets opened against Colgate and Penn State and won 28–0 and 41-7. They continued with an impressive 27-6 win over Michigan in Yankee Stadium. The fourth game and fifth games were both shutouts, 49-0 over Harvard and 34-0 over Columbia. Army then went to Philadelphia and beat Penn, 28-13.

The season wrapped up against Stanford in Palo Alto and against Navy in Philadelphia. Prior to the Stanford game, Army stopped in Albuquerque and whipped New Mexico, 51-0.

It was then onto the West Coast where the Stanford game was played in terrible conditions triggered by a record 48-hour downpour. Army won, 7-0, on a Blaik-to-Foldberg pass in the third quarter. That was all the scoring and as Blaik said in his autobiography, *The Red Blaik Story,* "on such a day, seven seemed like seventy, and it was just as good."

44

In preparing for the final game against Navy, Army encountered bad weather and was forced into the fieldhouse to practice for nearly two weeks. Blaik later cited that as a major reason for the only loss of the year.

"No matter what the weather, I should have ordered some outdoor work," he wrote later. "The lack of it dulled our timing and our precision and we were a team that relied much on those qualities."

Navy was a decided underdog. Yet, the Midshipmen shut down Army completely allowing just five first downs, 77 yards on the ground and only 60 in the air. They scored their two touchdowns in the first half, then kept Army pinned down the rest of the game.

The failure to pull off another unbeaten season and the loss to Navy caused a funk among the Cadets and their followers. But that was to be nothing when compared to the setback that was to come in the summer of 1951.

# Seven

On Aug. 3, 1951, the news broke that 90 Cadets had been dismissed from the U.S. Military Academy for an infraction of the strict honor code. That code says no cadet shall cheat, steal or lie or tolerate those who do. Even the slightest infraction is cause for dismissal.

Much has been written regarding the famed "Cribbing Scandal" and the fact that 37 of the 90 cadets were members of the varsity football team. Over 40 years later, many people close to the situation then still contend that the infractions were questionable and the response by the academy was perhaps one of overreaction.

"There was a good deal of jealousy and resentment toward Blaik and the football program by members of the military and by some people in high-level administrative positions at West Point," Warmath believes. "I, for one, was very upset over the way it was handled, not just for our players but all of the kids who were cited."

Several prominent people shared Warmath's view. Blaik, in his autobiography, says he thinks the matter was poorly handled and states he was never allowed to enter his arguments into the official records. General Douglas MacArthur, a close confidant of Blaik's, officially wrote, "there was no real need for the cribbing scandal that wrecked West Point football. It could have been settled quickly, quietly and by a reprimand from the superintendent. That was all that would have been needed except in the case of perhaps two of the boys. And that could have been helped by a kick in the pants."

The infraction boiled down to this: cadets tipped off others to the subject matter of identical writs (written tests) given different sections of classes on different days. In most cases, the infraction involved only one subject. Those taking the test on the second day could benefit. The infractions didn't involve final exams, carrying illegal notes into class or exchanging information in classes. It did involve short daily quizzes or semi-monthly writs used primarily to post weekly grades.

Some of the 90 cadets dismissed did not take part in any of these activities, but had knowledge of them and didn't report them.

The divulging of the scandal and the subsequent internal investigation at West Point took place that spring and for Blaik personally, the matter struck at his heart when he was informed that his son, Bob, was involved.

The controversy lasted for weeks, months and even years.

Many military people and graduates of West Point were angry, feeling that the infractions were slight and the punishment unwarranted. Many also felt the football team was being singled out.

Shortly before the start of fall football practice, Warmath was called into the offices of the athletic board and informed that Blaik, feeling remorse and sadness over the chain of events, had resigned. The Board asked Warmath to take over as head coach.

"I felt very uneasy about that," Warmath recalls. "Obviously, I felt terrible for Coach Blaik and because I cared so much for him, did not want to see him leave the school he loved under such circumstances. I wanted to be a head coach someday, but not under those conditions.

Warmath went to Blaik and, along with arguments presented by others, including MacArthur, convinced him to stay on.

"I told him the team and the academy needed him right now more than ever and that we would regroup and make the best we could out of the 1951 season."

That would be a struggle because a team expected to have another fine year was now rocked by the loss of so many players.

As a credit to Blaik and his staff, however, the season was not as miserable as projected. They won only two of nine games, but were competitive in all but two of their losses, 28-6 to Southern Cal and a 42-7 drubbing by Navy. From the ashes of the 1951 season, Army came back in 1952 to go 4-4-1 and by 1953 was 7-1-1 and the Eastern champions. Blaik was the Touchdown Club of Washington D.C. Coach of the Year in '53. Warmath, alas, was not there for the resurgence.

Following the 1951 season, he was offered and accepted the head coaching job at Mississippi State.

"Naturally, it was a position I would take," Warmath said. "I had learned a great deal under Blaik, but I was angry as hell at the way he and the 90 cadets were treated during the cribbing scandal. I had a bit of a bad taste in my mouth regarding the academy."

Blaik regretted Warmath's leaving but never stood in the way of an assistant who had a shot at a head coaching job. As Warmath was very laudatory in his feelings toward Blaik, the opposite was equally true. In his autobiography, Blaik speaks highly of Warmath as a man and a coach. He tells about the time in March, 1951, prior to the scandal, when at a dinner at famed Mama Leone's in Manhattan, Warmath lashed out at the Commandant of Cadets at West Point, Colonel Paul Harkins, who had made derogatory remarks regarding Army players of Italian descent, saying they lacked the proper background to become officers. Blaik was moved by Warmath's outrage at such bigotry.

Years later, Harkins was the U.S. commander in South Vietnam prior to William Westmoreland.

"I knew we were in trouble over there when I discovered Harkins was running things," Warmath said.

In writing about his assistants, Blaik said of Warmath that he was "one of the best coaches I ever had on the Army staff, Murray was the defensive team coach from 1949 to 1951. Strongwilled, with fixed opinions in the mold of Bob Neyland, his Tennessee coach, Murray was a decided asset to our staff. He readily adjusted to ideas that were not in accord with his own, and thus became a coach's coach. To Murray, football was a rugged game, a fact that he instilled into the West Point defense. When he left the Point, he became head coach at Mississippi State and later for years coached at Minnesota. There, he laid the ghost of Bierman to rest, refused to be cowed, and impressed an initially hostile "M" Association with his ability. In every way Murray represented the fighting qualities of the Rebel soldier and the decency of the Southern gentleman."

# Eight

"It seems like I have just walked around the corner and came back home."

That was the opening quote in The Reflector, the student newspaper at Mississippi State in its article announcing that Murray Warmath was the new football coach. In its Jan. 8, 1952 issue, the paper gave front page coverage noting that Allyn McKeen's former top assistant was now heading the State program.

"You might mention I like to birdhunt and fish; maybe I'll get some invitations," the new coach told the publication.

McKeen's final season at Mississippi State had been in 1948. He was replaced by Slick Morton who came to MSU from VMI. Morton was 8-18-1. MSU athletic director Dudy Noble decided a change was in order, fired Morton and contacted Warmath.

"Like practically any young assistant coach, I felt I had the expertise and experience to take over a head coaching position," Warmath said. "Naturally, my long-time ties to Mississippi State were such that when the opening occurred, I jumped at the chance."

Still, Earl Blaik wanted Warmath to stay at West Point.

"I was pretty angry at the higher-ups at the academy for the way they handled the cribbing scandal," Warmath said. "I owed a great deal to Blaik who is, as I have said many times, a man to whom I was very devoted and forever grateful for the way he treated me and my family.

"I obviously was yearning for a head coaching job. The Mississippi State position was a natural."

Blaik, in his typically gracious manner, offered high praise for Warmath and extended his best wishes.

"Warmath is one of the most capable young coaches in college football today. During his three years at West Point, he contributed much to the Army squad. His success is assured at Mississippi State where we wish him well," said the Cadets' coach upon hearing that his defensive coach was leaving.

Warmath returned to Starkville amid discontent among some alumni groups. The poor performance by the football team during the three years under Morton had prompted one local alumni chapter to call for the ouster of Noble and the school president, Dr. Fred Mitchell. However, both men were backed by the majority of alums and the news media. Warmath was Noble's clear choice. So highly did he regard him that Warmath beat out two fellow Tennessee grads and head coaches—Bowden Wyatt at Wyoming, and Ralph Hatley at Memphis State.

"Blessed with thinking equipment which works constantly in overdrive, this young colossus has everything except proven ability as a commander-in-chief," wrote Walter Stewart of the Memphis Commercial Appeal. "Anyone who has watched him go about his daily labors isn't likely to doubt his ability."

The 39-year-old Warmath immediately went to work. His first step was to organize a coaching staff. He mixed a blend of old, trusted comrades, rising young football minds and a couple of holdovers from Morton's staff.

He lured two former players who were serving as assistants elsewhere. Billy Murphy, who had played for Warmath for three seasons at Mississippi State before the war, was an assistant for Hatley. Warmath hired him to coach the Bulldogs' backs. Denver Crawford was at Maryland with Jim Tatum and came to Starkville to be the line coach. Two Morton assistants, Jim Pittman and Bill Hildebrand, were assigned to be the freshmen coaches with Pittman helping the varsity receiver coach. Charley Shira, who had been involved in the cribbing scandal at West Point and was not eligible to play at State, was hired as an assistant to Crawford to help coach the line.

Shira later would become the Bulldogs' head coach from 1967 through 1972.

Warmath had been well-schooled in the T formation by Blaik. However, he was intrigued by the newly-created Split-T which was originated by Missouri's Don Faurot in the late 1940's and perfected by Bud Wilkinson at Oklahoma and Tatum at Maryland. The Split-T took the basic T formation, widened the spaces between the offensive linemen and incorporated a sliding (rather than spinning) quarterback with running pitchouts, sprint out passes and downfield laterals. It was more deceptive than the straight T, required average personnel, statistically got more yards per play and put more pressure on conventional defenses. It didn't require a great passing quarterback to operate it.

To teach the Split T, Warmath hired Darrell Royal, who had learned the system under Wilkinson as a player and assistant coach. Royal would go onto be one of the great college coaches during a 20-year reign at Texas from the late 1950s to the mid-1970s.

"What we really needed was a quarterback to run the system," Warmath said. "We were very fortunate to find Jackie Parker."

Two of Warmath's new assistants, Murphy and Pittman, spotted Parker who was, ironically, a native of Knoxville and not recruited by Tennessee. Instead, he spent his first two collegiate years as a quarterback at Jones County Junior College in Ellisville, Miss.

"Parker was somewhat of a wild kid," Warmath said. "He was an avid poker player and a late nighter. He also was married and had a car and I was personally against players being married and wanted them to have access to cars only on weekends."

Murphy remembers Warmath's hesitancy about bringing Parker to Starkville because he was married and had wheels.

52

"I kept telling him for a couple of weeks there was this kid down at a local junior college who was our answer at quarterback," Murphy recalls. "But, when Murray made up his mind about something, it wasn't always easy to get him to change it.

"Finally, one day in spring practice when it was obvious that our quarterback problem wasn't getting resolved, he ambled over to me and asked quietly out of the corner of his mouth, 'where did you say that Parker kid is in junior college?' "

Later that week, Murphy and Pittman drove to Jones County Junior College and brought Parker back to Starkville. It turned out to be a great reversal on Warmath's part.

"We spent one week that winter in the fieldhouse at MSU working with him on the fundamentals of the Split-T," Murphy remembers. "At first it was a struggle, but the coaching staff hung with Parker and later when he had a big preseason scrimmage in which he had a hand in seven touchdowns, we knew we had the right guy."

Warmath decided Parker was too talented a player, wife or no wife, not to use but did make the blonde-haired quarterback relinquish his car keys.

Another major task for Warmath and his staff was determining who wanted to play football for the Bulldogs. Warmath was adamant that people who played for him had to love the game and to love the game, you had to be able to dish out, as well as take hitting.

"From the first day of spring practice, Murray and the rest of the coaching staff put the players through tough, nose-to-nose drills," Denver Crawford said. "Murray and the assistants would get down in their stances and take those kids on. We wanted to see who had fight in 'em and who didn't.

"Murray was as tough as they came and he'd mix it up with kids 20 years younger and 20 pounds heavier than he was. He didn't give an inch even though the next day he could hardly raise either arm to get a phone receiver up to his mouth."

At the end of spring practice, those who didn't want to play the Warmath brand of football were either gone or riding the pine.

There was some returning talent. Fullback Joe Fortunato, halfback Zerk Wilson and center Bo Reid were among a fine group of players inherited by Warmath.

Fortunato, who would gain his greatest fame later as a superb Chicago Bears linebacker in the 1950s and 1960s, played fullback and linebacker for Warmath.

"I originally had been at Virginia Military Institute as a freshman in 1948 where Slick Morton was the coach," Fortunato recounted. "Morton took the Mississippi State job and talked me into coming along. I was from Ohio and at first, MSU didn't appeal to me, but I finally went."

Fortunato, who would marry a Natchez, Miss. coed and eventually settle in that historic Delta city where today he is in the oil and real estate business, recalled that Warmath was the tonic in Starkville needed to get back to the winning ways of the McKeen era.

"Coach Warmath quickly gave the football program both stability and credibility," Fortunato said. "He was a tremendous motivator who prepared us to win."

Fortunato would play only one year for Warmath, but was a major factor in a winning season in 1952. Warmath later called him "the big Daddy you need to win."

"Thanks to Warmath and his staff, I was well prepared to successfully pursue a career in pro football," Fortunato added. "Murray had a sharp mind, a necessity given the talent we had."

The enthusiasm for Warmath's arrival carried over to more than just the players as the 1952 season neared. Bob Hartley, who served nearly 35 years as the sports information director at Mississippi State, recalled his delight when the word arrived in Starkville about the new coach.

"Murray had a reputation throughout the American collegiate football scene as one of the country's best assistants,"

Hartley said. "He was well thought of in Starkville because of his four years with McKeen. He was a solid, fundamental coach who commanded respect from everyone and still is to this day a wonderful person."

# Nine

The 1952 season saw State open against none other than Bob Neyland and his defending national champions from Tennessee.

"Naturally, I was excited to take on my alma mater and my old coach," Warmath recalled. "Tennessee had graduated a sizeable number of its national championship players and I believed we had a good chance to win. Neyland also had announced it would be his final season as head coach.

"It would be my only chance to beat him."

The Bulldogs came close.

The game was played at Crump Stadium in Memphis. Tennessee and State played the kind of traditionally tough defensive game one would expect from Neyland and Warmath-coached teams. The Vols held onto a 7-0 halftime lead. But early in the third quarter, State's Harold Eastwood recovered a Tennessee fumble in Volunteer territory and a few plays later, Zerk Wilson took a Jackie Parker pitch out and scored. Parker's extra point tied the game.

The game was a battle of the fullbacks—State's Fortunato and Tennessee's Andy Kozar. Both had some nice runs, but it was Kozar who got the final moment of glory when he scored on a short plunge with three minutes left in the game.

Neyland & Company held on to win 14-7.

Neyland was so impressed by Fortunato at both fullback and linebacker, that he came across to the MSU side of the field after the game to congratulate him.

While Warmath, who always hated to lose, was off to an 0-1 start, his opportunity for victories came quickly and in succession.

The following week, the Bulldogs easily handled Arkansas State 41-14. Parker's 29 points (four touchdowns and five extra points) made a statement. It was a harbinger of things to come.

State scored on its first two possessions as Parker and Fortunato both scored on four yard runs. Parker's passing was erratic that day in Starkville, one of his throws being picked off and returned for a touchdown.

The following week, the Bulldogs hosted North Texas State and won 14-0 with Fortunato scoring twice.

It was Mississippi State's homecoming the next weekend. Paul "Bear" Bryant was bringing in his Kentucky Wildcats. Bryant already had established a reputation as an up-and-coming young college coach, first at Maryland, then in Lexington.

"We were ready for 'em," Warmath remembered. "We had a good week of practice and went into the game well-prepared."

Parker played a near-perfect game, After a scoreless first quarter, the blond State quarterback got things rolling when he sidestepped a severe Wildcat rush and uncorked a 39-yard touchdown pass to Wilson. The score came following a Kentucky fumble by fullback Joe Paolone which was recovered by State end John Santillo. Runs by Wilson and Fortunato worked the ball down to the UK 39 where Parker connected with Wilson.

Kentucky handed the Bulldogs another opportunity when Wallace Mitchell fumbled the kickoff at the 28 and Dennis Fulton recovered. Three plays later, Parker threw a second TD pass to Wilson which first bounced out of the arms of teammate Norm Duplain.

Kentucky came back and cut the lead to 14-7. Parker and State quickly countered with Fortunato and Wilson making good runs to take the ball to the Wildcat one where Parker scored to make the lead 21-7.

Parker's passing again proved a major factor as the second half started. A 16-yard throw to John McKee set up a two-yard

Parker run for the fourth Bulldog touchdown and MSU went on to a 27-14 victory.

Warmath's record was now a respectable 3-1.

•   •   •

State's lack of depth came back to haunt them in the fifth game against Alabama in Tuscaloosa. 'Bama's two star halfbacks, Bobby Marlow and Corky Tharp, led the way for a 42-19 Crimson Tide victory by scoring five touchdowns between them. Jackie Parker scored three touchdown for the Bulldogs. However, Parker was hurt during his final touchdown run in the third quarter and State, trailing 28-19 at that point, never got its offense moving again.

The final score didn't reflect how close the game was. As long as Parker and Fortunato were playing, the Bulldogs made a fight of it. State took a 7-0 lead in the first quarter, but Alabama came back and scored three times before the half. Parker scored the second of his eventual three touchdowns to narrow the gap to eight points at the start of the second half. The Tide scored right after that, but Parker answered with his third TD.

Parker's injury, however, broke the back of the Mississippi State offense and other than two Alabama touchdowns in the fourth quarter to put the game out of reach, the only other highlight was a brawl which erupted with 12 seconds left in the game. It took place right in front of Warmath and the Bulldogs' bench.

"Ralph Carrigan, an Alabama linebacker, got mad at one of our tackles, Joe Cimini, over something and kicked him while he was on the ground," Warmath said. "Within seconds, about a dozen players in all were going at it and our staff and the officials had to break it up."

The Bulldogs played Auburn the following week and the Tigers were the clear favorite. However, the outcome was far different than anyone really expected. The game propelled Parker into the national limelight.

"Jackie Parker of Mississippi State gave one of college football's greatest performances Saturday to lead his club to a wild 49-34 victory over Auburn," reported the Associated Press.

Parker scored three touchdowns on runs and passed for three others. He had scored 90 points in six games and was just eight points shy of the Southeastern Conference record set by LSU great Steve Van Buren in 1943. And there still were three games to play.

The Bulldogs put the Tigers away fairly easily. Parker's play gave the "Dogs" a 14-7 lead through the first 20 minutes. Then the scoring floodgates opened with Mississippi State adding 21 points before the half, the highlight being a 26-yard touchdown pass from Parker to Joe McKee. Auburn scored once before halftime, but State countered with 14 points in the third quarter to make the lead 49-14. Auburn scored three fourth quarter touchdowns after the game was out of reach.

The following Saturday State suffered a natural letdown after the big win over Auburn. Their record fell to 5-3 as they got outplayed in the second half by Tulane and lost 34-21 in New Orleans.

"I was concerned going into the game that we might not play as well as we could, although Tulane was a good team," Warmath said. "We played only 30 minutes of good football."

State led 14-13 at the half on TDs by Wilson and Parker in the second quarter. The Green Wave was tough in the third and fourth quarters and they scored 21 points and allowed MSU one lone score in the fourth quarter.

Hard hitting on the field and unruly fans were the hallmarks of the game the following Saturday. LSU was in a down cycle when the Bulldogs came into Baton Rouge that Saturday night.

LSU gave the visitors all they could handle in the first half, leading 14-7 at intermission.

Billy Murphy and fellow assistant, Darrell Royal, were in the stands serving as spotters for Warmath.

"Then, as now, Baton Rouge was a wild place during a Saturday football game," Murphy said. "Visiting coaches didn't sit in the press box when they were spotting, but instead in a special section in the stands with two seats, a table and phone lines.

"The area was surrounded by railings. But some LSU fans who were pretty heavy into the booze that night got into a fist fight with some other fans and the next thing you know the fight spills over into the area where I'm sitting with Royal. I'm on the headset talking to Murray. Suddenly, a couple of people are falling on top of me. I handed the headset to Royal and said, 'Darrell, it's for you' and started throwing these people out of our way."

Like their coaches in the stands, the Mississippi State players decided to take control and in the second half scored 26 points and shutout the Tigers the rest of the way to win 33-14. Parker reached the 106 point mark and had the pleasure of setting the new SEC record in Steve Van Buren's backyard. He did it by scoring one TD and kicking three extra points. He also threw one touchdown pass.

The 1952 season closed with the traditional battle against intra-state rival Mississippi in Oxford. Parker scored all of State's 14 points in a game marked by rain, snow and sleet. It wasn't enough, however, as the Rebels won 20-14.

Warmath's first season ended with a respectable 5-4 record. Parker and Fortunato were named to the All-SEC team and Parker was the Conference MVP.

• • •

The 1953 season required Warmath and his staff to make adjustments. Several key players—Fortunato, Reid, DeLoe and Cimini—had graduated.

However, Warmath and the assistant coaches (now minus Royal who left to go to Edmonton in the Canadian Football

League), pieced together another respectable squad in the spring and refined them in the fall.

The Bulldogs, who would play an expanded 10 game season, opened against Memphis State and easily won 34-6. Parker picked up where he left off the year before by going seven for seven in passing including three for touchdowns as MSU rolled up 344 total offensive yards to Memphis State's 164.

It was a good tune up for the following Saturday, a game that was important to Warmath and Parker.

The Tennessee Volunteers were no longer a Bob Neyland-coached team. The famed general had stepped down from the position he had held off and on since 1926 to become the full-time athletic director.

He named Harvey Robinson as his replacement. Robinson was a former Tennessee teammate and assistant coach in Knoxville with Warmath.

"Clearly, the Tennessee game was one I wanted to win and win badly," Warmath said. "So did Jackie Parker because Knoxville was his home town and Tennessee hadn't recruited him."

The Vols were coming off an 8-2-1 season and the Mississippi State game was their opener. Warmath and the Bulldogs were ready.

"I told the team in the locker room before the kickoff that I didn't want to have to go through the courtesy of extending a congratulatory handshake to Coach Robinson after the game because they beat us," Warmath said. "I looked at Jackie and said Knoxville was sorta' home for both of us and I was sure he felt the same way. Parker jumped to his feet and called out, 'coach, I guarantee you and the team that you won't have to shake his hand.' That got everybody pretty fired up."

The game was no contest. MSU won 26-0.

Parker, behind a line that outmanned Tennessee's front, scored two touchdowns and passed for a third. The mood of the game was set midway through the first quarter when State's Hal

Easterwood blocked a punt by Volunteer Pat Shire on the UT 33. Given Tennessee's reverence for the kicking game, one can imagine the humiliation the Vols must have felt following that play.

Seven plays later, Parker scored on a keeper from seven yards out. A few minutes later, Parker hit Zerk Wilson on a 56-yard pass, Wilson sprinting the final 30 yards to score.

The Bulldogs continued to shut down the Vols and in the final quarter added another 13 points on a two-yard sneak by Parker and a short plunge by sophomore back Lou Vernier.

The final score was Mississippi State 26, Tennessee 0 and it was the most satisfying victory to date for Warmath.

"When the game ended, I started to take a few steps toward the middle of the field to shake Robinson's hand, but Parker and some of the other kids stopped me," Warmath said. " 'Make him come to you, coach. Make him come over here' they were saying. They held me back and Harvey came to our bench to offer his congratulations."

Later in the visitors' locker room, Warmath was hanging back as the team boarded the bus to leave the stadium. One of the equipment managers was packing the team's items when Neyland walked in.

"He was a bit unhappy," Warmath remembered. "First, we had whipped 'em pretty good and Robinson had to come over and shake my hand. Neyland said he didn't like that. I tried to explain what happened, but he didn't seem to be all that satisfied with the answer."

The meeting was brief and Neyland left quickly.

Warmath took his team back to Starkville to host North Texas State the next week. Parker scored two touchdowns, kicked two conversions and directed his team to its third touchdown (scored by Wilson) and a 21-6 victory.

Mississippi State was off to its best start in the post-World War II era and prepared to welcome Auburn with visions of going 4-0. It almost happened.

The Tigers came to Mississippi State in the second year of Ralph "Shug" Jordan's long and successful reign at the Alabama school. The way the MSU-Auburn game started, it looked as if a repeat of the '52 State victory was in the making.

As usual, Parker got things rolling, deftly running the Split-T with George Suda and Wilson scoring the first two MSU touchdowns which gave the Bulldogs a 14-0 intermission lead. Parker scored in the third quarter and it looked as if the game was on ice. But a reserve Auburn back, Bob Duke, took the ensuing kickoff and returned it 100 yards for the first Tiger score.

Victory still seemed fairly certain late in the fourth quarter. Auburn held State and Parker was back to punt. However, George Aitkins broke through for Auburn and blocked the punt at the 30. The ball bounced back to the six where Tiger defensive end Jim Pyburn grabbed it and went into the end zone. The conversion was good and suddenly it was only a 21-14 for the Bulldogs.

Again, Mississippi State couldn't move the ball. Jordan earlier had put in second-string quarterback Bobby Freeman, who now engineered a closing drive and took the ball in on the last play of the game. The conversion was good and a certain State victory evaporated into a 21-all tie.

"It was a terrible disappointment and it seemed to set the tone for the rest of the season," Warmath recalled.

"Some of our students were so upset, I sadly recall they vandalized cars belonging to Auburn fans," said Bob Hartley, the MSU sports information director at the time.

Seemingly demoralized after letting a certain victory slip through their fingers, the Bulldogs went without a victory in their next three games. Bear Bryant's Kentucky Wildcats easily won 32-13 in Lexington the next week by taking an insurmountable 26-0 lead at halftime.

Alabama, led by Bart Starr, earned the Crimson Tide a 7-7 tie.

In the second quarter, State started from its own 24 and in 16 plays, Parker marched MSU in for its lone touchdown which he scored from the two, He added the extra point. Starr led the Tide to its touchdown right after the second half kickoff. He threw three passes for 44 yards in the scoring drive. Corky Tharp, Alabama's leading rusher, scored on a two-yard run. The kick was good and although that would be all the scoring, Alabama tried a 34-yard field goal on the last play of the game which was low and wide.

The next week's game against Texas Tech was in "neutral" Jackson, Miss. and it turned into a long afternoon, especially for Parker. Tech had superior line play and some fine offensive work as they won 27-20. The score was not indicative of the lop-sidedness of the game. Tech took a 20-7 lead at the half, the Bulldog's only score being a fourth down, six-yard pass from Parker to Davis.

In the second half, Tech scored its last touchdown in the fourth quarter. Bobby Collins was put in for Parker who was harassed and battered all day by the Red Raiders' defenders. Collins hit Bucket Joseph for a touchdown that trimmed the score to 27-13. Parker returned late in the game and Joseph grabbed a 26-yard scoring throw, but the visitors held and won 27-20.

State, which started out in such fine fashion, was 3-2-2 with three games left.

"We needed some wins badly to salvage the season," Warmath recalled.

He got pretty close to what he wanted in the three remaining contests.

Parker got back in the groove the next week against Tulane when he led the 'Dogs to a 21-0 win over Tulane. Dinky Evans got the first State score on a 37-yard touchdown run in the first quarter. Later in the half, Don Morris' run, also of 37 yards, set up an eventual eight-yard sprint out TD run by Parker. In the second half, Parker hit John Katusa with a two-yard throw and a touchdown.

It was back to Baton Rouge for the second year in a row. Parker's season, while still outstanding, was not up to the level of his great 1952 performance. At LSU, where he set the SEC season scoring record that year, he suffered a big setback.

LSU was still not on par with the Bulldogs, yet at halftime the score was tied at 13-13. Parker scored the game's first touchdown on a short run, but missed the conversion. LSU came back to tie it, then Parker retaliated with a spectacular pass to Arthur Davis for 32 yards. Two plays later, Parker got whacked hard and fractured his left cheekbone. He stayed in long enough to hand off to fullback George Suda who blasted up the middle for an eight-yard scoring run. Parker, however, was too woozy to continue and Warmath replaced him with Collins.

Collins picked up the slack scoring both the fourth touchdown for MSU and sealing the victory by sneaking in for a touchdown from inside the Tiger one yard line. The final was 26-13.

The season finale in Starkville was against Mississippi. The Bulldogs had a shot at their sixth victory, the Rebels a shot at the SEC title. Neither team achieved their goal as the game ended in a 7-7 tie. Parker finished his career by hitting 9 of 9 passes, one for a touchdown to Davis.

Parker had the advantage of a two week layoff as State had a bye the week before. Still, he was expected to make only a token appearance in his final collegiate game due to his busted cheekbone. Mississippi hurt its chances with fumbles, two of which occurred inside the State five-yard line. It was a State fumble in the second quarter which led to the Rebels' lone touchdown, a short plunge by Earl Blair.

Mississippi State closed the season with a 5-2-3 record. Parker was named to both the Look Magazine and Associated Press first All-America teams as well as All-SEC and was named the Conference M.V.P. for the second year in a row. Center Hal Easterwood was also named All-SEC.

Parker was, in Warmath's words, "one of the great players of the post World War II era and it was his leadership and performance that was critical to whatever success we had. I was honored to coach him."

The 1953 season was over and State fans said good-bye to Parker who went on to play many years in the Canadian Football League. What they didn't know at the time was they were about to say good-bye to their head coach.

# Ten

 While serving as an assistant at Army, Warmath was asked to apply for the head coaching position at the University of Minnesota. It was the winter of 1951.

"I flew to Minneapolis and as the plane taxied to the terminal, the first thing I noticed were that the snow drifts and piles as high as the wing tips," he said. "When I stepped off the plane, it was as cold as anything I had ever experienced. Now as a Southerner, I was not one to take a quick likin' to the cold. I had experienced some cold weather at West Point and in Knoxville where the winters can be damp and chilly. But Minneapolis—well, that was damn cold to me."

Warmath also found out that Minnesota was offering a limited number of full-ride athletic scholarships which were quickly becoming the norm throughout most colleges.

"I thanked them for asking me in, but between the cold weather and what I perceived to be less than a full commitment to a big time program, I declined," he said.

Three years later, he again was asked to take the job.

Golden Gopher football had slipped somewhat by then.

The pre-World War II glory years were vivid in the minds of Minnesotans. Five outright or shared national championships and six outright or shared Big Ten titles had the school's faithful expecting more of the same once the war was over. The war's end and the return of the legendary Bernie Bierman as coach for the 1945 season had most fans believing future U of M football would pick up where it had left off.

It never quite happened.

Bierman had taken the Gophers to the pinnacle when the game called for powerful, strong, raw-boned, homegrown players to run his single-wing and run over opponents. His ability to teach fundamentals and to get his players to perform to perfection was unparalleled from the early 1930s through the 1941 season.

Like Neyland, he knew single-wing football inside and out and relied on the kicking game to keep his opponents bottled up deep in their end of the field. He was one of the greatest college football coaches and one of the major reasons the University of Minnesota gained national stature.

There were some significant changes taking place in college football when Bierman returned to the Twin Cities.

He continued to operate as he had before. First, was his reliance on the single-wing. As Warmath had noted when he decided to leave as a Neyland assistant and to go with Blaik at Army, the T-formation and its various derivatives, were clearly where offensive football was headed. To successfully run that new formation, a new type of player was needed—not necessarily the type in the traditional Minnesota mold.

Second, was Bierman's open displeasure with the advent of full athletic scholarships used to recruit players. To Bierman, any high school kid from Minnesota (and a few from surrounding states) would kill for a chance to play Golden Gopher football. From 1945 to 1950, he was able to field teams comprised of local kids who felt that way and he didn't have to entice them with scholarships. Certainly, there were some forms of financial help for Minnesota players dating back to the early Twenties. Bierman, however, was not about to get caught up in having "professionals" play football for him. He fought the new trend and by the end of the 1950 season, Bierman decided to step down.

In the six seasons from 1945 through 1950, Bierman had only two teams, the '48 and '49 squads, which even approached the halcyon days before the war. Both teams, particularly the one in 1949, seemed destined to go to the Rose Bowl. But the '49 squad suffered two devastating mid-season losses to Michigan and Purdue and didn't go to Pasadena. The 1950 team, hard hit by graduation losses that took the likes of Leo Nomellini, Clayt Tonnemaker, Billy Bye and Bud Grant, won only one game.

Despite finishing on a sour note, Bierman still was so popular that many thought he would become the athletic director and recommend his former All-American guard, Bud Wilkinson, to be the new Gopher coach. Wilkinson had forged a name for himself in the late Forties when he made Oklahoma a gridiron powerhouse. In the minds of the fans and the media, the tandem of Bierman and Wilkinson was a foregone conclusion.

Enter James Morrill, the University of Minnesota president. Morrill, who was named president at Minnesota in July of 1945, was not keen on big time intercollegiate athletics. He wanted to de-emphasize athletics and, to his way of thinking, Bernie Bierman and Bud Wilkinson were not the way to do it. Instead, he named Ike Armstrong the new athletic director. Armstrong, who was an accomplished football coach at Utah in the Thirties and Forties, selected Wes Fesler to replace Bierman.

Fesler came to Minnesota after coaching at Ohio State. He had wanted to retire from coaching, but Armstrong talked him into taking the Minnesota job in 1951. Thanks to Paul Giel, who served as his magnificent tailback in the primarily single wing offense, Fesler's teams were competitive, at least in 1952 and 1953. But Fesler's heart was not into coaching and he tendered his resignation after the '53 season.

Armstrong, who had first interviewed Warmath in 1951, again turned to the Tennessee native. At the NCAA meetings in January of 1954, Armstrong talked to Wilkinson, former Gopher assistant John Roning, who was then head coach at Utah, and Kansas State coach Bill Meek. But, he really wanted Warmath.

"I later flew to Chicago to meet Armstrong and Dr. Morrill who wanted to keep the media away from the interview process," Warmath recalled. "Minnesota had changed the situation enough to the point where I now was very interested. Dr. Morrill was up front with me in terms that he felt all intercollegiate sports should be relegated to the intramural level, but he wasn't going to push his personal views on me, the athletic department or the school.

"While I would encounter resistance by the administration to some things I wanted during my 18 years at Minnesota, I did respect Dr. Morrill. We disagreed about the role of football and sports at the college level. However, he was honest and straight with me and we generally got along fine."

In 1954, the Big Ten was regarded by many as the premier conference and Minnesota, despite the so-so years after the war, was a school with an excellent reputation.

"Mississippi State was a good situation for me and my family as well as my assistant coaches," Warmath pointed out. "I had many wonderful years there with some great people. However, the chance to coach at a school like Minnesota was a tremendous opportunity."

That being the case, the announcement was made that Murray Warmath was the new head football coach at the University of Minnesota.

The Mississippi State reaction was one of shock.

"A stunning surprise" was how the student paper, The Reflector, reported it. Dudy Noble was sad, adding that "we wanted Coach Warmath to stay with us for many, many years."

"I was personally devastated," recalled Bob Hartley. "I felt that with Murray at the helm, we could continually improve."

Billy Murphy remembered Warmath breaking the news to him.

"Rumors were circulating for days. I personally wanted to make a change in my career and asked Murray to give me a referral to Army and a position with Red Blaik. Then, one morning in January, he asked me to hop into the jeep he used for hunting and fishing and we drove to a lake outside of Starkville. He broke the news to me about Minnesota and asked me to come with him."

70

Murphy, along with Denver Crawford, Jim Camp and Bill Hildebrand decided to make the move to Minneapolis. Mississippi State hired Darrell Royal to replace Warmath. His stay was as brief as Warmath's (two seasons). Royal left in 1956 to take the job at the University of Washington and later he went to Texas where he attained his greatest fame.

By the middle of February, the new Minnesota coaching staff was in place and Warmath looked ahead to the first year in an 18-year reign.

# Eleven

When the 1954 spring football practice sessions began, Warmath and his staff took a close look at what they had inherited and realized they had their work cut out for them.

"We knew that Minnesota didn't have the number of quality players we would have liked, " Murphy remembered. "Yet, they were a good group who wanted to win."

Murphy, as backfield coach, also knew the Split-T was going to present problems because the returning players, under Fesler, had operated out of the single-wing with a bit of the straight T thrown in.

"I was delighted when we found a kid who could run the Split-T from the quarterback's position," Murphy said.

That kid turned out to be Geno Cappelletti who was Fesler's quarterback.

Murphy fondly remembers the delight the coaching staff experienced when they also discovered the all-around talents of Bob McNamara, a halfback who would go on to earn All-America honors in the fall of 1954.

"McNamara was in a class of elite three or four ballplayers I have been associated with in my years as a coach," Murphy declared. "He had played end and wingback in the single-wing and defensive safety prior to our arrival."

The spring of 1954 was devoted to instilling the new Split-T and impressing upon the squad the Warmath philosophy of football.

"When practice was over, I was fairly confident we had some kids who wanted to play and understood our expectations of them," Warmath said.

Minnesota opened the 1954 season by hosting Nebraska at Memorial Stadium in Minneapolis on Sept. 25th. It was sunny and warm that day and both Warmath and Nebraska coach Bill Glassford used two full teams to combat fatigue. A crowd of more than 55,000 was on hand to see the first of Warmath's 172 games as Gopher coach over the next 18 seasons. Warmath's 10-year-old daughter, Carol, had a goodluck card and a rabbit's foot delivered to her father before the game.

The Gophers took the field for the start of the Warmath era in new uniforms.

The teams struggled throughout most of the game as they both committed errors and had several penalties. The Gophers scored midway through the first quarter when Cappelletti took it in on a short run following the recovery of a Nebraska fumble. The Gopher's missed the extra point and the 6-0 lead held up until late in the first half. In the second quarter, Minnesota had other scoring chances, but fumbles by Cappelletti and halfback Dale Quist nixed Gopher drives. The 'Huskers came back and took a 7-6 lead on Ron Clark's 48-yard TD run and successful conversion.

In the second half, the failure to convert a fourth down play deep in Gopher territory stymied Nebraska. Minnesota scored on a Bob McNamara run and made the extra point kick. Six and nine- man defensive fronts and excellent punt returns by Shorty Cochran and Richard "Pinky" McNamara sparked the Gophers in the fourth quarter. Pinky's one-yard plunge added six more points for a 19-6 lead.

The line play by center Chuck Stamschor, tackles Gordie Holz and Bob Hobert and ends Jim Soltau and Ron Smith were singled out by Warmath.

"Both teams hurt themselves, but we got some good punt returns and played strong pass defense," Warmath said in first post-game comments as a Gopher coach.

"Minnesota is very talented and their defensive alignment, especially in pass situations, confused us," said Glassford.

The Gopher staff and players were happy with the season opener. They were even happier a week later after traveling to Pittsburgh and soundly beating the Panthers, 46-7.

Again, the day was hot (mid-80s) and humid and the Gopher conditioning, always a trademark of a Warmath team, wore down Pitt. A third quarter scoring burst of three touchdowns was the capper. Yet, Minnesota dominated from the opening kickoff even though it took a while to get going.

Cappelletti hit "Pinky" McNamara on a 24-yard scoring toss following a fumble by Pitt's Henry Ford. Minnesota came back and marched 83 yards with Cappelletti finding Frank Bachman on a three-yard touchdown throw. Pitt countered with Ford scoring before halftime on a four-yard run.

In the third quarter, Minnesota put the Panthers away as Bob McNamara returned a punt 65 yards for a touchdown. Cappelletti came back with a 13-yard TD run and "Pinky" went six yards for the fifth touchdown of the day for Minnesota. The fourth quarter saw Minnesota widen the gap further when Cochran ran 16 yards for one score and reserve quarterback Don Swanson hit end Tom Juhl on a 27-yard touchdown play.

"Our kicking game kept Pitt deep in its territory," Warmath said afterwards. "We used the running pass play, which is my favorite way to score a touchdown."

Minnesota averaged more than five yards a play and kept Pittsburgh to less than two yards. Pitt's Ford called the problem, "too many McNamara's. Last year we had to only worry about Paul Giel."

Pitt coach Red Dawson was so upset by his team's performance that he left the locker room before the media showed up.

Another 55,000 were on hand the following Saturday when a good Northwestern team came to Minneapolis. The Wildcats scored first on a short run by back Jim Troglio. Minnesota came back with two TDs in the second quarter and two in the third quarter. Bob McNamara had another great day scoring twice while rushing for 120 yards on 12 runs. Fullbacks John Baumgartner and Frank Bachman had 84 and 53 yards respectively with Bachman getting a TD. Reserve halfback Ralph Goode scored the other touchdown in the 26-7 victory.

Warmath utilized his second team led by Dale Quist to wear down the Wildcats and Holz and guards Mike Falls and Bob Hagemeister were dominate in the line.

The great J.C. Caroline, Illinois' All-American halfback, came to Minneapolis the next week and 63,000 filled Memorial Stadium for what the Minneapolis Tribune's reporter Dick Cullum called "a magnificently played contest which was every bit as close as the final score and might have been closer." He referred to the fourth Gopher victory, 19-7 over the Illini.

Illinois arrived with a 0-3 record having lost to Penn State, Stanford and Ohio State. Still, it had a great offense led by Caroline, an explosive runner, and fellow backs Abe Woodson and Mickey Bates. But Gopher ball control was the story and Minnesota built a 19-0 lead. Illinois helped by fumbling. Woodson turned over the ball on the Minnesota 33 in the first quarter. Hobert recovered and a few minutes later Bob McNamara scored on a two-yard plunge.

In the second quarter, Ken Yackel intercepted a pass by Bob Gongola (later a Warmath assistant) and along with Quist and Cochran from the second unit, drove to the Illini one where Cochran took it over the goal line.

In the third quarter, Gary Francis of Illinois returned the opening kickoff to the Minnesota 48, but a few plays later another fumble killed the drive. Cappelletti hit Bob McNamara on a 35-yard pass to set up a Baumgartner 10-yard scoring run. Caroline, who had a fine day, scored in the fourth quarter on a one yard plunge for the only other tally of the game.

"I thought we looked sharp," Warmath said afterward. "I'm pleased because Illinois had the fastest group of backs I've ever seen."

"Minnesota was just what you'd expect from a Warmath team," commented Jack Chamblin, the Illinois center. Chamblin had spent the spring of 1951 at Army before transferring and had been there for practices when Warmath was Blaik's assistant. "Minnesota hits hard and is well-drilled in the fundamentals. He's a great defensive coach and Warmath will make Minnesota tough for the rest of the Big Ten."

Warmath was off to a 4-0 start, the media was laudatory, the alumni happy and the country was taking notice. At Ann Arbor the bubble burst.

•     •     •

"OUCH! Michigan 34, Minnesota 0.

That was the headline in the Minneapolis Sunday Tribune's sports section the morning after the Michigan game.

"Minnesota was outclassed in every phase of the game," wrote the Tribune's Charles Johnson. "Our team was outcharged, outblocked and outfought," Warmath said after the rout. Leo Johnson, scouting the game for Illinois which was to play Michigan the next week, commented that the Wolverines "could have beaten any team in the country today."

Michigan came into the game with a 3-1 record having lost to Army and beaten Washington, Iowa and Northwestern. They were led by their great end, Ron Kramer, who scored one of the two first-half touchdowns against Minnesota. Bennie Oosterbaan's team had scoring drives of 80, 66, 63 and 37 yards and allowed the Gophers to penetrate only to their 25 and that was on the last play of the game.

"We simply were never in the game," Warmath lamented.

Bob McNamara said the Gophers lacked desire and fire and senior tackle Chuck Kubes recounted that the game was "decided in the first minutes of play."

76

The Little Brown Jug, which had been in Minneapolis for a year thanks to Paul Giel's great performance in the 1953 upset of Michigan by 22-0, now made its way back to the Wolverine trophy case and the Gophers staggered back to Minneapolis to get ready for Michigan State, the 1953 conference champions.

It was homecoming at Minnesota and 63,575 were in attendance as the Spartans came to town. Duffy Daugherty's young team had a 1-4 record. The efforts of Cappelletti and Bob McNamara were to add to the Spartan loss column.

State scored early as Earl Morrall engineered a drive capped off by John Matsock's 22-yard TD run. But Minnesota came back as Bob McNamara scored on a two-yard run to put the Gophers ahead 7-6 at halftime.

Two big defensive plays in the third quarter allowed Minnesota to pull away. A partially-blocked Morrall punt gave Minnesota the ball on the State 42 and in 13 plays, the Gophers scored on a one-yard sneak by Cappelletti. A few minutes later, Bob Wilson, the Spartans' reserve quarterback, was hit as he rolled out to his left and the ball popped loose. As he fell back, he inadvertently kicked the ball in the air and it came down in the hands of Bob McNamara who went 40 yards for his second touchdown and a 19-6 Gopher lead. State scored late in the game and the final was Minnesota 19, Michigan State 13.

"McNamara was the best player on the field," said Gopher assistant Murphy.

Warmath made special mention of both McNamaras and guard Mike Falls for playing both ways for nearly 60 minutes, and end Jim Soltau for his defensive efforts.

The next opponent, Oregon State, drew a reduced crowd of 49,000 to Memorial Stadium. Bob McNamara had what Johnson wrote was "the greatest day of his career so far." McNamara netted 161 of the Gophers' 492 offensive yards on just 14 carries. He played fullback as well as halfback and scored two touchdowns.

The other Minnesota offensive weapon was Cochran who scored all three of Minnesota's first-quarter touchdowns. Cappelletti was six-of-eight passing and the Minnesota defense was solid. The Gophers scored 21 points in both the first and third quarters and added a two point safety in the fourth quarter when reserves, end Franz Koeneke and safety Gerry Eisenberg, tackled Oregon State's QB Bob Clark in the end zone.

After the game, Beaver coach Kip Taylor called McNamara a sure All-American, the Gopher Split-T the best he had seen and Minnesota as being close to Pacific Coast perennial powers UCLA and USC in terms of talent.

"McNamara has outstanding speed, quickness and power."

That fact was very evident the next week.

•   •   •

The 1954 Minnesota-Iowa football game still is considered by long-time Gopher football fans to be one of the greatest in U of M history. The reasons are two-fold: a close-fought battle by two old rivals that went down to the wire and the individual performance of Bob McNamara.

The final was Minnesota 22, Iowa 20.

"For every 42 points scored there was a story to unfold for the 65,429 fans who Saturday watched one of the best played and most dramatic games Memorial Stadium has ever had," wrote the Tribune's Dick Cullum.

Iowa coach Forest Evashevski started his second unit. The Hawkeyes kicked off and Minnesota returned the ball to midfield. Five plays later from the Hawkeye 36, McNamara scored on a touchdown run off left tackle. Cappelletti kicked the extra point to give Minnesota an early 7-0 lead. Iowa came back quickly and Eddie Vincent, the fine Iowa back who had a great game that day, made a 68-yard run to the Minnesota 12 where Hawkeye quarterback Jerry Reichow scored a couple of plays later on a keeper. It was 7-7.

Seventeen seconds later came the play of the game. McNamara took the kickoff at his 11 and started up the middle.

"My intent was to bring the ball up the middle of the field and try to get as close as possible to the 50-yard-line," McNamara recounted. "A hole opened and I made it all the way to our 45."

There McNamara made two spectacular moves that Warmath called "the greatest example of one man against eleven."

Iowa tackle Bob Deasy hit McNamara at the 47 and all but pulled him down, but the determined Gopher kept his feet, shaking off the Hawkeye. Earl Smith of Iowa hit McNamara up high, but a well-timed twist sent the would-be tackler flying. McNamara broke for the sideline in front of the Gopher bench. All this time, his brother "Pinky" was stride-for-stride as Bob streaked down the sideline. Bob Hobert threw a good block on a Iowa defender at about the 30.

At the Minnesota 10, Reichow was closing fast on McNamara, but "Pinky" took him out with a beautiful cross-body block and his brother went into the end zone. Warmath later said, "it was finest example of brilliance and desire I have ever seen."

The extra point was good and Minnesota now led 14-7.

While McNamara's run was the highlight play of the game, it was one of just many fine efforts by the two teams. Iowa came back, but Bob McNamara picked off a Reichow pass at the Minnesota 41 and returned it 22 yards into Hawkeye territory. Minnesota couldn't take advantage. Iowa hit back in the second quarter and Smith and Vincent marched the Hawkeyes to the Gopher 13. There, Cappelletti went down with an elbow injury and was taken out of the game. It was his last play as a Gopher.

Smith scored and the extra point once again tied the game.

The Gophers came back. "Pinky" returned the kickoff to the Minnesota 32. Don Swanson filled in well for Cappelletti and led a scoring drive which went to the Iowa 32. There, he hit "Pinky" down the left side at the 22. End Phil McElroy threw a key block and the younger McNamara was in for the third Gopher TD of the game. The extra point was wide and it was 20-14 at half.

Iowa took the second half kickoff and Reichow marched his team to the eight with a mix of runs and passes. Eddie Vincent scored on a short plunge, but a strong Gopher rush blocked the conversion attempt.

The next series was another major turning point. Minnesota was penalized twice and Dale Quist was forced to punt from his own 22. Smith took the kick at his 15 and then made a spectacular run for a touchdown—or so it seemed. A clipping penalty brought the play back to the Hawkeye three.

Two plays netted one yard. Then on third down, the Hawkeyes tried a Reichow-to-Vincent pitch out for a sweep left. The lateral was behind Vincent and into the end zone. The Iowa back had to turn and fall on the ball, giving Minnesota a safety. It was 22-20 which would be the winning margin. That was all the scoring for the day, but not all the excitement.

With four minutes left, Iowa got to the Minnesota 37. Vincent got four yards, then in two plays took the ball to the Gopher 23. Dean Maas hit Reichow for a two-yard loss, but on the next play Minnesota was offside. The Hawks were at the 20. A Reichow pass to Frank Gilliam was fumbled at the 15 and "Pinky" McNamara recovered. On second down, Bob McNamara fumbled the ball away and Iowa had life with 1:53 left. But on the next play, a Reichow-to- Binkey Broeder pass was deflected by Cochran and Swanson intercepted at the goal line, taking it to out to the six. The Gophers then ran out the clock.

The jubilant Minnesota players carried Bob McNamara off the field on their shoulders. Mac played one of the finest all-around games in Minnesota football history. In the first half alone, he amassed 209 total yards: 98 on rushes, his 89-yard touchdown run on the kickoff return and a 22-yard return of an intercepted pass. All together, he had 115 yards rushing and played the full 60 minutes. Vincent was magnificent as he had 154 yards rushing and Smith had 117 as the Hawkeyes put up 321 total rushing yards to Minnesota's 174 and outpassed the Gophers, 77 to 33 yards.

Warmath, also carried off, temporarily lost his hat and coat on the bench. "The kids just wanted this game," he told the press. "We beat a really good team in Iowa."

"I waited 12 months for this," yelled tackle Gordie Holz in the jubilant Minnesota locker room, referring to the shutout suffered in 1953 at Iowa City.

Evashevski was dejected, saying his team played its best offensive game of the year, yet still lost. "Actually, the game didn't prove much other than there were two really good clubs on the field," he said."

Minnesota was now 7-1 and had just won the biggest game of the year. Ohio State wrapped up the Big Ten championship the same day with a 28-6 win over Purdue. The Buckeyes would go on to an undefeated season, a Rose Bowl victory over USC and the national championship. Minnesota got ready to go to Wisconsin.

In Madison, Minnesota ended the first year of the Warmath era on a down note. With Cappelletti out and in cold weather with 51,000 fans on hand, the Badgers shutout Minnesota 27-0. Seven passes of backup quarterback Don Swanson were intercepted. Still, the Gophers played well in spots, holding that year's Heisman Award winner, Alan Ameche, to just 26 yards on 13 carries. In fairness to Ameche, however, he was playing on a bad ankle. The Wisconsin defense was outstanding, allowing Minnesota only 19 total yards in the first half and 69 in the game, 68 of which were made by Bob McNamara.

"Their defense was the best we saw all year," "Pinky" McNamara said afterward.

Regardless, Warmath had shown the Gopher faithful his abilities as a coach and Minnesota finished third in the Big Ten. It had been a good year.

# Twelve

The Gopher coaching staff had hit the road in the winter of 1954 and recruited their first class.

"We grabbed up some good players like Dick Larson, Mike Svendsen, Dave Burkholder, Bob Rasmussen, Jon Jelacic, Dick Borstad and Bob Schultz," Warmath pointed out.

The 1955 season was the first varsity year for these recruits and because of heavy graduation losses from the 1954 team, Warmath and his staff had to rely on these young players to fill the void.

The 1955 season turned out to be a transition year. The Gophers took their share of lumps for nine games, but they grew in the process.

The squad hosted Washington at Memorial Stadium in the opener. Led by quarterback Steve Roake, the Huskies won handily, 30-0.

Dean Derby, later a Minnesota Viking, kicked a first-quarter field goal set up by a pass interception by teammate Jim Houston. Roake later hit Houston with a short TD pass for a 10-0 Huskies lead at halftime. In the third quarter, Washington capitalized on further Gopher miscues by falling on a muffed pitch in the Minnesota end zone for another touchdown. A Huskie touchdown by Jim Jones in the third quarter and a fourth-quarter Jim Harryman TD run ended the scoring.

Warmath kept the locker room doors shut for 45 minutes to give his team a post-game lecture and then publicly stated that his kids didn't look like a football team except for "maybe five minutes all afternoon."

Captain Mike Falls called Washington the best team he had faced in three years.

The next week Minnesota played a much better game, but still lost to Purdue 7-6.

The Gopher pass defense was tenacious as it picked off four Len Dawson passes in the first half, three by "Shorty" Cochran. All of the scoring took place in the third quarter. Purdue marched 64 yards with fullback Bill Murakowski scoring on a one-yard plunge. Dawson kicked the conversion. Minnesota came back quickly and went 80 yards in 14 plays with Dick Borstad scoring on a one-yard plunge. "Pinky" McNamara bobbled the conversion snap and Swanson couldn't get off the kick.

"A great pass defense," said Dawson of Minnesota's effort.

"As hard a hitting team as I've ever played against," added Boilermaker tackle Dick Murkey.

"I have no complaint about our effort," Warmath summed up.

The first win came the next week in Evanston, Ill. Dick Borstad, the sophomore fullback, was the hero as he rushed for 142 yards in 22 carries in an 18-7 victory over Northwestern.

However, the Gophers were sloppy in the opening quarter when they fumbled twice, once at the Wildcats 16, then again at the 18. Northwestern had a 7-0 lead going into the second quarter, but sophomore quarterback Dick Larson threw a 40-yard touchdown pass to McNamara. On the next Gopher series end Jon Jelacic made a spectacular catch and Borstad scored on a four-yard run to give Minnesota a 12-7 lead at halftime.

Minnesota secured the win in the third quarter when a 52-yard drive culminated in another Borstad score. It was a sloppy game with Minnesota fumbling nine times, losing three. Northwestern coughed up the ball six times and lost two of them.

Lou Saban, the peripatetic Northwestern coach, said the second Minnesota touchdown, highlighted by the Jelacic catch, "killed us."

Illinois, led by their stellar back, Abe Woodson, took advantage of four more Minnesota fumbles to post a 21-13 victory. The

Gophers also committed numerous penalties. The Illini led 7-0 on Harry Jefferson's touchdown run in the first quarter.

Illinois scored again in the second quarter by going 90 yards with quarterback Em Lindbeck scrambling on a blown play and scoring.

The Gophers, however, were undaunted and after stopping Illinois at the Minnesota 34, put together a drive that saw Larson hit end Franz Koeneke on a long pass caught at the 20 which the St. Paul Murray graduate ran the rest of the way into the end zone. The PAT attempt by Mike Falls was no good.

Minnesota made it 14-12. Larson, on an option, pitched to halfback Bob Schultz who went 65 yards for the touchdown.

It was back and forth in the fourth quarter, but with 1:40 left, Abe Woodson picked off an option pass by Gopher halfback Ken Bombardier at the Illini 39 and went to the Minnesota 45. Five plays later, Woodson scored on a pass from Hiles Stout.

"The little things ( fumbles and penalties) stopped us in the first half," Warmath said in an understatement.

Minnesota was 1-3 nearing the halfway point of the season and went home to face Michigan.

•     •     •

There were 64,434 at Memorial Stadium when the Wolverines came in as the No. 1 team in the country. It looked like a long afternoon was in store for the Maroon and Gold, but the Gophers gave Bennie Oosterbaan's Michigan squad a scare by taking a 13-0 lead after the first 11 minutes. Bob Schultz and Ken Yackel scored touchdowns for the Gophers. The Wolverines' Terry Barr scored on a five-yard run with 1:43 left in the half. The second half belonged to Michigan. Playing without All-American end Ron Kramer who was hurt, the Wolverine defense adjusted to Minnesota's Split-T and held the Gophers to just 41 yards and two first downs. Again, fumbling plagued Warmath's team and

Michigan took advantage when their quarterback Jim Van Pelt hit end Tom Maentz on a 10-yard pass for a third-quarter touchdown. The conversion was good and that was the deciding point in a 14-13 Michigan victory.

In a downcast Gopher locker room, Warmath said that Michigan's first touchdown at the end of the first half was the key to the Wolverines getting back in the game.

Oosterbaan agreed. "Minnesota was very tough, but we commanded the last two quarters and the first touchdown we got in the second quarter was critical for us."

The Gophers needed a win badly. With the help of mother nature they got it.

When the USC Trojans came to town on Friday, Oct. 28th, it was a typical Minnesota fall day, overcast with temperatures in the mid-fifties. When they woke up on Saturday morning, it was "Welcome to Minnesota, this ain't Tinsel Town."

Twenty mile-per-hour winds with temperatures just above freezing made for a miserable mix of rain, sleet and snow. Southern Cal must have wondered why 64,592 people would sit and watch the game that was about to take place.

The weather continued to sour as the game progressed. Snow was the prevailing form of precipitation. It was the perfect equalizer to USC's speed led by its great backs, Jon Arnett and C.R. Roberts.

The Warmath philosophy that the kicking game is critical proved true in Minnesota's first two touchdowns. In the first quarter, Franz Koeneke blocked a Trojan punt that set up an ensuing 15-yard TD scamper by Bob Schultz. The PAT was no good. USC came right back and Arnett took the kickoff, cut in front of the Minnesota bench and angled laterally at about midfield. Dick Larson, who had missed a tackle in front of the Gopher bench, doubled back and brought Arnett down at the Minnesota eight. Three running plays lost five yards and Don Swanson intercepted a Trojan pass in the end zone which he returned to the 15 to kill the USC threat. Minnesota's lead remained 6-0 at halftime.

Again, punting and defense were the keys in the second half. Borstad deflected a third-quarter Trojan punt and scored several plays later on a three-yard plunge. Gordon Duvall took the Minnesota kickoff and went 73 yards up the middle for a touchdown.

Swanson got that touchdown back on a 65-yard keeper play for a touchdown. USC couldn't get their running game going, but punt and kickoff returns posed few problems. Ernie Merk returned a punt 93 yards for a Trojan TD at the end of the third quarter to cut the Gophers' lead to 19-12.

In the fourth quarter, Southern Cal fumbled at its 27 and Borstad scored his second TD on a four-yard run. The weather showed some slight improvement and the Trojans, behind quarterback Ells Kissinger, hit on five passes, including a scoring toss to end Chuck Leimbach to make the score 25-19 for Minnesota.

The Gophers gave USC one more chance when Rhody Tuszka fumbled at the Minnesota 25 with 56 seconds left. But Swanson, made another interception, this time on a pass from Frank Hall and the Gophers ran out the clock for the victory.

The Minnesota line play was the difference in the minds of both Warmath and USC coach Jess Hill. Mike Falls, Bob Hobert, Koeneke and reserve end Bob Schmidt were singled out. Arnett called Minnesota the "hardest hitting team we played all year." Braven Dyer, the LA Times reporter covering the game, said it was played before "64,592 prospective pneumonia patients" adding "there was no fluke about Minnesota's triumph and they handed Jess Hill his first loss against a Big Ten team in regular season games."

The victory was costly, however, for McNamara and Schultz both were banged up and couldn't play the next week in Iowa City. The Hawkeyes, seeking to avenge the loss the previous year, took the opening kickoff and marched 80 yards for a touchdown. End Jim Gibbons scored on a halfback option pass from Eddie Vincent. Minnesota fumbled twice in the second quarter and Iowa capitalized on both mistakes with Vincent scoring both times. Hawkeyes quarterback Jerry Reichow was 12 for 16 in passing and his substitute, Ken Ploen, got the fourth Iowa TD in the third quarter on a 19-yard scramble. The final was 26-0.

"Iowa deserved to win," was Warmath's terse assessment.

Things were equally as bad the following week in East Lansing, Michigan as Michigan State whipped Minnesota 42-14 thanks to a defense which blocked two Gopher punts and picked off three passes. State scored all its points in the first three quarters. It was a team good enough to represent the Big Ten in the 1956 Rose Bowl.

Earl Morrall led the Spartan attack which featured halfback Walt Kowalczyck, end Dave Kaiser and backup quarterback Jim Ninowski. Minnesota did have a brief shot early in the game when Bill Garner scored on a 16-yard sweep. But it wasn't until the Gophers were down 42-7 in the fourth quarter that Don Swanson snuck in for the next Minnesota score.

"They are the best all-around team we played in two years," Warmath stated.

It was a clear day in the mid-twenties when Minnesota met the Wisconsin before a crowd of 62,717 at Memorial Stadium. Sophomore back Bob Schultz was the Gopher star in a 21-6 victory. The Badgers were trying to win one for retiring coach Ivy Williamson, who would be replaced by one of his assistants, Minnesota native and former Gopher star, Milt Bruhn.

Warmath threw Wisconsin off-balance by going with the straight-T and Schultz ran for 117 yards, scored two touchdowns and picked off two Badger passes. Gopher punter Kelvin Kleber bobbled a snap in the first quarter, but made a 23-yard run out of it to pickup a first down at the Wisconsin 26 and set up Schultz's first score, a plunge in from the two.

Schultz continued to lead the Maroon and Gold attack as he capped off a third-quarter drive of 72 yards in 12 plays with an eight-yard scoring run. The Pelican Rapids native sealed the victory in the fourth quarter when he intercepted a Badger pass at their 27. Five plays later quarterback Don Swanson snuck in from the two. The Badgers got their lone score with 2:27 left and Minnesota had its third win of the season.

Tom Juhl, Bob Hobert, captain Mike Falls, Erle Ukkelberg, Bob Rasumussen and Dean Maas were cited by Warmath for their tough line play which contributed to the victory.

"It was the best line play of the year," remarked line coach Denver Crawford.

"Minnesota was the superior team. We were just outplayed," lamented the departing Williamson. The loss left the Badgers' with a 4-5 record for the year, the first losing season in nine years for Williamson.

The Gophers finished 3-6, but looked ahead to 1956 with a more mature team to work with and a flashy, cocky transfer quarterback from Walla Walla, Wash. waiting in the wings.

# Thirteen

 Robert deLafayette Cox was a handsome, confident, curly- haired, part Latino originally from Los Angeles, who grew up as a smart-street kid with an instinct for survival. He left home as a young teenager, escaping an unhappy family life. Years later, a mentally ill brother killed his father in an argument. Cox was the kind of kid that most sociologists would have predicted was headed nowhere. But he had a few things going for him: he was a great athlete, very competitive, intelligent and had a burning desire to be successful.

"I wound up with friends of the family in Walla Walla, Wash. after my own family situation went to hell," Cox said. "I played high school football and ran track. I was recruited by the University of Washington. In 1954, my sophomore year, I started at quarterback after three games and I threw three TD passes and we almost beat UCLA which was undefeated that year and shared some No. 1 rankings with Ohio State."

But Cox wasn't happy with the situation at Washington. He made a connection through a local family with roots in Duluth to then-assistant Minnesota athletic director Chet Roan and inquired about coming to the U of M.

"I decided to transfer to Minnesota, but told Roan that I needed money. I had no family to speak of and was working as well as playing football and going to school. When I was at Washington, Dave Beck, the president of the Teamsters Union, would give me money under the table.

"I first met Warmath in the winter of 1955 and told him I needed at least $400 a month. He was emphatic and said there was no way, that he didn't pay players on, or under, the table. I learned early that he was ethical and a man of principle."

Warmath did arrange for him to get a night job on the railroad. Cox registered for class and reported for spring practice even though he wouldn't be eligible for another year.

When the 1956 season rolled around, Dick Larson, by then a junior and who had shared some quarterback duties in 1955 with Don Swanson, was the experienced signal-caller. Larson was a fine athlete, equally as strong as a defensive safety. In 1956, he and Cox would share quarterback duties. Warmath would use two full units interchangeably and, therefore, it was often difficult to distinguish first and second teams. But it was Cox who was the flashy gambler and the one who almost took the Gophers to the Rose Bowl.

The team had Bob Hobert returning who was an outstanding tackle and would make All-America that season and was the first of four academic All-Americans Warmath would coach.

"We felt confident going into the 1956 season because we had a lot of guys returning. Spring and fall practice was at its usual intense level. Murray Warmath was the most intense person I have ever known and I am in the business of measuring intensity," said Hobert, who today is a business psychologist in Minneapolis. "Murray pounded in and pounded in the basics and harped and harped that the team with the fewest mistakes wins."

Warmath was looking at a pretty good backfield of not only Cox and Larson, but Dick Borstad, Bob Schultz, Ken Bombardier and Dave Lindblom. His line included Hobert, center and captain Dean Maas, guards Dave Burkholder and Bob Rasmussen, tackle Frank Youso and ends Jon Jelacic, Tom Juhl, Bob Schmidt and Perry Gehring.

Washington was again the opening opponent, this time in Seattle where Warmath went against his old Mississippi State assistant and Split-T aficionado, Darrell Royal.

The Gophers took the opening kickoff and went 65 yards in 14 plays with Larson hitting end Dick Fairchild on a three-yard touchdown yard pass. Washington came back and tied it with Jim

Jones scoring on a two-yard plunge. Minnesota took a 14-7 lead into halftime after another three-yard scoring pass, this time from Cox to Lindblom.

The Gophers widened the margin in the second half on a short TD run by Dick Borstad in the third quarter, a Rhody Tuszka interception return of 32 yards for a score and a Larson-to-Schultz touchdown toss in the fourth quarter. Washington's Bill Snyder scored on a quarterback sneak in the closing minutes of the game.

Minnesota headed home with a 34-14 victory.

The next Saturday, Purdue came to Minneapolis and Len Dawson, now a senior, was the Boilermaker quarterback. He marched his team 68 yards for the game's first score. Minnesota had driven in the opening quarter to the Purdue 32, but was stopped. From there Dawson took the Boilermakers down to the Minnesota one where Tony Fletcher scored on a plunge.

In the second quarter, Larson picked off a Dawson pass and returned it to the Gopher 46, but was hurt on the play. Cox came in at quarterback and moved the Gophers to the Purdue six where Tuszka scored. The Boilermakers' Dawson threw a 40-yard scoring pass to Erich Barnes and Purdue led 14-7 at halftime.

Minnesota scored twice in the third quarter. First, Dick Borstad recovered a Fletcher fumble at the Purdue 28 and combined with Bob Schultz to move the ball to the two where Borstad took it in. A few series later, Dawson punted to the Gopher 40. Dick Larson returned to engineer the Gophers' next touchdown drive. With 57 seconds left, Bombardier scored on an eight-yard run.

Minnesota's pass defense kept up the ball-hawking as both Bombardier and linebacker Mike Svendsen picked off Purdue throws to preserve the 21-14 victory. Bombardier hadn't played at all in the Washington game. Against Purdue, he was one of the best players on the field.

In the post-game summary, Jack Mollenkopf, the Purdue coach who would have many classic battles with Warmath over the next dozen years, praised Minnesota saying its pass defense, poise and savvy were the difference.

"Our kids were in great shape. Several of them played 60 minutes," Warmath commented.

"The coach made adjustments at the half to Purdue's shifting from seven and eight-man fronts to five-man fronts and that was a big help," Larson told the media.

The next week, however, things bogged down as Warmath and his team faced Northwestern now under the direction of a young Armenian-American fresh from the "cradle of coaches", Miami of Ohio.

•   •   •

Ara Parseghian brought in his Wildcats for what turned out to be a scoreless slugfest. Parseghian had come to Evanston from Miami of Ohio and was in the first of eight successful years there. In 1964, he left for South Bend and fame as the Notre Dame coach for 12 seasons.

The Minnesota-Northwestern clash started out in eighty degree heat and turned into a downpour that paralyzed both teams. Unlike the week before, it was the Gophers who were cursed with turnovers as they fumbled three times and threw two interceptions. Bombardier fumbled at the Northwestern one and Bob Blakley at the Wildcats 18, both miscues occurring in the second quarter.

Northwestern never threatened to score, but played inspired defense and in the fourth quarter, a punt rolled dead on the Gopher one which seemed to take the fight out of Minnesota. The game ended 0-0.

Having "kissed their sister", the Gophers hosted Illinois the next week, a team with a cadre of excellent players.

With just over 63,000 on hand in Memorial Stadium, Minnesota relied on the toe of Dick Borstad and the running and passing of Bobby Cox to pull off a thrilling 16-13 victory. Both players accounted for all the Minnesota points that afternoon. A great defensive play by Minnesota's Mike Svendsen on the last play of the game preserved the triumph.

In the first quarter, a quick kick by Illini fullback Ray Nitschke went 52 yards to the Gopher 41. Cox came in with the second team and went down to score. The extra point was no good. In the second quarter, Illinois' Abe Woodson scored a touchdown after a fumble by Larson. After the Illinois score and an ensuing Gopher punt, Bobby Mitchell coughed up the ball and a few plays later Cox raced in from the 23 to give Minnesota the lead at 13-7.

In the final quarter, the Illini tied it 13-13.

An ineligible receiver downfield nullified a Gopher pass play at the Illinois 16. Illinois took possession, couldn't move and punted to Cox who returned it 30 yards to the Illinois 44. With 4:14 left, he hit Dave Lindblom on a pass to the 22. Blakley made a 15-yard run to the seven for a first down. Two plays gained three yards and a pass was incomplete. Borstad split the uprights with the game-winning field goal.

Illinois came back and moved to the Minnesota 49. With time for one play, Illinois pulled a fake field goal attempt, hit Woodson in the flat who then criss-crossed the field several times. Svendsen sniffed out the play and stopped the Illinois back at the 43 as the game ended.

"Cox had the heart of a lion," said Warmath afterwards. "We had to play our best because Mitchell and Woodson are so dangerous."

"I waited two years for a chance like this," Cox said and praised the second-team effort by Svendsen, Ed Buckingham and Ev Gerths.

"Cox was the difference," Nitschke added. A week later in Ann Arbor, the Michigan Wolverines would learn the same thing.

# Fourteen

"One of the most glorious victories in the history of Minnesota football," was the description by Dick Cullum in his Tribune report on the 1956 Minnesota-Michigan game.

It was certainly a victory long remembered by Murray Warmath.

"When we went in that day, I remembered my first trip in '54 and how soundly we were beaten (34-0), so I wanted a win bad," the Gopher coach said.

One of the things Warmath recalled about the first game was that the Minnesota players were intimidated by Michigan even as the teams prepared to come out the famous tunnel unto Michigan Stadium. The Gopher players had stepped back and let a charged up Wolverine team run past them. Warmath vowed that sort of thing wouldn't happen in 1956.

"I remember we were in the locker room waiting to go out and Warmath had one of the student managers watching through the front door to make certain Michigan already was taking the field," recalled Dick Larson.

"We aren't going out of this goddamn locker room until they are out there," Warmath growled to his team and assistants. A warning from the officials made the Gophers move, but Warmath made his point for the Michigan players were standing in front of their bench waiting for the game to start.

Michigan had the ball at its eight with several minutes to go in the opening period and put together a 92-yard march with Terry Barr scoring the Wolverine touchdown on the first play of the second quarter. The conversion was good and the score stayed at 7-0 until halftime intermission.

In the locker room, Warmath urged his team to stick to the game plan and in his second inspirational move of the afternoon, told his players "we've had our scrimmage, now let's play the game." They did just that.

The Gophers took the opening kickoff and went 92 yards with a 30-yard TD run by Bob Schultz being the big play. However, some luck was involved as earlier, Cox had been confused and thinking it was third and six when it was fourth and six, hit McNamara with a first down pass to keep the drive alive.

"I remember afterward that Murray chewed my ass out for not punting on fourth down," Cox said years later.

Cox mixed his play calling and scored the next touchdown after Michigan turned the ball over at its 28. He drove the Gophers in eight plays and took it in from the three.

Larson, McNamara and Svendsen were excellent on pass defense, especially in the fourth quarter when the Wolverines were trying to hit end Ron Kramer to get back in the game. Minnesota, meanwhile, again looked to Cox and he came through as he put together a 55-yard drive and scored from the seven on the 10th play of the series.

Michigan made a late move and drove 78 yards, but Svendsen intercepted a Wolverine pass at the Minnesota two and Minnesota had a 20-7 victory. Jubilation and the Little Brown Jug was the story in the Gopher locker room.

"I was never worried about the outcome," Warmath said. "Cox was inspirational."

"I wanted this game more than anything in my life," Cox told the media which heralded him as a "swashbuckling ball handler."

"The scribes were screaming in the press box for Minnesota to slow down so they could keep up with the game," reported Joe Falls of the Detroit Free Press.

Bob Blakley also was singled out for his great play both offensively and defensively and Warmath again cited Larson and McNamara.

"The second half was the best half of football we've played in three years," said Hobert.

"This game was just like back in the golden Thirties," reflected assistant coach Butch Nash, a star Gopher end before World War II.

The Gophers returned home to a crowd of more than 5,000 at the old Wold-Chamberlain Field in Richfield. Pittsburgh was coming to town next, but everyone was thinking two weeks ahead when Iowa would be in Minneapolis for the battle that likely would determine the Big Ten champion and Rose Bowl representative.

• • •

The Minnesota-Pitt game was "savage and hard-hitting" reported the Tribune's Johnson.

Like the Illinois game, Minnesota relied on the toe of Dick Borstad to win 9-6. This time he kicked a 23-yard goal with 2:34 left and did it after sitting out most of the game with a pinched hip nerve.

Joe Walton, years later coach of the New York Jets, returned the opening kickoff 77 yards for an apparent touchdown but it was called back because of a clipping penalty. In the second quarter, Bob Soltis intercepted a Pitt pass and Cox drove the Gophers 99 yards in 12 plays, capped by an eight-yard scoring pass to Jon Jelacic. The conversion failed.

Corny Salvaterra's five-yard pass to Walton tied the score in the third quarter. The extra point attempt was no good and the score remained 6-6 until the final minutes. Pitt had a fourth and one at its 32 and risked going for it. The gamble backfired when the snap was fumbled and Minnesota gained possession. Five plays later, Borstad made the winning field goal.

"We were lucky to win," Warmath commented afterwards. The Gophers had to be looking ahead to the next Saturday. Iowa was coming to town, but Michigan had just beaten the Hawkeyes in the last 66 seconds, 17-14. The Minnesota-Iowa game was set for national television and Minnesota fans smelled roses.

•      •      •

Neither school had ever been to the Rose Bowl and the winner of the '56 game would have the inside track. Minnesota had a tie, Iowa a loss in the Big Ten. A Gopher win would given them a real shot for the championship and the trip to Pasadena. A Hawkeye loss would have virtually ended any chance for them. Ohio State was still very much in the running with one loss.

A crowd of 64,531 at Memorial Stadium on a clear, crisp November day, sat back expecting to see a fast-paced, possibly high-scoring battle. What they saw instead was a defensive slugfest and a slew of Minnesota mistakes.

The game came down to turnovers and Minnesota had them by the truckload. The Gophers fumbled six times, lost four and had two passes intercepted.

The Hawkeyes did all the game's scoring in the first quarter. Bob Schultz fumbled at the Minnesota 38 where Frank Gilliam recovered. In the ensuing Iowa drive, Gopher captain Dean Maas suffered a concussion and was lost for the rest of the game. On fourth and one from the eight, Iowa quarterback Ken Ploen hit end Jim Gibbons at the one. Fred Harris plunged over on the next play. The kick was good and that Iowa led 7-0.

Minnesota drove to the Hawks 39, but Schultz fumbled again.

Schultz fumbled a third time in the third quarter. Bill Jukich intercepted an Iowa pass and went from the Hawkeyes' 43 to their 31. Minnesota marched to the Iowa 11 and Gopher fans felt a tie was forthcoming. But an offside and then Bill Happel's interception of Dick Larson's pass killed the drive.

Minnesota got into Iowa territory late in the fourth quarter, but on fourth down Blakley fumbled and even though Larson recovered, it was short of the first down. Happel picked off a Cox

97

pass with only a couple of minutes left to secure the Iowa 7-0 victory.

In a dejected Gopher locker room, Warmath put it simply: "You can't give up the ball six times and expect to win. Iowa deserved the victory."

"We're grateful for the breaks, especially since we had several starters hurt and had to turn to our reserves," said Hawkeye coach Forrest Evashevski.

Minnesota had a loss and a tie and faced Michigan State. Iowa had a loss and traveled to Columbus, Ohio to meet Ohio State.

In a game that Warmath described as one where he "never had a team with more resolution, courage and poise than Minnesota had today," the Gophers beat Michigan State 14-13 before 62,478 in Minneapolis. But afterward, the Gopher team was down when it received word that Iowa had defeated Ohio State 6-0. Memorial Stadium public address announcer, Julius Perlt, withheld giving that score until after the Gopher-Spartan game ended.

Minnesota had opened the scoring in the first half as Cox ran and passed the Gophers to the Spartans' one where he made the scoring toss to Dave Lindblom. At the start of both quarters of the second half, State put together scoring drives of 78 and 86 yards respectively with quarterback Bob Wilson scoring on sneaks. The conversion attempt following the second Spartan touchdown failed and Michigan State led 13-7.

With 8:34 left in the game, Dick Larson moved the ball to the State 27-yard line. There Blakley, aided by a Dave Herbold block, bounced off tacklers and went all the way for the tying score. Bob Rasmussen missed the first PAT attempt, but a Spartan offside gave him a second chance. This time, the kick was good and Minnesota held on to win.

Spartan coach Duffy Daughtery said "Cox and Larson made the Split-T roll for Minnesota. No one marched like that on us all year."

Bart Smith, a State assistant, said "Cox is better than Paul Hornung of Notre Dame." That was quite a compliment since Hornung would be awarded the Heisman Trophy in 1956.

The Gophers went to Wisconsin for the final game and settled for a 13-13 tie. Six penalties killed Minnesota's play. One penalty was critical when with two minutes left and Minnesota leading 13-7, Ken Bombardier was called for pass interference on Wisconsin's Dave Howard in the end zone giving the Badgers first down on the one. The Badgers scored to tie, but a loss was averted when the extra point attempt by Jim Hobbs was blocked by Perry Gehring.

Wisconsin had opened the scoring in the first quarter when it marched to the Gopher one, a 48-yard pass from Sid Williams to Howard being the big play. From the one, Danny Lewis went in and the Badgers had a 7-0 halftime lead. In the third quarter, a bad punt snap by Wisconsin gave Minnesota the ball at the Badger six, Cox scored on the third play to tie the game at 7-7. Cox scored again when the Gophers went 56 yards in 14 plays to make it 13-7.

The conversion was good, but a holding call nullified it and the succeeding longer attempt failed. Minnesota ended the year 6-1-2 and tied for second place with Michigan.

"It was a pretty good year," Warmath reflected.

With Cox, Larson, Schultz, Borstad, Jelacic, Rasmussen, Burkholder, Frank Youso, Gehring, Svendsen, Bob Schmidt, Bombardier, Tuszka and a host of others back, Warmath, his team and the State of Minnesota looked ahead to 1957. The start of the next season was nine months away, but Gopher football was on everyone's minds, especially since Minnesota had been only a win away from the conference title and a Rose Bowl trip.

Nineteen fifty-seven. It was to be the year. Pasadena, get ready for a horde of Golden Gophers. A sixth national title for the school was a real possibility. Everybody was fired up.

However, by the time the 1957 season ended, the Gopher faithful would instead be asking what went wrong and for nearly three years, Murray Warmath would experience the toughest time in his football life.

# Fifteen

Murray Warmath's long-time friend from the University of Tennessee, Herman Hickman, was the prognosticator on college football for Sports Illustrated when the 1957 college preview issue came out. He told the readers the Gophers were in his top 11 picks and the game in November against Michigan State would undoubtedly decide the Big Ten championship, the Rose Bowl representative and maybe the national champion.

However, by the time the two met, the Gophers already had three conference losses and were fighting to just have a winning season.

Prior to the season opener against Washington, Gopher football was the hottest sports topic in the state. Bobby Cox had appeared on the covers of many of the pre-season college football magazines and local writers and the national media were picking the Gophers to be the team to watch.

Warmath was extremely confident about the 1957 squad, so confident, in fact, he turned down invitations to interview for both the Texas and Arkansas head coaching jobs.

"I remember when Murray told me about the Texas job, I urged him to talk to them because I felt it was a place where a real powerhouse could be developed, " recalled Billy Murphy. "But he said he wasn't interested because he felt that in 1957 Minnesota had a real shot at the national title."

Everybody in the state was so fired up that during the summer, Bobby Cox took advantage of the frenzy. "I decided to make money off the interest," he recounted. "I went to Paul Foss, a local printer and big-time Gopher booster and had him print 5,000 posters rimmed with pictures of the returning players and our 1957 schedule in the middle. The last listing on the schedule was the Rose Bowl."

Cox agreed to pay Foss back for the printing costs out the proceeds from the poster sales. He then put on his letterman's jacket, grabbed a bunch of posters and hit the streets. He introduced himself in the bars and barbershops and asked if they'd buy a poster for $10. He claimed the money was to help needy athletes.

"The needy athlete was me. I'd get home every night and my pockets would be stuffed with $10 bills."

The scheme worked until Warmath got wind of it.

"One day I was called into his office and he was waiting for me along with Ike Armstrong and Marsh Ryman, then the business manager of the athletic department.

"Murray raised hell with me saying that I was running the risk of getting the NCAA on us and having the team declared ineligible and put on probation. It looked as if my money-making scheme ended right there. However, I got my two brothers-in-law to help sell the posters. I gave them 50 percent."

Guard Dave Burkholder later heard of Cox's venture and demanded royalties since his picture was used on the posters.

There were other signs of the enthusiasm surrounding the Gophers in '57, none more evident than student season-ticket sales hit approximately 20,000.

"I remember that freshmen students were allowed to visit practice during Welcome Week," said Dana Marshall, a freshman himself that year and a student manager on the team for four years. "Warmath introduced the coaching staff to the freshmen and would give their names and their hometowns. I was struck by the 'southern' influence on the team."

Marshall pointed out it also was the last year that mass tryouts for the freshmen team were held and there were about 175 kids out for the team.

"Murray had a way with words and phrases. I remember at a team meeting, while announcing our plans for the weekend, he said we would be traveling 'incognito and incommunicado' to the Saint Paul Hotel."

The season again opened against Washington. There were more than 63,000 at Memorial Stadium and they watched the Gophers whip the Huskies 46-7.

Cox threw a 10-yard scoring pass to Jon Jelacic in the first quarter. He set up the score by recovering a Washington fumble at midfield. The Gophers built a 21-0 halftime lead on a Dave Lindblom 15-yard sweep of right end for one TD and a Dick Larson-to-Ken Schultz touchdown pass of three yards.

Washington's only bright moment of the game was when Jim Jones returned the second half kickoff 91 yards up the middle for a touchdown. It looked like they might have a shot to get back in the game when they intercepted a Gopher pass on the following possession and went to the Minnesota 19. The Gophers stopped them, however, then calmly marched the length of the field where Dick Borstad capped the drive with a six-yard scoring run.

Bob Blakley scored on a four-yard run to start the final quarter and later, third-team quarterback Jim Reese scored the last TD of the day. Minnesota amassed 522 yards in total offense to Washington's 105. The Gopher effort set a new single game yardage record up to that date.

On Oct. 4th, Minnesota fans awoke to get ready for the game with visiting Purdue and also to the shocking news that the Soviet Union had launched Sputnik, the world's first earth orbiting satellite.

At Memorial Stadium, more than 65,000 watched the Gophers squeak by the Boilermakers 21-17. Purdue might have won the game had they not been stymied by five lost fumbles. Dick Larson was the difference for the Gophers as he scored two touchdowns, one on a 72-yard punt return.

Purdue opened with an unbalanced line and marched to Minnesota goal line where Minnesota stopped them. Later in the quarter, Larson combined with Bob Soltis on a criss-cross and went 72 yards with the Purdue punt for the TD. Bob Schmidt and Mike Svendsen threw key blocks on the return.

Dick Brooks hauled in a touchdown reception to put Purdue back in it at halftime. Minnesota got a break in the third quarter when Bob Rasmussen recovered a Purdue fumble. Larson hit Bill Chorske on a 16-yard TD throw. Midway through the fourth quarter on a fourth-down play, Larson swept right end and scored from the six. Purdue argued that they stopped him just short of near the corner by the goal line, but the TD held up and Minnesota held on to win.

"Larson was the better quarterback today for us," said Bobby Cox, who had an off day completing only one pass.

Minnesota raised its season record to 3-0 the next weekend in Evanston as they routed Northwestern 41-6. They got off to a 27-0 halftime lead.

Cox marched the team 47 yards in the opening quarter and snuck in from the one for the first score. Another 47-yard march in the second quarter culminated with Borstad scoring from the one. Then Bill Martin, a Chicago native, debuted as a Gopher halfback and intercepted a Northwestern throw at the Minnesota 45 and took it back to the Wildcat 37. From the six, Larson threw a scoring pass to Bob Schmidt. A halfback option pass from Norm Anderson to Ken Bombardier gave Minnesota its fourth touchdown.

In the third quarter, Cox scrambled at the Wildcat 32 and hit Martin for the score. Two minutes later, Kelvin Kleber recovered a Wilmer Fowler fumble at the Northwestern 21 and Martin scored his second touchdown on a four-yard reverse. Northwestern finally scored in the last minute of the game.

"Frank Youso led with great line play and we had a solid pass rush," Warmath said "Martin was terrific."

Minnesota 2-0 in the Big Ten and with six games to play and maybe a seventh in Pasadena, prepared for Illinois. The following Saturday, before a national television audience, a pre-game speech by a football legend and a big disparity in team speed, were factors that dashed the dreams of the 1957 season.

•   •   •

"The biggest upset in Illinois football history since the 1924 game against Michigan when Red Grange scored five touchdowns." That was the opinion written by the Chicago Herald American's Leo Fischer in summarizing the 34-13 rout of the Gophers by the Illini in Champaign, Ill.

In many ways, the shellacking was over before it began.

"I remember when we were down on the field for pregame warmups, I saw Red Grange over by the Illinois players. He then left with them and went into their locker room," Billy Murphy remembered. "I mentioned this to Warmath who said he wasn't worried unless Grange was planning to play in the game."

The Galloping Ghost had no plans to suit up, instead choosing to give his alma mater a pep talk before taking the field against the Gophers. It was a talk many of the players said later inspired them to go out and pull off the upset.

In 1924, Grange made football history when he scored five touchdowns, most on long, spectacular runs, against highly-favored Michigan. He led Illinois to one of college football's greatest upsets. A few weeks later the Illini came to Minneapolis for the dedication game of Memorial Stadium and were upset. Grange never forgot and 33 years later used the memories of that experience to urge Illinois to go out and take it to Minnesota.

Ray Eliot's Illini were blessed with great team speed. Minnesota wasn't and that was the difference. Before the second quarter was four minutes old, the Illini were ahead 21-0. Minnesota had taken the opening kickoff and gotten to the Illinois 47, but had to punt. Twelve plays later the Illini scored on Jack Delveaux's two-yard smash over tackle.

On the next series, Bill Martin fumbled at the Gopher 28 and Bobby Mitchell recovered for the Illini. Mitchell then ripped off an 18-yard run and Delveaux scored the second touchdown. Minnesota couldn't do a thing on offense and punted again. Mitchell capped a nine play drive when he scored from the one just 18:35 into the game.

The Illini scored twice in the third quarter on Dale Smith's run from the two and Tom Haller's 37-yard pass to Ron Hill. The fourth quarter scoring was by Minnesota. Cox hit Lindblom on a 16-yard TD toss and on the game's last play, Jim Reese threw a 14-yarder to end Jerry Friend.

The physical toll on Minnesota was as bad as the score. Larson injured his Achilles tendon and missed most of that game and the next two. Tackle Frank Youso had battled the flu all week, left the game in the second quarter and didn't return. Svendsen and Blakley were banged up and played little.

Warmath kept the locker room doors shut for 45 minutes to the media. Finally, he let them in and said simply that the Illinois team speed was tremendous and that was the difference.

"It's obviously the best Illinois team I've seen and their passing was surprisingly effective," he stated.

"I never expected to win this easily," said Illinois' Eliot.

The Gophers returned home and everyone knew the game the following week against Michigan was critical. Preseason co-favorite Michigan State had been beaten by Purdue the same day Minnesota fell in Champaign. Clayton Tonnemaker, the captain of the 1949 Gophers which was that year's pre-season Big Ten favorite, wrote an open letter to '57 captain Jon Jelacic and urged the Gophers not to make the same mistake the '49 team made when after rolling over Ohio State 27-0 in Columbus, they lost two consecutive games to Michigan and Purdue.

A cartoon appeared that week in the Minneapolis papers showing a Gopher about to attempt to vault over a standard with the word "Michigan" on it. The attached article pointed out that the fate of the '57 season hinged on that outcome. However, the 1957 team had been so severely pounded by Illinois that it never did recover. When Michigan left with the Little Brown Jug that next Saturday, the title and Rose Bowl hopes were over.

The Wolverines used an excellent blend of running and passing on a regionally-televised game to seal Minnesota's fate. The game was only eight minutes old when Michigan quarterback Stan Noskin threw a 37-yard pass to Dave Bowers for a touchdown.

In the second quarter, Michigan scored again marching 65 yards in nine plays with Jim Van Pelt hitting Jim Pace for a 13-yard score. Van Pelt then kicked a 34-yard field goal with 34 seconds left in the half.

The Gophers came back and outplayed Michigan in the second half, but they were too far behind. Jim Reese made it 24-7 on a short run in the third quarter to finish the scoring.

"Something's wrong, something's missing," was the sentiment in the Minnesota locker room afterward.

"Had we scored on the first possession, it might have been a lot different," muttered Butch Nash.

"Michigan was simply excellent, especially passing," Warmath lamented.

•    •    •

Minnesota came back the next week against an undermanned Indiana team coached by Warmath's former Tennessee teammate, Phil Dickens. The Gophers won 34-0 scoring 27 points in the second half.

Rhody Tuszka got the first touchdown in the first quarter on an eight-yard run right after Indiana fumbled at its eight. In the third quarter, Bob Schultz and Jim Reese each scored on short runs, Bob Blakley and Dave Lindblom each added a touchdown in the fourth quarter.

"We just wore them down," Cox said after the game.

"We played near-perfect football today," Warmath added.

The Gopher coach would have to relish the moment for it was to be the last victory of the season.

The Iowa game the next week was a 44-20 disaster. The Hawkeyes had 58,000 in the stands at Kinnick Stadium and quarterback Randy Duncan directed the Hawkeye offense. Using several formations, the Iowa squad amassed 535 offensive yards. End Jim Gibbons was outstanding, catching nine passes for 164 yards. Duncan completed 11 of 19 passes.

Minnesota was in the game early as they countered Iowa's first score with a Blakley two-yard run to tie the game. Things came apart after that as Iowa scored on a 10-play, 69- yard drive. Then on third down with many yards to go, Minnesota tried to punt from its own end zone. Kelvin Kleber dropped the snap, picked up the ball and scrambled out to the one yard line. He dropped the next snap as well and Iowa's Bob Prescott fell on the loose ball for a touchdown.

Minnesota got to the Iowa 19 before a Jim Reese pass was intercepted by Kevin Furlong and returned to the 48. Duncan hit Gibbons on the next play and it was 27-7. A field goal made it 30-7 at halftime for Iowa.

In the third quarter, Cox came back in and took Minnesota on a 53-yard, eight-play scoring drive, sneaking it in himself from the two yard line.

Earlier that week, Cox had appeared on the cover of Sports Illustrated and was called the best college quarterback in America.

"The Iowa fans were on him badly after the Hawkeyes got way ahead," remembered Dana Marshall. "They kept yelling, 'Hey, Cover Boy' at him."

Reese intercepted a pass at the Minnesota one but the Gpohers couldn't move the ball. From the Minnesota 34, Duncan led Iowa to the two where he took it in. Later in the quarter, Bill Happel returned a Kleber punt 63 yards for a touchdown.

Blakley added a meaningless touchdown for Minnesota on a two-yard run late in the game and the final was 44-20.

A dejected Minnesota squad was shellshocked. Warmath again kept the locker room closed to the media for some time.

Minnesota's Kleber blamed himself for the botched punt snaps in the first half and Jon Jelacic said he thought the Gophers were as high for a game as they had been all year, "as high as we were for Michigan in 1956."

"Iowa passed us dizzy", Warmath muttered.

"There was a reference in Time magazine this past week that we quit in the tie with Michigan last Saturday," pointed out Hawkeye end Gibbons. "That inspired us to play well today."

The Gophers were 4-3, 3-3 in the Big Ten.

The floodgates stayed open the next week in East Lansing, the game Herman Hickman predicted earlier might be for the title. Using 51 players, Duffy Daughtery's Michigan State Spartans, blitzed Minnesota 42-13. State was up 21-0 after the first quarter, the big play being Spartan end Dave Kaiser's picking off in mid-air a Soltis-to-Lindblom lateral on a reverse play and going 77 yards for the score. Walt Kowalczyk and Art Johnson scored the other two MSU touchdowns in the half.

In the second quarter, Don Gilbert and Henry Young each scored on two-yard plunges and it was 35-0 at halftime. Cox hit Bob Schultz on a 14-yard touchdown throw in the third quarter, Kowalczyk countered with a 32-yard TD run and Blakley scored the only other Minnesota touchdown from the one.

"It's been the same all year," said Warmath in reflecting on the lopsided loss. "We make mistakes early, get in a hole and can't get out."

Mistakes were again the story in the season finale, a 14-6 loss to Wisconsin in Minneapolis. In the second quarter, Cox fumbled at the Minnesota 22 and five plays later sophomore quarterback Dale Hackbart scored from the one. Minnesota came back on an 80-yard drive as Borstad went in from the three.

109

The extra point was no good and Wisconsin led 7-6 at the half.

In the third quarter, the Gophers got to the Wisconsin one, but Cox was stopped on a fourth down attempt. In the last quarter, Hackbart iced the game with a 54-yard scoring run.

"It was my most disappointing year as a coach," Warmath said reflecting back 35 years later. "We never recovered after the Illinois game."

"I think we were a team lacking mental toughness when we needed it, especially against Michigan," said Mike Svendsen.

"We really lacked team speed," Dick Larson remembered. "We were overrated because of the '56 season."

Regardless, 1957 was over and the two years ahead weren't much better.

# Sixteen

Following the 1957 season, Warmath and his staff began to make recruiting moves which would pay enormous dividends three years later.

"It always had been evident to us from the time we arrived at Minnesota that we couldn't win consistently with teams comprised almost entirely of home-grown players," he pointed out. "There simply were not the speed players coming out of the Upper Midwest."

In late 1957 and early 1958, the staff began to go to places like Pennsylvania, Delaware, North Carolina and Illinois to seek top high school football players. When school started in 1958, Minnesota had secured players who in 1960 and 1961 would lead the school to its finest years since the Bierman era. They included Sandy Stephens, Judge Dickson, John Mulvena, Bob Frisbee and Tom Hall from outside the Upper Midwest. Players from the Upper Midwest such as Dave Mulholland, Tom King, Dick Enga, Robin Tellor, Tom Loechler and Jim Wheeler were also cogs in the upcoming years.

Not only was Warmath flying in the face of tradition by recruiting kids who were non-Minnesotans which irritated a lot of the old guard from the Bierman era, but he recognized the talents of the black athlete and made an effort to land them.

"Its tough enough for any kid to go away to school, but if you are black and going to a place like Minnesota with a very small minority population, it's doubly intimidating," said Stephens. "One of the key people who made the transition easier was Carl Rowan, a black columnist for the Minneapolis papers. He impressed upon me and the other black recruits that the Twin Cities was a decent place to live and as a graduate of Minnesota, gave very high marks to the University."

111

"Rowan was instrumental in making the black athletes feel at ease and telling them that an education from Minnesota and life here was worth the commitment," Warmath added.

"I was up front with Warmath when I first met him," Judge Dickson remembered." I told him that I had some doubts. I was black and he was a white Southerner. This was 1958, remember, and the South was still steeped in Jim Crow.

"But Coach Warmath was straight with me as he was with everybody. He said if I played by the rules, went to class and put out, he'd treat me fairly and didn't give a damn what color I was. He always kept his word on that in my four years there."

Both Dickson and Stephens were highly-recruited. As stars out of the very competitive Western Pennsylvania prep scene, they had schools such as Michigan, USC and Ohio State recruiting them. Minnesota was chosen for a variety of reasons, Warmath being the most important.

"Murray told me from the beginning that he'd give me a shot at quarterback," Stephens remembered. "There were no black quarterbacks to speak of at the major collegiate level in the late 1950s. I was taken by his honesty."

The 1958 in-coming class was not only a turning point for Warmath and Minnesota football, it was a major milestone in the development of college football. That year and in the years that followed, Warmath and his staff were at the vanguard in the advancement of black high school players into the college football scene, particularly when it came to recruiting players out of the South. It wasn't until nearly 10 years later that Southeastern, Atlantic Coast and Southwest Conference schools would knock down the segregation barriers. Until then, it was the northern schools, while not without their elements of racism, that offered the only chance for the black collegiate players.

Warmath was a force in starting that process. True, he needed their athletic abilities to turn his program around. At the same time, he gave them opportunities they wouldn't have gotten elsewhere.

"Coach Warmath gave us opportunities not just on the football field, but in the classroom and later life that we would otherwise not have had," Stephens added. "I will always be indebted to him for what he did for me."

•    •    •

For the fall of 1958, Warmath had to suffer while his talented freshmen, ineligible to play in those days, served as the scout team and scrimmaged each other. His fifth year at the helm was a miserable one, at least in the won-loss column. Gone were Cox, Larson (now the backfield coach after Billy Murphy had left to become head coach at Memphis State), Jelacic, Schultz, Borstad, Lindblom, Schmidt, Tuszka, Rasmussen and Burkholder.

It was a long season and when it was over the first wave of howling wolves were at Warmath's door.

"We still suffered from lack of speed," Warmath said. "Yet, there were some talented kids on the team and the seniors were an especially tough, big-hearted group who played all out. I have fond memories of them."

If one were to look at the 1-8 record for 1958, it could be called one of the worst in Minnesota history. What is not apparent is that the Gophers could easily have won from two to five more games. Regardless of the record, the team had talented sophomores who would blossom in 1960.

The first six games of the '58 season were particularly frustrating because, while the Gophers lost all six, they were not far from winning each of them.

For the fourth year in a row, the opening opponent was the University of Washington, this time back in Seattle.

With Cox and Larson gone, the quarterbacking duties fell upon senior Jim Reese, a native of Long Island who had transferred to Minnesota when Fordham dropped football. While lacking speed, Reese was smart, had a good arm and was a good defensive safety. Washington came out passing and on the opening drive the Huskies quarterback Bob Hivner threw the first five times he had the ball. He hit six out of seven for 60 yards in a 73- yard scoring drive. He capped it with a four yard TD run and Huskies were ahead 7-0 less than three minutes into the game.

The Gophers tied it with a 66-yard drive with sophomore fullback Roger Hagberg scoring from one yard out. The Gophers struck again the second quarter when Reese threw a 10 yard scoring pass to end Perry Gehring. Washington's Luther Carr had a 44-yard gain on the ensuing Huskie drive and Hivner took it in from three yards out to tie the game 14-14.

Later, Hivner completed a short pass to halfback Mike McCluskey to give Washington a 21-14 lead. A fumbled punt by Gopher Tom Chandonnet set up a George Fleming field goal with two seconds left before the half.

In the fourth quarter, Reese hit Bill Kauth for a 25-yard TD to narrow the margin to 24-21. Minnesota then drove to Washington's 12 and with 1:17 left, Reese went back to pass but was blindsided by Washington's Kirk Wilson and fumbled. The ball bounced out to the 27 where a swarm of Huskies fell on it to preserve the victory.

The Gophers returned to Minneapolis to face Pitt. What ensued was the first of two consecutive Minnesota losses that turned in the final two minutes.

There were 56,450 fans on hand as Pitt beat Minnesota for the first time in this 10-game series, 13-7. It was a game of incredible frustration for Minnesota. The Gophers put together first-half drives that went to the Panthers' 21, 35, 3 and 11, yet failed to score. In the third quarter, Pitt's Fred Riddle fumbled and Arlie Bomstad recovered at the Panther 32. Six plays later, Hagberg went over the right side from the six and into the end zone. Ev Gerths' PAT was good.

In the fourth quarter, Pitt drove 96 yards to the Gopher one, but was stopped. Pitt kept Minnesota bottled up and took a short punt at the Gopher 33. Quarterback Bill Kaliden snuck in a few plays later. Pitt went for the two-point conversion (the two-point rule was put in effect in 1958), but failed and Minnesota held a one point lead.

Pitt regained the ball in the closing minutes at the Gopher 37 and nine plays later, Kaliden scored again. This time the PAT was a successful kick with 1:34 left giving Pitt a 13-7 victory.

Afterward, Warmath told the media he was not ashamed of the loss insofar as his team had performed gallantly.

"We never gave up," said captain Mike Svendsen.

Pitt coach John Michelosen said the tough Gopher defense forced his team to adjust at halftime and throw. He noted a 14-yard completion to end Mike Ditka on the first scoring drive as being critical. Panther back Ed Sharockman, later a defensive back with the Minnesota Vikings, called Minnesota a "very hard hitting team."

The Gophers frustration increased the next Saturday when they entertained Northwestern and lost with 58 seconds to play.

In the second quarter, Gerths kicked a 23-yard field goal to give Minnesota a 3-0 lead that held until the final minute. Guard Jerry Shetler set up the field goal by recovering a Wildcat fumble at the 32. Reese took the Gophers to the 15 before a tough Northwestern defensive stand forced Minnesota back and the Gophers settled for the field goal.

Minnesota was driving late in the fourth quarter when fullback Jim Rogers fumbled and Northwestern recovered at its 41. Four minutes later, sophomore quarterback Dick Thornton slanted off to his left from the one and barely got in for the game's only touchdown. The extra point was good. The Gophers had lost 7-3.

"I thought we had this one," a dejected Warmath said.

"We've beaten the hell out of three teams and lost three times," Svendsen muttered.

•    •    •

The next week against Illinois, the Gophers fell again. This time they were at least spared the heartbreak of losing in the closing seconds. They continued to demonstrate toughness and spirit and were leading at one point in the second half.

The difference was a fine Illini end named Rich Kreitling who caught two long bombs from quarterback Bob Hickey that resulted in a 20-8 victory, the first for Illinois in Minneapolis since 1919. The other difference, as witnessed by 58,000 home-coming fans in Memorial Stadium, was seven Gopher fumbles, four of which Illinois recovered.

In the first quarter, Bill Burrell, the great Illini guard and linebacker, recovered a Minnesota fumble at the Gopher 29. A field goal attempt a few plays later was no good. Another Minnesota fumble gave Illinois the ball at the Minnesota 21. Again Illinois failed to score. Minnesota then drove to the Illinois 16, but it was the Illini's turn to play good defense and they held. Two plays later, Hickey's long bomb connected to a wide-open Kreitling for 83 yards and a TD.

In the third quarter, sophomore quarterback Joe Salem (Gopher coach from 1979 through 1983) came in with the second unit (except for starting halfback Bill Kauth) and put together a drive that culminated in a short TD pass to end Bruce Hammond.

"Smoky Joe" followed up with a two point conversion run for a brief 8-7 lead.

Hickey and Kreitling combined again, this time striking from 66 yards out and a touchdown.

A few series later, Burrell picked off a Gopher pass and returned it to the 20. Bill "Boom Boom" Brown, also a Viking in the 1960s and 70s, made two runs that got the ball to the Gopher eight. Halfback Dick McDade ran for the touchdown.

Following the 20-8 loss, Warmath pointed out the obvious: fumbles killed the Gophers, but he added, "our line play is the best in the Big Ten."

Minnesota returned to its old ways in Ann Arbor the next week, losing a close game and letting victory slip away in the closing seconds. This time, the Wolverines prevailed 20-19 in what the Tribune's Dick Cullum reported was "one of the finest efforts seen on this field".

Again fumbles (three in the first half alone) stymied the Gophers. Tom Robbins fumbled at the Minnesota 42 and Michigan's Bob Ptacek later scored from the one for a 7-0 lead. Minnesota tied it in the second quarter when Kauth capped a 58-yard march with a six-yard TD run. Michigan quickly countered on a 69-yard drive with Ptacek again sneaking over from the one. The two-point attempt was no good.

The Wolverines went ahead 20-7 on a beautifully-executed trap play by Darrell Harper for 58 yards and a touchdown. Minnesota was valiant, however, and Bob Soltis scored to cap a 77-yard Minnesota drive to cut Michigan's lead to 20-13.

In the fourth quarter, Kauth, Hagberg and halfback Gary Melchert led an 80-yard drive. When it was fourth and 10 from the Wolverine's 14, Reese hit end Ken Schultz at the one and then snuck in to make it 20-19. Warmath went for the win, but the pass attempt was nixed by a strong Wolverine's rush which forced Reese to tuck it away and run. He was knocked out of bounds at the one.

The Gophers again drove deep into Michigan territory, but Kauth was stopped by Walter Johnson for a nine-yard loss. Two pass attempts failed. Michigan got the ball and the victory.

Michigan Athletic Director Fritz Crisler stopped in the Gopher locker room afterward and told Warmath, "Your kids fought their hearts out."

"That's getting to be a habit," Warmath responded, undoubtedly thinking such virtue should be rewarded with a victory. "I thought the two-point play was a good call given how well we moved the ball today."

Then-Michigan assistant Bob Hollway (also later a Viking as an assistant coach and team executive) seconded Warmath's opinion of the Minnesota line, calling it "the best" in the conference.

The Gopher frustration level cranked up a couple of notches the next week when they went to Bloomington, Ind. and left 6-0 losers to the Indiana Hoosiers. Penalties, fumbles and interceptions were Minnesota's undoing this gloomy, overcast Saturday in early November. Indiana got its first Big Ten win in 12 tries with what Cullum reported was "greater desire and resourcefulness."

Indiana, under coach Phil Dickens, deployed a lot of old Tennessee-style single wing. Ted Smith's one-yard plunge in the third quarter was the only score of the game. The statistical difference was amazing. Minnesota got only 94 yards and one first down on the ground compared to 223 yards and 21 first downs for the Hoosiers. In addition, Minnesota had four drives inside the Indiana 25 in the first half that resulted in no points. The Gophers also had 11 penalties.

The biggest play for Minnesota came in the fourth quarter when end Tom Moe caught a pass for 68 yards to the Hoosier 14. Alas, the Gophers came away empty as Larry Johnson was intercepted.

"We were just simply outplayed, despite the close score," Warmath stated.

Nothing changed the next week.

Iowa was No. 2 in the nation when it came to town for the battle for Floyd of Rosedale. The Hawkeyes had an explosive offense and their only non-win was an early season tie against Air Force. The Hawkeyes used halfback Willie Fleming, a burner, who scored two first half touchdown on runs of 63 and 46 yards to give Iowa a 21-0 lead. In the first half alone, the Hawkeyes amassed 319 yards in total offense.

The Gophers scored in the third quarter on a Larry Johnson-to-Bill Kauth pass of 30 yards. In the fourth quarter, Iowa's great quarterback, Randy Duncan, flipped a one-yard pass to end Don Norton to make the final score 28-6.

After the game, Minnesota athletic director Ike Armstrong called the Hawkeyes the best Big Ten team he had ever seen and Warmath added he knew of no team that year which could beat them.

"They were terribly quick and there was no way to contain them," offered Mike Svendsen.

Meanwhile, the Hawkeyes learned after the victory that they were the conference representatives in the Rose Bowl of 1959.

The Gophers were now 0-7 and in bad need of a victory. They finally got it the next Saturday against Michigan State.

The team was "finally repaid for their determination and spirit", reported the Tribune's Johnson and Warmath was rewarded with "a trip across the gridiron at the finish on his players' shoulders."

Minnesota's victory was the result of six pass interceptions and four fumble recoveries. Roger Hagberg's recovery of a muffed punt snap in the first quarter at the State 28 resulted in the first score—Larry Johnson's one-yard sneak to culminate a nine-play drive. Shortly thereafter, the Gophers went ahead 13-0 on a Hagberg plunge from the three. A two-point conversion pass by Johnson failed.

Spartan Al Luplow returned the kickoff to the Gopher 43. A few plays later, Herb Adderley made an 11-yard sweep into the end zone. In the second quarter, it looked like another Gopher loss was possible. Reese was intercepted at his 32. Mike Panitch, the MSU quarterback, snuck in from the one and the Minnesota lead was 13-12.

To the Gophers credit, however, they continued to demonstrate their never-say-die attitude and stopped two late first-half MSU drives, the first on an interception by Reese, the second when a fourth down pass was batted away by Svendsen.

In the second half, the Gophers put State away. A Tom Robbins punt bounced off State's Greg Montgomery and Norm Sixta fell on the ball at the four. Robbins scored in two plays. Then lineman Jerry Wallin picked off a Panitch fumble in the air at the Michigan State 29. Four plays later Kauth scored from the 12 to put the Gophers ahead 26-12.

In the fourth quarter, Arlie Bomstad intercepted a State pass at the 27 and went to the one. He was rewarded on the next play when he scored the TD. Later, Herschel "Pepper" Lysacker returned a punt for 36 yards to the MSU 11 and Johnson hit end Dick Larson (not the former QB) on a touchdown throw.

The final was Minnesota 39, Michigan State 12.

Joy reigned in the Gopher locker room and Warmath called the win his "biggest thrill in my coaching career. We won it for this great group of seniors. We've had every tough break this year. I have never coached a group of kids with more poise and character."

Perry Gehring disagreed somewhat with his coach saying "we won it for Warmath."

Sadly, they couldn't close the season on the same note.

The traditional finale against Wisconsin was in Madison and again, Dale Hackbart led the Badgers to a 27-12 victory. Hackbart ran for one touchdown, threw for another and picked off three passes as the Wisconsin safety.

The first touchdown was scored by the other Wisconsin quarterback, Sid Williams, who led the opening drive and scored on a 20-yard keeper. A few minutes later, Hackbart picked off a Reese pass and took the Badgers inside the Minnesota five. Mike Svendsen led a strong defense that left the Badgers a foot short of a score. Minnesota couldn't move, punted and Hackbart put together a drive that saw him score on a run from the seven.

Bill Kauth returned the ensuing kickoff 61 yards, but a few plays later, Hackbart again intercepted a pass and returned it to the Badger 37. Another Minnesota march late in the second quarter was stopped by a third Hackbart interception.

In the third quarter, a 74-yard Wisconsin drive resulted in a two-yard TD run by Bob Zeman and it was 20-0. Minnesota countered when Larry Johnson hit end Dick Johnson with a 77-yard touchdown pass. The two-point attempt failed. In the fourth quarter, Hackbart connected with Bill Hobbs for a 44-yard scoring toss. Minnesota came back and went 90 yards, featuring two outstanding receptions by Kauth and Tom Moe. Larry Johnson snuck in from the two. The two-point attempt again failed and the last game of the long, painful 1958 season ended.

The post game review focused on Warmath.

"I plan to coach at Minnesota the rest of my career," was his answer to how he felt about the season and the inevitable pressure that was mounting from Gopher fans over the disappointment of 1957 and only one win in 1958.

Within days there was the first wave of what would be two seasons of Monday morning quarterbacking and the call for the Gopher coach to step down. Behind the scenes, Warmath continued business as usual, including some successful recruiting that would have the nay-sayers whistling a different tune a couple of years later.

# Seventeen

Following the 1958 season, Warmath and his staff once again had a great recruiting year. The high school seniors who committed to Minnesota were as fine a group as the previous class that consisted of Stephens, Dickson and Company.

From Minnesota came players such as Julian Hook, Paul Benson, Duane Blaska, Jerry Jones, Al Fischer, Jack Perkovich and John Campbell. Uniontown, Penn., Sandy Stephens' home town, sent halfback, Bill Munsey. Bob Prawdzik was a fullback from Berwyn, Ill.

But the premier player of the freshmen class of 1959 was Bobby Lee Bell of Shelby, N.C. Many experts believe Bell was the finest all-around athlete to ever play at the University of Minnesota. Recruited as a quarterback, he was converted to a tackle by Warmath. He spent 13 years with the Kansas City Chiefs and was the first outside linebacker ever named to pro football's Hall of Fame.

"I never played with or coached a player any better than Bobby Bell," Warmath said.

Bell was the classic physical specimen. It's hard to imagine today that at 6-foot-4 and 215 pounds, he was a two-way tackle. Bell played in an era before the behemoth linemen of today. What separated him from his peers was his incredible strength, amazing speed and quickness. He had no weaknesses as a player.

"We got wind of Bell through my old friend Jim Tatum, who was at North Carolina at the time," Warmath recounted. "Jim called me one day and said there was a black kid playing in a small town in western North Carolina who was the talk of the state.

"In those days, of course, Southern schools still were segregated, so Jim was alerting his friends in the North about Bell. I remember Jim saying, `if you're lookin' for films, there ain't any, if you're lookin' for scouting reports, there ain't any, but take my word for it, this kid is something and if you aren't interested I'll call Forrest Evashevski at Iowa.'

"No, God don't do that, I shot back," Warmath said. "We'll get somebody on this kid right away."

Bell made his first airplane trip ever when he came to the Twin Cities.

"I also was being recruited hard by Notre Dame and Michigan State," Bell said. "I fell in love with the Twin Cities and the U of M and called my Dad back in Shelby and said I wasn't coming back. I wanted to stay."

"Warmath was the first big time coach I ever met and I was both very impressed and also scared of him," Bell remembered. "The other person who was key in my time at Minnesota was Don Knutson, a local construction company owner and Gopher booster and friend of Murray's. He took me under his wing and served as a second father. He rarely asked me about football, but more about how things in general were going."

Bell also served as the team court jester, the guy who kept everybody laughing and loose, remembered Dana Marshall, senior student manager of the 1960 team.

"One afternoon at spring practice in 1961 after Bobby's sophomore season Warmath was talking to the team on the practice field. He was reading an announcement that the undergraduate chapter of the M Club was holding a dinner dance in a few weeks and all of the varsity teams were invited to sponsor a queen candidate for the event.

"He suggested that maybe the team should consider putting up a queen candidate.

"Bobby was standing nearby and as Warmath said that, he called out, 'Hey, I got a candidate.' With that he took both hands and pulled out the front of Warmath's sweatshirt to make two points and added, 'but, I don't think she's got much up here.'

"I remember thinking that Warmath would jump all over him. Everybody was standing with their mouths open. Nobody would have dared do something like that to Murray. But he just smiled and brushed it off. Then everyone laughed. It was obvious that Murray gave Bobby a little more latitude, but I think it was a psychological ploy to keep everyone loose when it was appropriate."

Before Warmath and the rest of the team could enjoy Bell's sense of humor, not to mention splendid play, they would have to endure the 1959 season. While the won-loss record was a slight improvement over 1958, the seeds were being planted for the future. The first signs of the bountiful harvest to come began to show in the fall of 1959.

•     •     •

Nebraska replaced Washington as the opening opponent. It was the first meeting between the two since Warmath's initial year in 1954. Sophomore Sandy Stephens had demonstrated his talents and Warmath was comfortable naming him the starting quarterback against the Cornhuskers. In his first game, Stephens was impressive, throwing for one touchdown and returning an interception for another. He had a part in all of Minnesota's 12 points, but it wasn't enough. Nebraska, a slight underdog who had been shutout the week before by Texas, won 32-12.

Less than 51,000 fans endured a game-long drizzle in Memorial Stadium to watch the debut of Stephens and a group of talented sophomores. The Gophers gave them hope as they were only down 13-12 at halftime.

Minnesota opened the scoring near the end of the first quarter when Stephens found end Dick Johnson open in the end zone. The kick was no good. Pat Fischer, Nebraska's left half-back and later a fine NFL defensive back in the 1960s, got

Nebraska's first score in the second quarter. The Cornhusker possession was set up on a questionable call when a Stephens-to-Dave Mulholland pass bounced out of the sophomore's hands just as he was hit and Nebraska recovered what was ruled a fumble. Minnesota felt it was an incompletion, but the officials ruled otherwise. Five plays later, Fischer scored from the 12 and the PAT put Nebraska ahead 7-6. Three minutes later, Nebraska scored again. Noel Martin picked off a Stephens pass at the Gopher 38 and went to the 16. Four plays later quarterback Harry Tolly scored, but the conversion attempt was no good. Then Stephens intercepted a pass and went 55 yards for a touchdown aided by a fine block by another sophomore, end Tom Hall. Jim Rogers point after attempt was blocked.

In the second half, Minnesota fell apart. Fumbles and interceptions were turned into opportunities for the visitors. Stephens showed his great natural talent early in the third quarter when he returned a punt 78 yards to the Huskers' 12. But the Gophers came away empty. Then Stephens fumbled a punt at his 16 and the Gophers lost possession. Clay White scored a few plays later to put Nebraska ahead 19-12.

Another Stephens fumble gave Nebraska the ball at the Minnesota 47. Despite a 15-yard penalty for holding, the Cornhuskers scored anyway. The touchdown was a nifty piece of running by White who reversed his field on a 34-yard jaunt.

A Nebraska interception in the fourth quarter gave the Cornhuskers' the ball at the Minnesota 18. On fourth and three at the three, Tolly hit White for the score. The two-point PAT pass attempt was batted down.

"Too many fumbles," Warmath said. "We also lost guard Tom Brown just before half and that was a blow. I was impressed with Stephens play in general insofar as it was his first start as a varsity player."

"Stephens will be a great player some day," said Husker coach Bill Jennings.

This would be a year of learning and sophomore mistakes, but there was no doubt that the talent was there.

The Gophers turned things around the next week against Indiana for only their second win in 14 games dating back to 1957.

Minnesota operated successfully out of the winged-T with Indiana using primarily the single wing and some T-formation.

The tone of the game was set on the first play when Indiana's Mel Ross fumbled the opening kickoff at his 27 and Stephens recovered. Kauth, Bomstad and Stephens moved the ball to the four where Sandy scored on a bootleg play. The PAT attempt was wide. The Gophers kicked off and the Hoosiers fumbled again, but Stephens returned the favor. Despite a 45-yard run by Vic Jones, Indiana couldn't score. Minnesota wasn't able to move the ball and Tom Robbins boomed a 71-yard punt all the way to the Hoosier eight.

Indiana's Willie Hunter tried a wide run on a fake quick kick, but the Gophers' Dick Johnson nailed him in the end zone for a safety. The Hoosiers' free kick from the 20 went only to the 50. In eight plays, highlighted by Stephens' run for 21 yards and a pass to Jim Rogers for 24, the Gophers scored with sophomore halfback Tom King leaping over from the four. Minnesota led 14-0 at halftime.

The Gophers expanded the lead in the third quarter. Tom Brown recovered a Hoosier fumble at the 44. Bomstad, Kauth and Larry Johnson contributed to the drive with Kauth getting the touchdown. Later in the quarter, Judge Dickson kicked a 20-yard field goal and Minnesota led 24-0. The Hoosiers finally got things going through the air and scored twice in the last quarter to make the final 24-14.

The entire defensive effort, especially the end play of Dick Johnson, Hall and Bob Deegan, was lauded.

"As good a line play on the defensive side as we have ever had at Minnesota," Warmath said.

Captain Mike Wright said the coaching staff had scouted Indiana well. "We knew what to expect."

"We needed this one," added end Tom Moe.

The next week at Northwestern, the Gophers came within a play of winning another game.

Northwestern was undefeated when the Gophers traveled to Evanston for the game on Oct. 10th. The Wildcats were without their star quarterback, Dick Thornton, so Chip Holcomb, son of the former Purdue coach, Stu Holcomb, took charge. The Wildcats star halfback, Ron Burton, missed the second half of the game.

The contest was a classic Warmath-Parseghian battle, one of many the two would have in the eight years they coached against each other. This time, Northwestern prevailed 6-0 in another struggle that went down to the wire.

Trailing 6-0 with 2:24 to play, the Gophers passed their way from their 17 to the Northwestern 17. Thirty-seven seconds were left when Gopher quarterback Johnson's 11th pass of the drive was picked off by Northwestern's Mark Johnston in the end zone as the clock ran out. Nevertheless, the game was a virtual draw and proved that despite the team's won-loss record, the Gophers were talented and had a bright future.

It was third-string Northwestern quarterback Bob Eickhoff who took over for Holcomb and got the only score the Wildcats needed for the win. Eickhoff directed an 85-yard march that resulted in a seven-yard TD pass to end Paul Yanke early in the fourth quarter. Prior to that, the Gopher defense had played superbly and Stephens continued to show his skills.

In the first half, Minnesota held the Wildcats to just 27 yards on the ground. Yet, two costly penalties killed the Gophers. Early in the first period, Stephens ran a punt back for 73 yards for an apparent touchdown, but Arlie Bomstad's block was ruled a clip. Then, with Northwestern backed up deep in its territory, a Holcomb pass was picked off by Robbins, but it was ruled the Gopher rushers had roughed the passer.

In the second period, Minnesota moved to the Wildcat 23 but a fourth-down pass was batted away and the Gophers came up empty.

Robbins had an active day punting, kicking 10 times for 337 yards. A couple of those were for more than 50 yards. Northwestern also punted 10 times, but for a just 284 yards.

The Wildcats, ranked No. 2 in the country that week, had a hard-fought victory.

"We're just thankful we won. We knew they'd (Minnesota) be tough and they sure proved it today," Parseghian said in his post-game interview.

The talk in the Gopher locker room was whether there was a clip on the Stephens' punt return for an apparent TD and the roughing the passer call on the Robbins' interception. Regardless, Minnesota certainly could have won the game.

It was more of the same the following week against Illinois for the young Gophers.

At Champaign, the Gophers put on a masterful defensive display and took a late gamble. The result was Illinois posting a 14-6 victory.

"On merit, it was a 7-6 game in favor of Illinois, but the Gophers gambled in the last few minutes by trying a fourth down pass from their 21-yard line. The pass failed and Illinois took the ball on downs. From this start, it scored its second touchdown against the disheartened Gophers," reported Dick Cullum.

Illinois got the game's first score midway through the second quarter. After recovering a Larry Johnson fumble, Ethan Blackaby scored a few plays later on a 19-yard run. The conversion was good.

The Gophers came back when Tom Brown recovered a fumble by John Counts. Stephens hit Dickson twice on passes, Hagberg took it three yards to the one and on the second try, Stephens scored. A debate then ensued as to whether to go for one or two points on the PAT. It was decided to go for the tie.

128

However, the ball was not properly marked by the officials and Dickson was forced to try a conversion from a slight angle. It was wide and the Gophers trailed 7-6 at halftime.

The Gopher defense kept the team in the game when the offense couldn't sustain any drives. Illinois threw a lot of trick formations at Minnesota including the "lonesome end" look popularized the year before by Earl Blaik at Army. Still, the Gophers held.

Illinois put the game away late when Minnesota failed to get out of a fourth-down situation when backed up to its 21. A few plays later, Jim Brown scored for Illinois from the three as time ran out. The final was 14-6.

"We've been playing a man-sized game and still losing" Warmath said, taking this defeat harder than any during the season. "These kids of ours are real fighters."

It was the second-quarter fumble, not four interceptions, that hurt Minnesota, he pointed out.

Illinois coach Ray Eliot called the Gophers a typical young team that would give people trouble. He praised Brown and Stephens, adding "one of these days he's (Stephens) going to run and pass an opponent right out of the park."

Several of the Illini players expressed surprise the Gophers didn't try for two points after their touchdown. The following week when Michigan came to Minneapolis, reference was made to the kick attempt instead of the two-point try. One of the medical fraternities hung a large cartoon on the front of its frat house. It showed a buxomly coed with a football bouncing off her cleavage and the caption, "next time, go for the two points."

# Eighteen

The Gophers were a slight favorite when Michigan came to town for the battle for the Little Brown Jug, which the Wolverines regained in 1957.

The game was reflective of the frustration of the past two seasons: a statistical victory, but a scoreboard loss. This time, Minnesota fell 14-6. The Wolverines won on two quick third- quarter scores. Otherwise, the Gophers more than held their own.

The game was scoreless until a couple of minutes into the third quarter when Michigan's Darrell Harper took a punt at his 17 and went down the sideline for an 83-yard touchdown. Two minutes later, Fred Julian raced 42 yards on the first play from scrimmage after the visitors recovered a Gopher fumble.

Larry Johnson led a Gopher scoring drive in the closing minutes when he hit Tom Hall with a 16-yard throw. The two tried to combine for a two-point conversion, but failed. An onside kick was recovered by Michigan, which ran out the clock.

Minnesota dominated many facets of the game including 20 first downs to Michigan's nine and 371 offensive yards to 186.

The line was outstanding as usual, but the first seven times the Gophers got inside the Wolverines' 35 they couldn't score.

"We let down on a couple of plays", observed assistant Minnesota coach Jim Camp, "When they got that quick touchdown on the punt return and then we fumbled, they were sky high. We naturally let down and bingo, they get another."

"I don't want to alibi, but the fact is we were playing with a patched up line," Warmath added. He pointed out the failure to capitalize on being in Michigan territory so many times as another factor in the loss.

The Gophers were 1-4 and the fans were becoming restless. Warmath was hung in effigy in front of a fraternity house across from Memorial Stadium as thousands of downhearted fans left the game late that afternoon.

•   •   •

The Gophers left conference play the next week when they hosted Vanderbilt from the SEC. Minnesota needed a victory badly and they got it. The Minnesota defense hemmed in the Commodore's great running back, Tom Moore, and the offense finally got untracked.

"Spook the House that Vanderbilt" was the 1959 homecoming slogan on Halloween Day before 49,000 fans at Memorial Stadium on an overcast afternoon. The story of the game was defense as the Gophers held Moore to a minus one yard rushing and only 28 yards on pass receptions.

Both defenses played well, especially in the first half. The only score came in the second quarter when Vandy quarterback, Jim McKee, tried to hit end Fred Riggs on a square out pattern to the left. Tom Robbins, playing outside linebacker, stepped in front of Riggs and intercepted the throw. He went untouched for 62 yards and the touchdown.

The third quarter was one of ball control, but no scoring. In that quarter, however, Minnesota ran 25 plays to Vanderbilt's nine. It wasn't until 11:32 was left in the game that Minnesota got its next score. Thanks to a holding penalty, the Gophers faced third and 22 from their 41. Joe Salem threw deep to halfback Tom King. Vandy's Russ Moore tipped the ball, but King caught it for the first down at the Commodore 30. From there, King, Dave Mulholland and Salem finished off the drive with Salem scoring from the three. The Gophers led 13-0.

Vanderbilt clipped on the kickoff and had a pass interference call go against it on the first play from scrimmage. Unable to get out of the shadows of its own end zone, Vanderbilt punted to the Minnesota 34.

Roger Hagberg got five off tackle, quarterback Larry Johnson picked up three on a right end keeper and Hagberg went 26 yards off left guard for the TD. Dickson made the conversion and it was 20-0 for the Gophers. Late in the game, the Commodores put together a drive of 48 yards with McKee scoring on a six-yard run. The two-point pass try was no good.

"Their line never gave us a chance to get started," observed Vanderbilt coach Art Guepe. "That 76 (Gopher tackle Frank Brixius) really socked us in the line."

Tom Moore was asked if he'd ever been held in check like he was by the Gopher defense.

"Well, Mississippi held me to 13 yards but I've never been held to any minus yards," he answered.

Asked if there was any one particular Gopher who was in his hair, he answered "no, they all seemed to be there."

Salem, who had played only five minutes all season prior to the homecoming game, was the locker room hero.

"Salem didn't surprise me," Warmath pointed out. "He's always been a fine field general and the best ball handler on the team."

Warmath went on to cite the breaks the Gophers finally got, especially Robbins' interception return for the touchdown and the reception by King of the tipped pass.

"When the game was in question, the defense did the job," Warmath said.

Asked about the future (namely his), Warmath gave a terse, reply: "It always helps to win."

The next week at Iowa, that axiom wouldn't come true and the Hawkeyes thrashed the Gophers, 33-0. It turned out to be the only real drubbing the team took all season. Even then, it was a close game for the first half as Evashevski's team led only 7-0 at halftime before wearing down the Gophers.

Minnesota was missing Wright and Brown from the line due to injuries. Nevertheless, the Gopher line remained tough for almost three quarters.

Iowa scored its first half touchdown in the second period. Sophomore quarterback Wilburn Hollis led the Iowa second unit on a drive from their 26 to the Gopher 14. Evy put the first string back in and with third down on the seven, Olen Treadway hit Jeff Langston for the touchdown pass.

Midway in the third period, Treadway led another drive, highlighted by 22 and 14-yard runs by halfback Tony Jeter. From the three, fullback Gene Mosley punched it in for the Hawkeyes who were now ahead 13-0.

In the fourth quarter, the Gophers, battered and with thinning ranks, began to crumble. A 47-yard, nine play Iowa drive was capped by Jeter's six-yard scoring run. The two- point attempt failed. A couple of exchanges later Iowa had the ball at its 40. Hollis passed for 26 yards to Mosley and ran on a roll out for 17. Halfback Larry Ferguson scored from the one. Another two-pointer was no good, but Iowa was comfortably ahead 25-0.

The last score came as a result of an interception by Jerry Mauren of a Sandy Stephens' pass late in the game. A couple of quick plays took the Hawkeyes to the Gopher 18. John Brown went around end from there for the score with nine seconds left. Finally, a two-point conversion was good and the clock mercifully ran out on the ensuing kickoff.

Warmath pointed out the depth and speed of the Iowa backs and the fact his line was decimated by injuries as contributing to the one-sided loss.

"We aren't going to quit," proclaimed reserve end Bob Deegan. "But the squad is lower today than it has been after any defeat this year."

Although he didn't openly let on, Warmath was feeling as low as he ever had in his 29 years as a player and coach.

Mike Wright, the team captain, who missed the Iowa game, recalled receiving a note afterward from Mary Louise Warmath.

"She wrote to me saying Coach Warmath was so down after the Iowa loss that he was mumbling about maybe resigning. But then upon realizing we were all rallying as a team and stood behind him and the rest of the coaches, he quickly changed his mind.

"Our problem that year was we were so young in a lot of positions and made dumb mistakes. We didn't know how to win."

Wright added that years later in looking back, the incredible part about Warmath was his "ability to rise above all of it."

•    •    •

"Fund Sought to Payoff Warmath Pact."

That was the headline to the lead story in the Nov. 12th edition of the Tribune. Written by Sid Hartman, the article was surprisingly brief and it did not give any names of the so-called downtown Twin Cities business leaders who were trying to put together a $40,000 package to pay off the 1960 and 1961 years of Warmath's contract.

At a banquet at the Amateur Sportsmens' Club later in the week to honor the 1959 state high school football champions, Minneapolis Washburn, Warmath joked about his status.

"The trick when you're being run out of town on a rail is to make it look like you're heading the parade."

Meantime, it was back to the "close-but-no-cigar" style of 1959 Minnesota football, this time against Purdue. In the second-to-last game, the Gophers fell 29-23 and were marching for a possible winning score when the game ended.

Playing with a patched-up squad still racked by injury, the Gophers fell behind 21-7 at halftime, but fought back with two TDs and two two-point conversions in the second half. It was quarterback Larry Johnson, end Tom Hall and center/linebacker Greg Larson who were the keys to the Gophers' success. Minnesota opened the scoring midway through the first quarter when Bill Kauth picked off a Boilermaker pass on his own 45 and went to the Purdue 40. From there, passes to Hall for 14 and Tom Moe for 15 yards were the key. From the four, Tom Robbins hit the line twice for the score. Dickson made the extra point kick.

Minnesota then began to self-destruct as they had so many times before. Two interceptions and a fumble resulted in three Boilermaker scores. From the Minnesota 49, Purdue quarterback Bernie Allen (later the second baseman for the Minnesota Twins), scrambled and just as he was hit at the line of scrimmage, unloaded a throw to a wide-open Dick Brooks at the Minnesota 21 who ran in for the score.

A fumble recovery by Purdue at the Gopher 26 resulted in a Clyde Washington 10-yard touchdown run on a pitch play. Then on the last play of the first half, Ross Fichtner picked off a Stephens pass and went 66 yards to score.

The Gophers completely dominated the third quarter. The first score came after Minnesota moved from its own 33 to the Purdue two. The offense stalled, but Larson broke through on Purdue's first play from scrimmage and nailed Boilermaker quarterback Maury Guttman for a safety. The free kick followed and the Gophers got the ball at midfield. Johnson hit Hall on a 10-yard scoring throw, but the two-point conversion pass attempt to Hall was no good and the Boilermaker lead was cut to 21-15.

Purdue came back in the fourth quarter and Washington scored on a one-yard plunge. The two-pointer was good and it was 29-15.

Sandy Stephens took over and marched the Gophers 62 yards in eight plays with Hagberg scoring on a short plunge. Stephens swept end for the two points to make it 29-23. A Minnesota march was stopped with Fichtner's third interception locking up the Purdue victory.

The Gophers played "a man's game, a helluva game. They were on Purdue's neck all afternoon and that's all you can ask," Warmath was quoted by the Minneapolis Star's Dick Gordon in his post-game story.

Gordon reported Warmath didn't comment on whether the Gophers were more inspired because of speculation on his perhaps being forced to resign.

But Mike Wright addressed the issue.

"We fought especially hard because of all that stuff that happened during the week. Of course, we've been fighting hard every game. But this one we really wanted to win. You know why."

They had one last chance to try and win one more for their coach. Once again, they only came close.

•    •    •

Wisconsin arrived in Minneapolis for the 1959 season finale in an absolute must-win situation to have any chance for the Big Ten title. The Badgers, Northwestern and Michigan State all had four wins and two losses in conference play. When the day was over, it was Wisconsin who won the title and headed for the Rose Bowl. Minnesota, however, didn't make it easy for them.

Once again, the Gophers took it down to the wire and once again, mistakes and failure to execute killed the young team. Wisconsin won 11-7.

The Gophers struck early and quickly. With just 1:43 gone in the first quarter, Stephens hit Arlie Bomstad on a 57-yard touchdown pass on the fifth play of the game. The kick was good by Hall and the Gophers led 7-0. Minnesota showed its usual tenacity on defense when it stopped Wisconsin twice in the same quarter, both times at the Gopher 15.

No further scoring took place until the third quarter when the Badgers' Karl Holzwarth kicked a 12-yard field goal. That kick set a NCAA record for the most consecutive field goals (seven) by a player. Later that day, George Grant of Colorado College tied Holzwarth's record in a game against Fort Hayes State with his seventh consecutive field goal.

Wisconsin came back in the fourth quarter when Dale Hackbart marched the Badgers 80 yards in 10 plays, scoring the go-ahead TD himself on a short sneak with 8:41 left in the game. He then hit Henry Derleth on the two-point conversion and the Badgers had an 11-7 lead.

Minnesota fought back. Tom King returned the kickoff to the Gopher 28. Larry Johnson was intercepted by Jerry Stalcup, but a personal foul before the throw nullified the play and Minnesota kept possession. Johnson took the Gophers to the Badger six. However, Stalcup knocked down a fourth-down pass. Minnesota threatened one more time, but once again, as in 1958, it was Hackbart intercepting the pass, this one on the last play of the game.

Northwestern lost to Illinois and Michigan State played one less conference game than the Badgers, so it was Wisconsin who went to the Rose Bowl. It was a trip best forgotten as Washington routed the Badgers 44-8.

In his post-game comments, Warmath, feeling the heat from a sizeable number of alumni and media, boldly stated that in 1959, Minnesota was close to being a championship team, not just a good team.

Senior end Tom Moe commented that "we could have been 8-1 this year."

In retrospect, both men were accurate. Perhaps 7-2 was more realistic since both the Nebraska and Iowa losses were sizeable. Despite the malcontents, the hanging of Warmath in effigy and the garbage that was tossed on the front lawn of his Edina home, the loyalty of the staff and especially the players remained strong.

"I felt the team would be a good one the next year," remembered Mike Wright. "Don Riley of the St. Paul papers told me we had the material for a national championship team in 1960."

Judge Dickson, Dave Mulholland and Sandy Stephens all recalled 1959 vividly.

"I remember one day during the week when we were scheduled to practice in the fieldhouse because of bad weather," recounted Dickson. "I think it was right after the Iowa loss and there were rumors every day about Warmath being out. That day, some of us heard that he was going to be fired and one of the assistants was taking over immediately and would finish out the end of the year.

"It was a few minutes before practice and I was standing by the door leading into the fieldhouse from the tunnel that comes over from Cooke Hall. Suddenly the doors swung open and Murray came in. I looked at him and said 'what the hell are you doing here. We heard you quit?' He sorta glared at me and said 'nobody is quitting on this goddamn team, now get ready for practice.' I remember being struck by how much he was sticking by his beliefs and the confidence he had in us."

"That year was very painful for me because I was not used to losing like that," Stephens said. "There were rumors they might shift me to halfback. I also was very interested in playing baseball. But before spring practice in 1960, Murray asked me to forego baseball for spring football, saying that I was his quarterback. He said we'd have a great team that year and I totally believed him . . . and in us."

"Coach was not quitting on us and that was very important," Mulholland said. "Looking back, there wasn't much difference in talent between 1959 and 1960. Warmath never deviated from what he believed in, including us, and that made the difference in 1960."

With a laugh, lineman Bob Frisbee recalled that "at Christmas in 1959, I bet my Dad a new car, we'd go to the Rose Bowl. He said it was a bet he'd gladly take."

By Christmas of 1960, Frisbee was driving a new Corvette.

# Nineteen

"My staff and I were very confident that we would have a good team in 1960," Warmath says today. His returning players agreed with him.

"Warmath set a great example in 1959 on to how to handle adversity and it simply rubbed off on us," Mulholland remembered. "We knew we were talented. We were young in '59 and seasoned going into '60."

"We never saw ourselves as losers," Judge Dickson said of the '59 team.

"Tom Brown had been awesome in 1959 and we knew that Bobby Bell and Bill Munsey were among a group of really good freshmen who were coming up to the varsity," recounted Bob Frisbee.

"One of the things I noticed was that Murray seemed to loosen up a bit after the 1959 season and was listening more to his assistants like Dick Larson," Frank Brixius pointed out. "I think his approach that year made a real difference in how we melded as a team."

The staff would have to replace Wright at tackle, Shetler at guard and Tom Moe at end. Critical to that was the decision to convert the outstanding freshman, Bell, to tackle. Bell had been a quarterback in high school and played that position, halfback and end on the freshmen squad.

"I remember when Warmath called me into his office to tell me about the change," Bell said. "It was just before spring practice of 1960. As a freshman, I was concerned with just holding my own on the team and staying ahead in my studies. I was in awe of Warmath.

"He asked me to sit down and started telling me that he and the coaches needed to shore up the line, especially at tackle with the graduation of Wright. He said the decision was made to move me to tackle. I was shocked, but didn't dare say anything. While he was telling me this, he reached into a drawer of his desk and pulled out a rolled up tube sock. In the sock was a pearl-handled revolver and he starting twirling it around his finger as he was telling me about moving me to tackle. I was listening, but I was distracted by that gun.

"I couldn't imagine being a tackle, but in no way was I going to argue. I just said 'yes, sir' and promised to do my best and left the meeting."

"Warmath's moving Bell to tackle wasn't a big surprise to many of us," Dickson recalled. "I've always contended that one of the things he did to turn around the program at Minnesota was to recruit a lot of high school backs with good skills and speed and convert many of them to linemen."

Those changes, an experienced group of juniors and a solid core of seniors such as captain Greg Larson, Brown, Brixius, Dick Larson, Joe Salem and Larry Johnson, were the perfect combination. The media called the Gophers a darkhorse and Playboy Magazine made the Gophers the title favorite. The 1960 season started in fine fashion.

•   •   •

As in 1959, Minnesota opened with Nebraska, this time in Lincoln. It was apparent in this game that the experience gained by the 1959 sophomores would pay off and that a couple of talented new sophomores were going to make an impact in 1960.

A strong interior line led by seniors Brown, Larson and Brixius, returning letterman Jack Mulvena at guard and Bell, showed that the line was where the Gophers would dominate.

Late in the first quarter, Brown and Bell led a tough defense which thwarted a midfield drive by Nebraska. The Gophers couldn't move themselves and Stephens punted to the Cornhusker two. But a few plays later, Minnesota had the ball again at the Nebraska 47 on another punt exchange. Stephens led the drive, primarily with the Gopher second team, that got to the opposition's six as the quarter ended. The rest of the first unit came back in and Stephens scored from the two on fourth down. Dickson missed the point after.

Later in the quarter, the Gophers took over at their 32 and overcame two penalties and relied on a much-improved Stephens passing game to get their second touchdown. Two big passes by Stephens, the first to end Bob Deegan for 17 yards and the second to Mulholland for 23 yards and the score, highlighted the march. Dickson kicked the conversion with 8:40 left in the half.

In the second half, Bell hit Pat Fischer hard enough to cause a fumble which Brixius recovered. The Gophers went 21 yards for the third touchdown, this one coming on a Jim Rogers one-yard plunge. The PAT was good and it was 20-0. The Gophers added to the score almost immediately. On the second play after the kickoff, Bill Munsey picked off a Nebraska pass and went 42 yards into the end zone. Dickson missed the conversion.

With a 26-0 lead, Minnesota played it conservatively, eating up the clock. The Cornhuskers got two late touchdowns to make the final 26-13.

"We were tough when we had to be tough," Brixius told the media afterward.

"Delighted," was Warmath's summation of his feelings. "Nebraska came in very optimistic. They had the advantage of opening the season last week (they beat Texas), so this win was especially satisfying since it was also in their stadium."

Bill Jennings, the Cornhusker coach, called Minnesota's passing game very good and their pass rush "terrific".

Dana Marshall, the senior student manager pointed out the victory was the first road triumph since the Northwestern game in early 1957.

The next week was against Indiana, which was on such severe probation by the Big Ten for recruiting violations that neither its wins nor losses counted in conference records. The Gophers scored only twice in the first three quarters, then four times in the fourth to win 42-0.

Minnesota struggled early and didn't score its first touchdown until only three minutes were left in the first half. The Gophers went 48 yards in 12 plays with Hagberg getting the final two.

At the start of the second half, Stephens returned the kickoff to his 33. Seven plays later on a run-pass option, he hit Dick Larson on the Indiana 15 who ran for the touchdown.

What seemed to be another touchdown pass to Tom Hall was called back because of a motion penalty. However, a fumble recovery by Stephens gave the Gophers another shot as the fourth quarter started. Hagberg gained 18 yards, then Stephens, who carried only four times all day, scored from the three.

Indiana moved into Minnesota territory, but reserve linebacker Jerry Annis intercepted a pass and went 68 yards to score. The final two scores were on a Rogers one-yard plunge and a Joe Salem-to-Dave Lothner pass of 28 yards.

Warmath had made a change in the kicking game and it was Jim Rogers who made six conversion attempts.

Stephens said the slow start was not a concern and Salem said defensive play was very encouraging.

"Minnesota's got two good units and that's what kills you," moaned Indiana coach Phil Dickens. "I didn't see one offensive mistake by Minnesota."

That same afternoon, Northwestern, the next Gopher opponent, was trounced 42-0 by visiting Iowa, one of the favorites for the Big Ten title. Warmath knew he would have a fight on his hands when the Wildcats, determined to get back into the win column, came to Minneapolis for the third game of the year.

For the previous few years, Ara Parseghian had molded a highly-competitive football program at Northwestern. Nationally ranked and almost always in the hunt for the Big Ten title, the Wildcats were reflective of Parseghian—tough, disciplined and always prepared to do battle with any opponent. So, in the third game, reeling from the lopsided loss to Iowa, it was not surprising that they came to Minneapolis ready to give the Gophers all they could handle.

Dick Thornton was in his "second" junior year as the Northwestern quarterback. He received an extra year of eligibility due to an injury in 1959. In 1958, he had established himself as one of college footballs' better signal callers. By the time the '60 contest with the Gophers was over, Thornton had been rocked by the Minnesota defense, but had demonstrated remarkable courage.

There wasn't a lot in the way of thrilling highlights since the game developed into a low-scoring, defensive slugfest. Yet, it was a classic battle between old rivals. Both teams played superb defense, the Gophers' just slightly better. The depth at the Gopher quarterback position proved to be crucial, as it would throughout the season.

Thornton not only stood tough against a relentless Gopher rush, but his superb punting kept Minnesota in check for much of the game. Both teams repeatedly penetrated the other's side of the field, only to be stopped short. Minnesota got to the Wildcats' 20, 46, inside the one and the 32 without scoring. Minnesota saw Northwestern get to its 45, 3, 31, 35, 10 and 42 and come up empty.

It was third-string quarterback Joe Salem who engineered the only score of the game. In the third period, Bill Munsey took a Thornton punt at his 12 and brought it out to the Gopher 42. Salem came in and handed off to Munsey who hit the left side three consecutive times for a first down. He had set up a perfect long pass situation and on the next play, faked another Munsey inside run, stepped back and hit Bob Deegan streaking down the right sideline. The pass covered 40 yards and Deegan was stopped at the Wildcat nine. In came Stephens and on second down from the six, he ran in for the score. Rogers' kick was good.

Three Gopher interceptions in the fourth quarter were critical including one late in the game when a hard rush by Annis, Brown and Bell forced a throw which Munsey intercepted.

Minnesota held on to a 7-0 victory.

After the game, it was revealed Brown had played with the stomach flu and Munsey fought a case of leg cramps, something that would bother him throughout most of his career.

"This game was hard fought and one in which we played their best and won," Warmath noted.

Warmath was relieved and called the game the hardest so far in the season.

"It was typical Northwestern-Minnesota game—mean as hell," Parseghian said afterward.

He felt the one play (the Salem-to-Deegan throw in the third quarter) was the only difference. "Our defensive backs got mixed up on the assignment. Other than that, it was a dead even ball game."

Thornton said the Gopher pass rush was critical and the Gophers pretty much shut down the running game as well.

"I know from experience every game with Minnesota is close," said the Wildcat quarterback. referring to 7-3 and 6-0 Northwestern victories the previous two years. "They've (Minnesota) always been tough."

The next week against Illinois, Minnesota showed the toughness needed to win when faced with adversity.

There was a lot of homecoming spirit on campus that week. June Wilkinson (no relation to the author), the buxomly blonde cheese cake queen, rode in the homecoming parade and 63,000 fans were at Memorial Stadium when the Illini came to town. They saw an aroused Gopher team, trailing 10-7 as the third period ended, and angry because Frank Brixius was ejected for retaliating against a late hit by Illinois' Ed O'Bradovich, score two fourth-quarter TDs to pull off a 21-10 win. The Gophers, ranked 10th in the AP poll the week of the game, began a climb that would see them take the top spot in the country at season's end. The Illinois game was critical to that process.

Illinois had a banty little 158 pound, 5-foot 8-inch quarterback, John Easterbrook, who baffled Minnesota in the first half with his deceptive ball handling, keepers, pitchouts and passes. He put together a 94-yard march late in the first quarter on 15 plays. The score came on a pitchout to Joe Krakowski for the final four yards. The conversion was good.

The Gophers came back as the second team, with Larry Johnson quarterbacking, moved to the Illini nine from its 34. Stephens came back in and scored on a nine-yard keeper.

A 33-yard field goal by Illinois' Gerald Wood made it 10-7 at halftime.

The Brixius ejection occurred on the third play of the second half.

"O'Bradovich hit me in the face with both hands on a block," Brixius recalled. "We had come out of the halftime locker room really fired up and I sorta' lost my head. I grabbed him by the face mask and gave him an uppercut to the jaw. The next thing I knew, I was gone."

Illinois had the ball and worked its way to the Gopher 18. But Tom Hall and sophomore linebacker Julian Hook, a fine backup, led a tough defense that denied Illinois a score. A few series later, Illinois was backed up deep in its territory and a hard Minnesota punt rush resulted in a meager 20-yard kick. The Gophers took over on the visitors' 43. Johnson and Stephens again combined with Stephens scoring from the two.

The Gophers, behind tough play from Hook, Hall, Greg Larson and reserve tackle Dick Miller, stopped everything Illinois tried. Minnesota began its third TD drive from its 26. It took just six plays to go the 74 yards. The key plays were Stephens hitting Deegan with a 41-yard pass and Larry Johnson connecting with Hall for 11 yards. On the next play, Stephens made a beautiful open-field run of 18 yards for his third touchdown. Rogers kicked his third PAT (and 10th in a row) and Minnesota went to 4-0 with a 21-10 triumph.

Illinois won the statistical battle of total yards and first downs, but Warmath's team won the scoreboard. That was because the Gophers were doing what they had not done in previous seasons—utilizing their fine talent and sound coaching and learning to win.

"I'm the happiest coach in the world," Warmath whooped after the game. "I've been waiting for this one for a long time. I'll never forget that loss in Champaign (the 1957 game)."

Larry Johnson said Warmath fired the team up at halftime. "I've never seen the coach like this."

Warmath praised his second unit and cited Hook and Miller (who had replaced the ejected Brixius) for their excellent defensive play, adding they made the first unit play better.

For the first time since 1954, Minnesota was 4-0. That year, the Gophers went to Michigan and were shut out badly. Six years later, they reversed the process.

• • •

Minnesota came into Ann Arbor as one of only two undefeated Big Ten teams (the other being Iowa) and ranked sixth in the nation. When it was over, they were still undefeated, along with the Hawkeyes and still sixth in the nation.

The battle with the Wolverines was a classic. Its focal points were the great defense and use of the kicking game, two traditional Warmath strong points. Dick Cullum's opening the next morning in the Minneapolis Sunday Tribune summarized the game  succinctly.

"Minnesota's football team scored a 10-0 victory at Michigan's homecoming here Saturday.

"That plain, unembellished statement of a simple fact will strike home to Minnesota supporters as forcefully as any wordy paean of joy.

"The Gophers simply whipped the Wolverines before 69,352 deeply impressed fans under perfect conditions for both players and spectators.

"The victory came by a formula which is becoming the hallmark of 1960 Minnesota football.

"It was done by an alert, hard-hitting defense which rushed the opponent's passers and harassed their ball carriers, causing interceptions and fumbles."

Minnesota got its first score less than two minutes into the second period. Michigan had a first down on its 44 when halfback Jim Ward attempted to sweep his left end. Gopher end Bob Prawdzik tripped up Ward who managed to stay on his feet only to be smacked hard by Bill Kauth coming up from the defensive corner. The ball popped loose and Stephens fell on it at Michigan 43. Hagberg and King went up the middle and got the Gophers 10 yards. Hall took a Stephens pass for 11 yards and a couple more runs by King and Hagberg got Minnesota to the Wolverines' eight. Munsey went to the two and Rogers smashed in for the touchdown. Rogers also kicked the PAT.

Later in the quarter, Michigan got to the Gophers 42. Wolverines quarterback Dave Glinka tried to go to the air three times, but a ferocious Gopher defense, which played nearly flawlessly all afternoon, stopped each attempt. Dean Odegard knocked down his first pass, Prawdzik dropped him for a 15-yard loss on the next play and Hagberg drove him out of bounds for a three-yard loss on third down.

In the third quarter, Stephens punted to the Wolverines' 25. Going to the air again, Glinka had his pass intercepted by Hagberg, who took it from the 33 to the 13. Minnesota got to the one, but a Stephens sneak for an apparent touchdown was called back because of a motion penalty. Minnesota had to settle for a Rogers field goal of 22 yards to make it 10-0.

The rest of the game belonged to the defense. Both the starters and the reserves were outstanding and Michigan never was able to get out of its end of the field. In the first quarter, Michigan penetrated to the Minnesota 37, but Bennie McRae fumbled and Rogers recovered. That was as deep as the Wolverines would get all day.

Warmath called it the finest line play he'd been associated with as a coach and was especially praiseworthy of Brixius and Brown. End coach Butch Nash received praise from players and coaches alike for the fine scouting report he prepared on Michigan and for the play of his ends such as Deegan, Prawdzik, Hall and Larson.

Bump Elliott, the Michigan coach, called Minnesota a "darn good football team," adding he had never seen better line play by a Big Ten team since becoming head coach at Ann Arbor.

"Their defense put so much pressure on us all afternoon that we couldn't get out of the hole."

A jubilant group of Gophers headed home with the Little Brown Jug in its possession for the first time since 1956. Ahead were the struggling and much less-talented Kansas State Wildcats. Then it was undefeated Iowa—No. 1 and lightning fast.

•     •     •

About the only down side to the 48-7 victory over Kansas State was the consecutive PAT string by Mankato native Jim Rogers ended at 14, and the first touchdown pass of the year was completed against the Gophers with less than 1:10 to play in the game.

The game proved to be a warmup for the big contest against Iowa the following week. Warmath used 51 players and the Gophers scored two touchdowns in each of the first three periods and one in the fourth before a relatively small crowd of 43,568.

The fullbacks—Rogers, Hagberg and sophomores Jerry Jones and Jon Jelinek—gained 223 of the 333 total rushing yards.

The first team played only about 14 minutes and second, third, fourth and even fifth stringers got in the game. Joe Salem scored the game's first TD on an 11-yard keeper and Rogers followed shortly thereafter with a one-yard plunge. In the second quarter, a short Kansas State punt into a strong wind set up a Gopher drive with Larry Johnson taking it over from the two. Johnson did the same thing on a six-play drive after Hall recovered a Wildcat fumble at the Kansas State 20.

In the second half, Dave Mulholland recovered a fumbled pass reception at the State 47, but it took 16 plays to score in large part due to penalties against Minnesota. Jones scored on a one-yard plunge.

Later, Jones picked up 33 of the 44 yards in a short drive and finished things off with a two-yard blast for the score. Minnesota topped off the scoring spree in the fourth quarter when Judge Dickson scored from the one to complete a 49-yard march. The big play was a 27-yard pass from Salem to sophomore end Dave Lothner.

State finally got on the board as the clock ran down when quarterback John Solmos hit end Willis Crenshaw on a 40-yard scoring play.

Warmath was relieved to have a breather after five tough games. He alluded to 1956 when Minnesota had to slug it out with Pitt for a 9-6 victory that resulted in three Gopher players being hurt and Minnesota being hampered the following week in the title game against Iowa. In 1960, Minnesota was in much better shape. Now, the attention of not just the two states, but of the country, turned to Minneapolis and Nov. 5th for the game of the year.

# Twenty

"The Twin Cities on the banks of the Mississippi will have a new big league baseball team next year, and they'll have a team in the National Football League, too. Minneapolis and St. Paul are very enthusiastic about this because they love baseball and pro football, but last weekend the transplanted Senators and the football Vikings could have raced down Nicollet Avenue astride giraffes with Nixon and Kennedy waiting at the finish line to kiss the winner, and no one in Minneapolis would have bothered to look around. The University of Minnesota was playing the University of Iowa and nothing was as important as this."

Thus wrote Sports Illustrated reporter Roy Terrell in his lead story in the Nov. 14th, issue of SI as he recounted the game for the Big Ten title and the No. 1 one spot in the polls.

Terrell was right. No game in recent memory had aroused such anticipation and passion as the Gopher-Hawkeye clash on the first Saturday in November. Memorial Stadium was sold out for weeks. Scalpers were getting $100 for a pair of seats between the 20 yard lines, an astronomical amount of money in those days. By game time, a record throng of 65, 610 was sandwiched into the old brickyard. Hotels and motels in a 20-mile radius were booked solid. Even Channel 2, the Twin Cities' public television station, broadcast the game. Long-time area sports announcer Rollie Johnson, who hosted Warmath's weekly TV show, did the play-by-play.

Terrell went on in the opening portion of his SI article to briefly recount Warmath's background as a player, an assistant coach and his ups and downs during his first six years at Minnesota.

"The team over which Warmath most frequently woke up screaming was Iowa. Warmath beat Evashevski in 1954 and then lost to him five straight times."

The Hawkeyes ranked No. 1 one in the country and the Gophers No. 3 when they met that chilly, overcast day. Iowa's first three teams of backs were all faster than anyone on the Minnesota team. Iowa had scored more than half their touchdowns on long runs. Quarterback Wilburn Hollis was a fine runner and an average passer, but one who seemed to connect on the long touchdown pass.

"If our team can contain their outside speed, we can win," Warmath proclaimed before the game. Warmath's defense, which had given up only 30 points in the previous six games, was the key. By game time, the oddsmakers rated the game even. It wasn't even at all. The key was the Minnesota line play which was magnificent. Guard Tom Brown had an unbelievable day, totally dominating the Hawkeyes. That performance sealed both All-American honors and the Outland Trophy for "Brownie" as the nation's top lineman.

The Gophers scored early, thanks to an Iowa miscue instigated by the Gopher line. The Hawks had the ball fourth down on their 46. Center Bill Van Buren made his only bad punt snap of the year and it sailed over John Calhoun's head and rolled back to the 14 where he picked up the loose pigskin but was immediately smothered by a swarm of Gophers.

On third-and-three from the seven, Stephens kept, then pitched to Munsey, who swept untouched around left end for the touchdown. Rogers converted. The game was five minutes old.

The two teams slugged it out into the second quarter when Iowa put together a march and got to the Gopher 12 but stalled. Tom Moore, a native of Rochester and years later an assistant coach with the Gophers, Steelers and Vikings, kicked a 28-yard field goal for Iowa to cut the lead to 7-3. The drive might have resulted in a touchdown were it not for Brown. On third down from the five, he blasted Iowa's left guard Bill DiCindio so hard he sent him flying back into Hollis who had pulled out with the ball to turn and handoff. So vicious was the force of Brown's hit that Hollis went down for a yard loss. Early in the second half and with the Gophers still ahead by four, Iowa made their last major offensive move of the day. From midfield, using some tricky trap plays that baffled the Gophers temporarily, Larry Ferguson, Hollis and Joe Williams ripped off runs of 18, 12 and 20 yards, the last by Williams being a run up the middle for the score. Moore split the uprights and Iowa led for the first time, 10-7, but only briefly.

Minnesota came back. Stephens took the kickoff to the 20, then moved the Gophers to the 36 where it was third-and- six. Joe Salem came in for the first time and in what was the crucial play of the game, hit Roger Hagberg along the left sideline for a 28-yard gain. Stephens came back in and connected with Tom King for four yards, then handed off Hagberg for a 19- yard run to the Iowa five. Mulholland went around right end for four. Stephens then followed a solid block by Brown over right guard and the Gophers were back on top.

Iowa made a brief fourth-quarter run getting to the Minnesota 42, but halfback Jerry Mauren was stopped short by Dick Larson and Dick Miller on a fourth and two play. The Gophers couldn't move and Iowa again tried to get something going. However, a fumble by Iowa which reserve tackle Jim Wheeler recovered, gave Minnesota the ball at the Hawkeye 41. A penalty temporarily slowed the Gophers down, but they struck again when Hagberg, who would wind up with 105 yards rushing, broke over left tackle and ran 42 yards to score. The Minnesota fans (there were between 10,000 and 15,000 Iowans on hand) went nuts. They sensed a victory not just because of the Hagberg score, but because it was evident that Minnesota was winning the battle in the trenches both offensively and defensively. Ends Bob Deegan, Tom Hall and Dick Larson kept the flanks under control, preventing any of the Iowa speed merchants from getting outside. The secondary would allow only six of 14 passes to be completed for just 46 yards.

With less than five minutes left, Iowa fumbled again at its 34. Salem was back in at quarterback and from the 15, pulled off three sneaks, the last one for Minnesota's fourth touchdown giving the Gophers a convincing 27-10 victory.

When the game ended, fans swarmed on to the field and for the third time in four weeks, Warmath was hoisted onto the players' shoulders. The previous rides weren't quite as thrilling as this one. Brown, Jerry Annis (who along with Greg Larson and Julian Hook, did a fine job of backing up the defensive line), Dickson and Salem were also carried off as the crowd went crazy.

The post-game remarks by both sides belied the obvious. For Minnesota, it was a combination of finally getting a shot at the top and using a great defense and opportunistic offense to do the job.

"This is the greatest moment of my life. Nothing comes close," yelled captain Greg Larson.

"I guess I got in my licks," Brown said modestly when asked about his superb play.

"Our kids were sky-high and the defensive play was outstanding," Warmath shouted over the roar in the locker room. He said the line play was magnificent and he never had a player perform like Brown did that day. He smiled broadly when someone in the media commented that it would be great to "feast on pork this weekend", referring to the return of the Floyd of Rosedale trophy, the traditional prize that went to the Minnesota-Iowa winner.

Evashevski was gracious in defeat, citing the all-too-often mentioned Minnesota line play and the inability of Iowa to move the ball.

"The Minnesota kids hit terribly hard. They got down and scrapped and dug in on every play. That's the way football is supposed to be played, you know," he remarked on what would be his last game ever against Minnesota. He had earlier announced his retirement at the end of the season and would become Iowa's full-time athletic director.

"Minnesota was the better team today. No question about that. It had more spirit, more power—it deserved to win."

The Gophers were 7-0 and took over the No. 1 spot in the AP poll. They needed to win one of their two remaining conference games to get at least a share of the title and a possible Rose Bowl invitation. That process would see them stumble and then recover before the season ended.

Terrell, in his Sports Illustrated article referred to Warmath's struggles in the 1950s and recounted a conversation from the past.

"Why do you stay here and take all this," an assistant once asked.

"Because, I'm a good football coach," said Warmath, "and I want to prove it."

•　　•　　•

For the week following the Iowa game, the people of Minnesota were giddy over the fact their team was No. 1 in the country. Warmath was a hero and those who a year or two earlier were calling for his scalp, were whistling a completely different tune. To this day, Warmath refuses to engage in conversations regarding those who tried to get rid of him or the fair weather fans.

"They had their opinions about me and I had mine," is all he will say.

Regardless, Warmath had proven what was known all along by those who knew the game of football—that he was a fine coach who received the respect of his colleagues and players.

154

The Gophers were sitting on top of the Big Ten with a 7-0 record, 4-0 in the conference while Iowa was 6-1 overall and 4-1 in Big Ten play. Purdue was next on the schedule and they came to Minneapolis with a 2-4-1 overall record and a conference mark of 1-4. The won-loss record did not reflect how good a team it was.

Most Gopher followers believed Minnesota would handle the Boilermakers even though it would be a tough fight. It turned out to be that and more.

Purdue took a 14-0 halftime lead and then staved off a gallant comeback effort to win 23-14.

Purdue took the opening kickoff and went right to work, marching 80 yards in 18 plays. Bernie Allen was back at quarterback for Purdue and he engineered the drive, mixing in three passes to go along with the fullback smashes of Tom Yakubowski. Yakubowski scored on a two-yard run and Allen kicked the PAT.

In the second quarter, Purdue scored with about six minutes left when it got the ball at Minnesota's 25. Three plays later, fullback Willie Jones scored from the five. Allen made the conversion.

Minnesota came out for the second half fired up. A 69-yard drive was highlighted by Larry Johnson's 40-yard pass to Bob Deegan, which got to the Boilermakers' 29. Stephens went for two, then Munsey scored on a reverse play of 27 yards. The Gophers went for two and made it as Stephens threw to Munsey.

Minnesota got the ball back shortly thereafter and looked like they might move, but Johnson had a pass picked off by guard Stan Sczurek. Purdue got to the Gopher 25 and settled for a field goal by Allen on fourth down to lead 17-8.

A few minutes later, Dave Mulholland intercepted a pass by substitute Purdue quarterback Maury Guttman and Minnesota was at the Boilermaker 37. Nine plays later, Hagberg scored from the two. Another two point conversion attempt was tried, but this one failed when Hall dropped a perfectly-thrown pass.

Munsey intercepted a pass, but the Gophers could not capitalize because Larry Johnson was sacked for a big loss by Purdue's Don Brumm.

Then came the critical play of the game. With the ball on the Gopher 49 and six minutes left, Stephens failed at his first two pass attempts. On third down, he unleashed a long throw down the left sideline to Hall. Covered by defensive halfback Dave Miller, Hall appeared to have a bead on the throw. However, Miller reached out and pushed him, but no flag was thrown and the ball sailed beyond the Gopher receiver. The crowd screamed for an interference penalty and Warmath stormed out onto the field, but to no avail. A fourth down throw went out of bounds.

Purdue couldn't move, so Minnesota got the ball again and still couldn't get anywhere. The Boilermakers took over with 1:33 left. Forced to punt, Allen hit one deep. Tom King bobbled the punt at his two and it trickled into the end zone where Jim Tiller of Purdue fell on it for a touchdown. The PAT was not good and the game ended 23-14 for the Boilermakers.

In a quiet dressing room, Warmath made no excuses.

"We knew in advance Purdue was going to be tough. They always are. Our boys weren't overconfident or complacent in the least. We just got beat, that's all."

Warmath felt the key to the Purdue win was their getting out of the blocks fast, taking the 14-0 halftime lead and then its play in the fourth quarter where they "outrushed" the Minnesota line.

Asked about the obviously missed pass interference call, the Gopher coach said, "you can write your own opinions if you saw the play, but I'm not going to be a cry-baby or alibi. I know Jack Mollenkopf (Purdue's head coach) has had a lot of bad breaks this fall."

The players now were looking ahead to the last game with Wisconsin. A win would get them a tie for the conference title and the inside shot to the Rose Bowl.

156

"One thing is sure," quarterback Salem added, "no one will have to worry about us getting up for that game."

Meanwhile, Mollenkopf was elated with his team's upset win, but added the only sad part was he had to beat his old friend, Warmath. "He's the nicest guy in this business."

•  •  •

The Gophers stay at the top of the national rankings was a short one. No. 2 Missouri beat Oklahoma 41-9 that same weekend and took over the No. 1 spot. Iowa, meanwhile, rebounded from the loss to the Gophers and beat No. 4 Ohio State, 35-12.

Now as the Gophers prepared for their trip to Madison, they had their destiny in their own hands. Iowa had finished Big Ten play and was to close its season against Notre Dame. A victory would give Minnesota a title share and an almost certain Rose Bowl bid.

At Wisconsin, the Gophers were not to be deterred. The Badgers, however, fought hard and the Maroon and Gold victory was a struggle.

The Gophers started as if they were going to run the Badgers out of Camp Randall Stadium. Wisconsin took the opening drive to their 37, but lost the ball on a fluke fumble that bounced into the air on the center snap. Minnesota's Bob Deegan grabbed it and went to the 21. Stephens, on third down, kept and just got the first down at the 11. The Gophers plugged away to the nine, then Stephens darted the final yards to score. Rogers missed the PAT.

The Gophers came back a couple of series later and went 67 yards for their second TD, this one coming on a Stephens sneak of two yards. Again, Rogers missed the conversion attempt.

While Minnesota had dominated the first quarter, they did not do a thing in the second or third quarters. In fact, they didn't get a first down for those 30 minutes.

Wisconsin drove deep into Gopher territory in the second quarter and it looked like they might score, but Gopher linebacker Dick Enga picked off a Ron Miller throw at the 15 and took it to the 33. The Gophers could only muster four yards and Stephens went back to punt. But he was kicking into a strong wind and as the ball left his foot, a sudden gust caught the pigskin and sent it backward. He had punted the ball for a minus four yards.

The Badgers took advantage of the misfortune by the Gophers. Five plays later, Wisconsin was back in the game as Miller hit end Henry Derleth for a 15-yard touchdown. The conversion was good. Late in the second quarter, the Badgers were again moving when Stephens intercepted at the 15.

Twice in the third quarter, the Badgers got into Minnesota's end of the field, but a fourth-down pass at the Gopher 11 wasn't long enough for the first down and a drive to the 34 fizzled when a fourth-down Miller throw was incomplete.

The fourth quarter began. Stephens got things going with a naked reverse that took him to the Wisconsin 39. A third down pass to Hagberg, a Stephens short run and a Mulholland smash for 12 yards had Minnesota on the 11. Hagberg went to the four and then Mulholland scored over the right side. This time Rogers made the conversion.

On the next series, Stephens, playing his best game of his two-year career at Minnesota, picked off another Miller pass at his 47 and took it back to the Badger 40. Dickson, King and quarterback Johnson moved the ball to the 18 where the senior signal caller from Edina went around left end and into the end zone. Rogers again hit on the PAT for a 26-7 lead.

In the dying minutes, Wisconsin got down to the Minnesota 20, but once again Stephens' brilliant defensive work stopped the Badgers when he intercepted another Miller throw, this one at the goal line. Stephens nearly went all the way as he returned the ball 51 yards.

Nine thousand Gophers fans were in attendance and the scene as the game ended was reminiscent of the Iowa win two weeks earlier. The players and coaches were mobbed and the visiting fans were feeling so good they tore down the goalposts.

In a jubilant Minnesota locker room, Bobby Bell pulled off Warmath's fedora and pulled it down over his ears and mugged for the cameras. All of the players, especially the seniors, called it their biggest thrill to be co-Big Ten champions, the school's first championship year since 1941. As for the Rose Bowl, that subject was somewhat mute insofar as it was uncertain if the Big Ten would go because the old agreement with the Pacific Coast Conference had expired.

Nevertheless, word reached the celebrating Gophers that Kansas had knocked off Missouri, 23-7. Immediately chants of "We're No. 1," rang throughout the locker room.

"Our kids never played so well as they did today," Warmath commented. "We were dead tired in the fourth quarter, but for some reason seemed to get stronger."

Line coach Bob Bossons was particularly complimentary of his players, adding that Brown had been playing for part of the season with a bum shoulder. Backfield coach Jim Camp called the secondary play outstanding, citing Stephens. Butch Nash said Deegan, Hall and Larson were "the best ends in the country."

That evening, more than 500 fans welcomed the Gophers home. The center of the attention was the Rose Bowl, scheduled Jan. 2nd because Jan. 1st fell on a Sunday and Bowl games weren't played on the Sabbath in those days. Because the Gophers tied Iowa for the championship and Iowa had gone to Pasadena in 1956 and 1958 and the Gophers never had made the trip, the natural expectation was that Minnesota would get the invitation. They would, but there were some rather strange reactions from the administration and faculty.

159

# Twenty-One

Three days later, the University of Minnesota accepted an invitation to be the Big Ten representative in the 1961 Rose Bowl. In doing so, however, they demonstrated less than enthusiastic response to the first-time-ever opportunity to take part in any bowl game.

The Gophers officially accepted the invitation on Nov. 22nd, the Tuesday after the Wisconsin victory. Tom Hamilton, commissioner of the Association of Western Universities (the scaled-back Pacific Coast Conference which in the late Fifties and early Sixties featured only the four California Schools and Washington), had talked to the U of M President O. Meredith Wilson, athletic director Ike Armstrong and Warmath after the Purdue game. There was a rumor that Navy might be invited since the contract with the Big Ten had not officially been renewed. The school hierarchy gave a preliminary OK, but added that the 168-member U of M senate would have to approve it. It did, but not before it instructed the 14-member Committee on Intercollegiate Athletics to "continue to strive as in the past for removal of the permissive clause from the regulations of the Western (Big 10) Conference." Other motions, including refusing to go to any more Rose Bowls after 1961 or to share in gate receipts from other conference schools going, were introduced.

Since the original pact, the U of M had voted against the Big Ten sending its representative to the game. For the 1961 game, however, the athletic committee agreed to go since in the past it had accepted its portion of gate receipts. In fairness, it concluded, it couldn't decline to go, and then deprive the other schools of their shares. The committee also acknowledged the mass appeal of the football program and the soaring interest in the success of the Gophers.

They also figured they'd probably be lynched if they turned down the offer.

Nevertheless, the anti-bowl sentiment was reflective of the struggle Warmath always had at the University—little enthusiasm or cooperation and the perception that the football program detracted from the school's main purpose. The ironic thing is that Warmath had an extraordinarily high number of players who were outstanding students and went on to successful careers in law, medicine, coaching, education and business, many becoming prominent members of their communities. It was extremely rare that any of his players caused embarrassment to the University or the community.

If anybody ran a clean program that turned out quality students, as well as athletes, it was Warmath.

Regardless of the backroom scenes, the Gophers were on their way to Pasadena to meet the University of Washington. When word of Minnesota's acceptance reached the squad, they were just leaving the annual team banquet at the St. Paul Athletic Club. Sid Hartman had gotten the official word to them, thanks to a confidant on the West Coast who telephoned him when Minnesota was officially named by Tom Hamilton and his people.

A celebration broke out and the media got quote after quote from the players and coaches. A similar celebration erupted in downtown Minneapolis and on campus with several thousand people at each site.

In the weeks leading up to the Rose Bowl, "Squash Wash" was the official slogan of the Golden Gophers.

•     •     •

The days and weeks leading to the Rose Bowl saw a combination of accolades for the Gophers and plenty of warning from the media that Washington would be a most formidable opponent. The overall achievement was the naming of Minnesota as 1960's national champions. Unlike today, when the final No. 1 ranking is made after the bowl games, the procedure was to vote for the champion after the regular season ended. Bowl games were viewed almost as an after-thought, sort of a reward for a good season complete with two weeks of fun-in-the-sun. In addition, there were only about eight or nine Bowl games in those days compared to nearly 20 today.

Supportive of the Gopher's No. 1 ranking was the awesome record by Big 10 teams against non-conference opposition—19 wins, 1 loss and 2 ties. Among the victims were Notre Dame four times, Penn State, Oklahoma, Nebraska and Southern Cal. The "cupcake" opponent had not appeared on the Big 10 schedule. The only loss was by Indiana to Oregon State which might be dismissed because Indiana's probation precluded counting its games in conference standings. Had the Gopher victory over Indiana counted in conference standings, Minnesota would have been the undisputed champion with a 6-1 record and Iowa would have been second with a 5-1 record.

Regardless, it was official and Minnesota was the national champion.

Warmath was the overwhelming choice as Coach of the Year by the National Football Writers Association. It was an obvious choice since he so dramatically turned around the Gopher program. From 1-8 and 2-7 seasons, he was the man who had gone to the top. There probably is no one in the history of college football who saved his job in such spectacular fashion.

Tom Brown also received his share of awards. A consensus choice on everybody's All-American teams, he was the winner of the Outland Trophy as the top collegiate lineman. The Chicago Tribune named him the Big Ten's most valuable player and he was second in the balloting for the Heisman Trophy to Joe Bellino of Navy. It was the highest any interior lineman ever finished in the vote. Football News named Stephens to its second All-American team. Frank Brixius was named an Academic

All-American, the second of four who would be honored during Warmath's 18 years at Minnesota.

After the Rose Bowl invitation was accepted, stories began to circulate about the plans for the game. When would the team leave for Los Angeles? Where the team would stay? What were the plans for Christmas?

The team left on Saturday, Dec. 17th, stayed at the Huntington Sheraton Hotel in Pasadena and had both Christmas Eve and Christmas Day parties. They did the usual sight-seeing, rubbing shoulders with Hollywood types and posing for endless photos and talking to countless reporters. They also practiced for the game. In retrospect, the practice facilities and the practice methods were more of a factor in determining their New Year's performance than were the distractions of Tinsel Town.

The Gophers practiced for the two weeks leading up to the Rose Bowl at East Los Angeles Junior College.

"The field was like concrete," recalled Frank Brixius. "It was warm the entire time we were there and the sun baked the field. I remember I had shin splints as did a lot of the guys. Others had blisters on their feet."

Warmath and his staff had conducted rather light drills back in Minneapolis, primarily to keep the team in condition. Once in California, they worked the players hard.

"If I had one criticism of the staff, it was that they worked us too hard before the Rose Bowl," Bobby Bell said. "It was like a pre-fall practice. We already knew what to do."

"Murray and the rest of the coaches ran too many tough practice sessions and were too strict in terms of the life we had off the field during time on our own," Bob Frisbee remembered. "I think it's to Murray's credit that the next year when we went back to the Rose Bowl, he listened to some of the complaints and suggestions made by the returning players and eased up. That helped us win."

"Like Minnesota the next year, Washington was coming into the 1961 game having been in it the year before. The Huskies drubbed Wisconsin 44-8 and that gave them an advantage," Sandy Stephens said. "I think we were pretty awe-struck our first year out there whereas Washington wasn't."

Another factor was the status of Tom Brown's shoulder, which had been bothering him all year. Everybody kept telling the media he was fine. In truth, the shoulder wasn't healing like it should and that would plague him during the game.

•　　•　　•

It was a beautiful afternoon when the teams took the field before nearly 98,000 in the stands and millions watching on television. There were approximately 15,000 Minnesotans in the stadium and while the day was beautiful, the game was not.

Washington came out smoking and Minnesota was flat. It showed as the Huskies took a 17-0 halftime lead. By the time Minnesota decided to play football, it was too late.

Bob Hivner and Bob Schloredt were the two Huskie quarterbacks. Schloredt, blind in one eye from a childhood accident, had received national attention the previous year by guiding the rout of Wisconsin. However, halfway through the regular 1960 season, he hurt his shoulder and was relegated to backup duties behind Hivner. Washington's coach, 33-year-old Jim Owens, decided to go back to Schloredt for the Rose Bowl and the crafty quarterback proved to be the difference.

The Huskies scored first when their fine halfback and place kicker George Fleming hit on a 44-yard field goal in the opening quarter. In the second quarter, Schloredt was in on two three-yard touchdown plays. The first was a swing pass to end Brent Wooten, the second was his own keeper. That made it 17-0 and Minnesota was reeling.

"We decided to spread out the Minnesota defense to take advantage of what we believed was our better speed," Owens told the media after the game.

To accomplish that, he deployed the "red eye" offense, a lone running back alignment with both ends split wide and two slotbacks. Minnesota finally adjusted to the new look, but not until the second half.

In that second half, the Gophers showed some fire and outplayed Washington. Minnesota marched to the Huskies' 33 in the third quarter, but was stopped. However, Bob Deegan recovered a Washington fumble on the next play at the 32 and from there Stephens led Minnesota to its only touchdown. He started out by keeping for nine yards. Mulholland went off tackle to the eighteen. On the next play, Stephens swept left end and pitched to Bill Munsey who streaked in for the score. Rogers connected on the point after kick and it was 17-7.

Minnesota had some life and had Schloredt not risen to the occasion a couple of series later, Minnesota could have gotten back into the contest quickly. After the Gopher score, Washington couldn't move, punted and gave Minnesota another chance. The Gophers got inside Washington territory, but a 15-yard holding penalty killed the drive. Stephens punted and the defense stiffened.

Washington had the ball on second down on their 28 when Schloredt ran a quarterback sneak and went to the 50. It may have been the turning point because Minnesota was starting to whip the Huskies along the line of scrimmage. That play put Washington in great field position and kept the Gophers in their end of the field for the rest of the third quarter and a good part of the fourth quarter.

Stephens got the Maroon and Gold down to the Washington six midway through the fourth quarter. On third and five he went back to pass but the Huskies' outstanding linebacker, Don McKeta blitzed and nailed Sandy for a 13-yard loss. The next play was a fake field goal on fourth and long and McKeta intercepted Stephens' pass at the goal line.

The Huskies controlled the ball and the clock the rest of the game.

"They hit us too hard and too fast and too early," said assistant coach Bob Bossons afterward.

"They got out ahead too quickly," Warmath said quietly in a hushed Gopher locker room. "We outplayed them in the second half but we were simply too far behind. They are the best team we played all year—better than Iowa, Purdue or any of the Big Ten teams we faced."

"Looking back on it today," student manager Dana Marshall reflects, "I recall the staleness that seemed to exist. There wasn't any of the real spirit we had displayed during the regular season against teams like Iowa, Michigan, Illinois and Wisconsin.

"The night before the game, we went to a movie and Jerry Annis bummed a cigarette from Dale Reisdorfer, one of the assistant student managers, when they were in the bathroom of the theater. Reisdorfer told me later, 'I knew when Annis wanted a smoke, that we weren't going to win the Rose Bowl.' "

Cigarette or not, the fact was that Washington was the better team. Sid Ziff of the Los Angeles Mirror, who had written late in November that Minnesota seemed "ingracious" for even debating whether to come to the Rose Bowl, now strongly suggested in his post-game story that Washington deserved to be the No. 1 team in the country.

Minnesota returned home a few days later and Warmath undoubtedly thought it would be a while before he would be able to redeem himself and his team with a return trip to the "grand daddy of them all".

What he or no one else knew at the time was that in less than a year, political infighting at the most unlikely of Big Ten schools would give Minnesota a chance to return to Pasadena much sooner than he or anyone else could have imagined.

# Twenty-Two

As the Gophers looked ahead to the 1961 season, several concerns were evident. Graduation had taken Tom Brown, unquestionably one of the greatest three or four University of Minnesota interior lineman ever. In addition, Greg Larson was gone and would eventually become a long-time center for the New York Giants. End Dick Larson, tackle Frank Brixius, backs Roger Hagberg, Jim Rogers, Bill Kauth and Tom Robbins, quarterbacks Larry Johnson and Joe Salem, center and linebacker Jerry Annis, guard Dean Odegard and fellow linemen Dan Powers, Paul Gorgas and Dick Miller also were graduated.

How good would the returning Gophers be? Would they be able to develop any depth?

The answers to these questions would eventually be answered. But the first game of the season raised more doubts than it did hope.

Minnesota opened the 1961 campaign against visiting Missouri, which was ranked No. 1 for one week in 1960. The Tigers' coach was Proctor, Minn. native Dan Devine. The game was played on Sept. 30th. It might as well have been Dec. 30th.

Cold, rain, wind, temperatures in the low 40s and eventually snow flurries greeted the Gophers and the Tigers in front of a crowd of 58,840 which diminished as the weather grew nastier and the outcome gloomier.

Never in the recent history of Minnesota football had lousy weather and poor execution resulted in such a bad offensive performance by two teams. Missouri won 6-0, lost the first down battle 7-5 and completed just one pass (albeit a critical one). The Tigers won because they kept Sandy Stephens penned up all afternoon. Missouri had some incredible luck including a third down punt that Minnesota blocked but the ball bounced back into the kicker's hands, who then ran for a first down.

The Missouri score was set up via a punt. Tiger punter Daryl Krugman put a kick out of bounds at the Gopher one. Stephens was forced to punt on the ensuing possession. Missouri took over at the Minnesota 30. Stephens nearly intercepted a Tiger pass on the next drive, but dropped it. From the 24, quarterback Ron Taylor pitched to sweeping halfback Mike Hunter who stopped and threw a pass to Carl Crawford who outleaped three Minnesota defenders and pulled down the pass at the six. It was the only Tiger completion all afternoon.

Andy Russell, later a Pittsburgh Steeler for many years, got to the one on two plunges and Bill Tobin took it in. The PAT attempt was no good.

In the third quarter, Minnesota marched 42 yards to the Missouri 20, but a botched pitch from Stephens to halfback Jim Cairns got away for a loss of six. The fourth down pass was out of Tom King's reach.

Late in the game, a Gopher punt put the Tigers on their 16. Russell had 25 and 19 yard runs, the only significant gains all day for Missouri as the clock ran out.

"Our plan was to keep Stephens from running the wide stuff and we did that," Devine said.

"The ball was so wet, I didn't throw it, I sorta' pushed it," offered Mike Hunter about his pass to Crawford to set up the only touchdown.

"We couldn't complete key passes when we needed them," Warmath added.

"Sandy never had a chance to get going," concluded Gopher end Bob Deegan.

•   •   •

The next Saturday, the elements and the outcome were reversed. Fifty-thousand-plus fans in shirt-sleeve weather were in Memorial Stadium to watch Minnesota come from behind in the second half to beat Oregon 14-7.

It was pretty clear from the beginning that the Gophers were a more mature and physically stronger squad. The Ducks, playing a lot of sophomores, nevertheless gave Minnesota all they could handle. In the first half, the Gophers went to the Oregon 21, 26, 29 and 24, but couldn't score, proving the offense wasn't as strong as the defense.

In the second quarter, Oregon got to the Minnesota 10. On fourth down, a fake field goal attempt failed. Minnesota, however, couldn't move and the Ducks got the ball back and moved to the Gopher 16. Quarterback Doug Post hit halfback Mike Goetcher in the corner of the end zone for the TD and Buck Corey kicked the extra point for a 7-0 lead.

In the third quarter, Oregon again moved, this time to the Minnesota six. On second down, halfback Derwin Jackson followed several blockers on a sweep to the right, but Bobby Bell, displaying his great speed, knifed through from behind and stopped Jackson at the five. A bad pitch out lost yardage and the fourth-down field goal attempt was missed.

Minnesota took over and held the ball for 48 of the next 53 plays. A 22-yard run by Munsey, along with some fine running by Dickson and King got Minnesota to the Oregon 24. Cairns took a pitch out from Stephens and sprinted to the eight. Two plays later, Stephens kept the ball and made a twisting run into the end zone. The Gophers got two points when Stephens pitched out to Cairns for a sweep into the end zone and an 8-7 Gopher advantage.

In the fourth quarter, Stephens, plagued since the Missouri game with sore ankles, sat down and backup quarterback Duane Blaska came in. Blaska did a nice job of guiding the Gophers to the Ducks five. Sandy returned and ran it in for another TD. The kick was no good.

The Gopher defense had now taken over. Oregon couldn't move. Minnesota closed the game by pinning the Ducks deep in their territory and running out the clock.

"At halftime, Warmath gave us the steamiest pep talk since last year's Illinois game," Julian Hook said after the game.

Warmath, for his part, told the post-game interviewers that he was pleased with the play of the reserve units and said if Bobby Bell "isn't the best tackle in the country, I don't know who is."

The next week in Evanston, Minnesota and Northwestern didn't deviate from previous years and were involved in another knock- down, dragged-out fight that was anybody's game.

The hard-hitting Gopher defense eventually took its toll on a tough, well-disciplined Northwestern team. The result was a 10-3 Minnesota victory.

The Wildcats took the opening kickoff and marched 58 yards in 10 plays to get a Dave Damm 22-yard field goal. After that, both teams got sloppy. In the second quarter, there were six pass interceptions, three by each side. The teams left the field at halftime with the Dyche Stadium scoreboard showing a 3-0 Wildcat lead.

Northwestern's sloppiness continued in the third quarter enabling Minnesota to get back in the game. Bell recovered an errant pitch out at the Wildcat 11. Minnesota looked like it would return the favor when it made a bad lateral and lost six, but kept possession. Stephens hit Tom Hall on a pass that got to the two. Stephens then made a third-and-inches sneak to get a first down. Sandy took it into the end zone on the next play. Dickson kicked the point after.

On the next series, lineman Steve Kereakos and end John Campbell smacked quarterback Fred Quinn who fumbled with Campbell falling on the loose ball. Minnesota couldn't move and Dickson connected on a 31-yard field goal.

Later, as the third quarter was nearing the end and Minnesota had a third down with the clock running. Warmath called a time out because he knew he would have to punt. The Gophers had a strong wind at their back and Jerry Jones, who kicked well all day, boomed a punt that rolled to the Northwestern five. Minnesota's defense grew stronger in the fourth quarter. Both teams made gallant attempts at getting one more score, but failed.

First, Minnesota sophomore back Jerry Pelletier took a punt at his 49, bolted to the Northwestern 29 and then as he was tackled, lateraled to a trailing Dave Mulholland who went to the Cats' 14. The offense sputtered, however, and a Dickson field goal attempt was wide.

Northwestern then got a chance to tie or win the game during the next series. Bill Swingle intercepted Stephens pass and returned the ball to the Minnesota 37. Two passes were incomplete and two runs were short and Minnesota got the ball on downs. Eight plays and a Jones punt to the Wildcat 11 sealed the victory.

"With all due respect to Missouri and Oregon, the Big Ten play always is very tough," Julian Hook summarized. "I feel like I've been through a meat grinder."

"I continue to be pleased with the play of our reserves," Warmath added, citing Pelletier and Jones for their efforts.

"I felt we had more spirit than Northwestern did in the second half and that might have been the difference," said end Bob Deegan.

Ara Parseghian was probably more on the mark when he said that against a team like Minnesota you can't fumble eight times and throw five interceptions and expect to win.

Minnesota was 1-0 in the Big Ten and there were six games left against conference foes. Years later, as the members of the 1961 team looked back on all of their opponents, they recalled that all but one put up a fierce fight.

Illinois, turned out to be the easiest win of the year and as fine a game as Stephens would have while at Minnesota. That day in Champaign, he threw for four touchdowns and ran for another. Nevertheless, Warmath went into the game still recalling the nightmare of 1957 when the wheels came off that year's team thanks to the thrashing they took at Illinois. All week, the media referred to the '57 debacle, but it turned out to be nothing. The Gophers romped 33-0.

Stephens had gotten off to a miserable start throwing the ball in 1961. In the Gophers' first three games, he was seven for 42. But in the Illini game, he was seven for 12 for 142 yards.

Minnesota had only a 6-0 halftime lead. In the first quarter, with just 49 seconds left, Stephens hit Tom Hall in the corner of the end zone on a third-and-goal from the Illinois eight.

In the third quarter Illinois, which was totally stymied all day by the Minnesota defense, punted from its 13 and Stephens returned it to their 43. On the second play from scrimmage, Judge Dickson ran 23 yards to the 19. On a bootleg, Stephens once again hit Hall for the score. Tom Loechler made the PAT and it was 13- 0.

Illinois couldn't get out of its end of the field and punted again. Pelletier returned the ball to the Illini 29. Five running plays were called before Stephens hit Bob Deegan on a 14-yard touchdown pass.

In the fourth quarter, Minnesota marched 55 yards, highlighted by a 23-yard pass from Stephens to Jim Cairns and reserve back Al Fischer's 11-yard run up the middle. Stephens got the touchdown on a two-yard run.

The final TD came on a 66-yard drive. First, Cairns got 12 of those yards and on the next play, Stephens covered the rest of the ground with a scoring pass to John Campbell.

"Sandy was always a good passer, but he has been hobbled by sore ankles since the opening game against Missouri," Warmath said in his post-game interview.

"I finally got things together. I felt I threw well last week against Northwestern, but was just slightly off target," Stephens said. "Tom Hall was great today and Jim Cairns made some fine runs."

Across the way, Illinois was reeling. Minnesota's fearsome defense held them to just 40 yards total offense, 37 of those on the ground, gave up just six first downs and let them cross the 50 only twice.

"I was trapped on every pass play," said Illinois quarterback Mel Romani.

"Their linebacker blitz was incredible," said Illini coach Pete Elliott. "We couldn't pick it up."

Minnesota was 2-0 in the Big Ten and went home to face Michigan. It was a superb game that was the confidence builder and turning point for what would be an outstanding season.

•   •   •

"Minnesota's utterly unbelievable fourth-quarter rally whipped Michigan 23-20 at Memorial Stadium Saturday afternoon.

"The miracle finish found fullback Judge Dickson plunging over with only 1:24 left.

"That turned a 20-15 deficit into the most thrilling triumph the Gophers have ever fashioned in this long, lustrous Little Brown Jug rivalry."

The Minneapolis Star's Dick Gordon was accurate. Up until that overcast afternoon in 1961, there probably had never been a more thrilling, down-to-the-wire game in the history of this great rivalry.

Minnesota never led until the final touchdown. The Gophers were behind 7-0 with the game only two minutes old, then 13-0 in the second quarter and 20-8 in the fourth quarter. They won, but gave the 63,900 in the stands cardiac arrest. It was a game featuring high drama. The biggest defensive play for Minnesota was the result of a gutsy effort by a virtually unknown reserve defensive back. The heroics were provided by Stephens who had gotten married two days before the game.

The Wolverines struck early when Dave Mulholland fumbled the opening kickoff on a double reverse and Michigan's Les Hall recovered. Three plays later, 230-pound Michigan fullback Bill Tunnicliff blasted over from the eight. The Gophers came right back and marched deep into Wolverine territory where a Stephens pass was intercepted by Dave Raimey at the five. Raimey fell backwards, but lateraled to Bennie McRae who went to midfield before Dickson stopped him.

In the second quarter, Stephens made a bad pitch to Cairns and Michigan's George Mans fell on the loose ball at the Gopher 27. Raimey scored on the next play when he went over left tackle into the end zone. Doug Bickle's conversion attempt was wide this time. With an early 13-0 Michigan lead, it looked like a long afternoon for Minnesota.

But Stephens got on track. After an exchange of punts and with just over eight minutes left in the half, he went 63 yards on a rollout to his right. Sprung by Cairns' block at the right flank, he cut inside at midfield, then pulled away from defenders Dave Kurtz and Jim Ward, who seemed to have him sandwiched for a tackle. He broke clear and went all the way. Stephens' pass to Campbell for the two-pointer made the score 13-8.

The Gophers marched again, but Raimey's interception of Stephens stopped the Gophers as the clock wound down to end the half.

Michigan "came out smokin'" in the second half and after an exchange of punts, put together a 60-yard drive without throwing one pass. Raimey scored, going over right tackle from the four for the touchdown. Bickle kicked the extra point to give Michigan a 20-8 lead with 10 minutes left in the third quarter. Minnesota got a break in the fourth quarter when defensive holding was called on the Wolverines after an incomplete pass.

On the next play, Campbell got behind the Michigan defense along the right sideline toward the open end of Memorial Stadium and caught Stephens' pass for a 46-yard touchdown. Loechler made it 20-15 with the point after kick. There was 10:32 left to play.

On the ensuing series, Raimey got a first down and then Mulholland was thrown out of the game for a personal foul. Things were looking bleak for Minnesota. But the Gopher defense held and forced a punt. Minnesota took possession at its 12.

King and Cairns each caught a pass. On a third down play, Stephens' keeper for 20 yards got just beyond midfield. Two quick passes to King and a Stephens sneak and a rollout got to the Wolverine 10. Sandy then sprinted into the end zone, but a motion penalty brought the ball back to the 15.

A third down pass was incomplete. On fourth down, Stephens threw a short pass in the flat to Cairns at the nine, but he slipped and fell at the four, still four yards short of a first down. The 84-yard march was for naught.

On the sidelines, Warmath grabbed Tom Teigen, a reserve back who had barely played all year.

"I don't care what you do, but get that ball back," the coach ordered. "Go into a goal line defense."

The Aberdeen, S. D. junior went onto the field. Michigan, wanting to run the clock down, played conservatively. McRae came off his right tackle and was clobbered by Teigen who put his helmet into the ball. It popped loose and Dickson, playing linebacker, fell on it just outside the five yard line. There was 2:45 left.

The Minnesota fans went nuts, but before they could cheer again, they would endure a tough Michigan stand for three downs. Stephens rolled to the one. Second down saw Michigan rise up and not give up an inch on Sandy's sneak. His next sneak got to the one foot line. It was fourth down.

"There was no question that we wanted to give it to Judge and have him blast over," Stephens said afterward.

With 1:23 left, the Clairton, Penn., senior slammed his 215 pounds over left guard and into the end zone. Not wanting to risk a loss by a field goal, Warmath elected for the two-point play and Stephens found Hall open in the end zone and Minnesota was out in front, 23-20.

Michigan wasn't through, but then neither was Stephens, who was having a magnificent game. Michigan got to midfield, before Sandy picked off a desperation throw at his two by grabbing it with one hand as he was falling back. There were just a few seconds left and the Gophers had an incredible homecoming victory.

"Sandy played a hell of a game. He must have been playing for his new wife because he never played that well for me," Warmath joked.

Everyone acknowledged it was a weird game, one in which Minnesota made the mistakes, yet won. The difference was Stephens who had 336 yards in total yardage—165 rushing, 144 passing and two punt returns for 27 yards.

Stephens and Campbell explained they made up the play that went for the second Minnesota touchdown. Realizing the Wolverine secondary was rotating, they designed a pass to catch them in the middle of the rotation. It was enough to spring Campbell down the sideline.

End coach Butch Nash said no one ever played a better game than Stephens had that day.

"Bump Elliott has done a great job at Michigan," Warmath added. "We needed some breaks to win."

Elliott praised his team and rightfully so. They had played a tough, gritty game and had done nothing to diminish the great Michigan football tradition.

"We didn't leave anything undone," Elliott said. "We shot the works, so did Minnesota. It was a great show of football.

When two teams fight it out like that, the little breaks make the difference."

Asked about the McRae fumble, the Michigan coach added that he didn't fault his ballcarrier. He just was hit "terribly hard".

As for Stephens, Elliott added, "he's just a heckuva football player. He ran and he threw and in the end, he beat us on defense, too.

"I can't understand why people keep saying Minnesota hasn't got an offense. They ran nearly every formation in the book and they must have passed on nearly half their downs. If that isn't wide open football, I don't know what is."

The Wolverine mentor summed it up best when he said, "I hope people realize this was a great football game."

# Twenty-Three

 "Hate State" was the chant on campus the next Monday as Minnesota prepared to host the Saturday, Nov. 4th game with the Michigan State Spartans, the country's top-ranked college team.

By then, the confidence of Warmath's team was extremely high and the campus and the entire State of Minnesota was tuned into the Gopher success after the great victory over Michigan. Interest was so high over the impending battle with the Spartans that the game was nationally-televised.

Both teams had versatile offenses and tough defenses. Michigan State had allowed no points in its previous three conference victories and only 10 in five games. The Spartans' offense was averaging more than 26 points per game.

The Gopher-Spartan game was well-played, but MSU never could cash in offensively. Warmath opened with an unbalanced line with both tackles on the same side of the center. It was confusing enough to keep the Spartan defense guessing. That, combined with the continuing excellent play of the Gopher defense and a core of 18 to 20 players who got stronger as the game progressed, was all it took to defeat the No. 1 team.

State took the opening kickoff, but the Gopher defense immediately established superiority. Bell and Hall threw halfback Sherman Lewis for a nine-yard loss. A punt was returned by Stephens to the Minnesota 29.

An important third down pass from Stephens to Hall got the Gophers to their 42. From there, the senior quarterback made a couple of nice rollouts, hit Hall again on a buttonhook pass and pitched to Dickson on a sweep. Minnesota was at the Spartans' eight when Stephens on a keeper around left end, pitched at the last moment to Bill Munsey. The pitch was so close to being forward it could have been ruled an illegal forward pass. Regardless, Munsey, playing for the first time in three weeks because of injuries, was untouched as he went into the end zone. The kick was no good.

For the rest of the half, Minnesota held off several deep drives. A 48-yard Lewis run was part of the march that brought the Spartans to the Gopher five. Two plays later on third and goal to go, Pete Smith missed the mark on a pass attempt. Wheeler, Bell and Mulholland then stopped Michigan State fullback George Saimes at the line of scrimmage on fourth down.

Later, the Spartans moved the ball again and got to the Gopher 12 where State again called on Saimes on fourth down. This time, he slipped trying to cut into the hole and Minnesota took over.

Minnesota came out in the second half and threatened. But the Gophers were frustrated as drives to the MSU 19, 32 and 13 came up short. Nine minutes remained in the game and Michigan State had plenty of time to overtake the 6-0 Gopher lead.

Three plays from their 13 got State out to its 38. After no gain, Lewis, trying to go outside end, got whacked by Hall. The ball popped out and Hall fell on it. The Gophers moved to the 23, but sputtered thanks to two penalties against them. It was third-and-11 when Stephens faded to his right and fired a bullet to the back of the end zone where Munsey leaped and came down with both feet just inside the end line for the touchdown. Loechler kicked the point after with 4:05 left in the game.

The Spartans came right back, however, and looked as if they at least might avert being shut out. From the Gopher 25, halfback Carl Charon took a pitch out on a sweep, stopped and threw into the end zone. Stephens who was having his third consecutive spectacular game, leaped and snared the ball with one hand, tucking in as he fell into the end zone for the touchback. That preserved the triumph.

179

In the victorious and loud Gopher locker room, an exhausted Warmath praised both teams. "State has a big, tough squad with the best collection of sophomores I've seen in many years."

"It was our hitting on defense that won it," said assistant Bob Bossons.

Everybody agreed that the defensive play was superb, especially in the clutch. Duffy Daugherty and his State staff had used nearly twice as many players as Minnesota, yet the Gophers seemed stronger as the game progressed. Bell, Mulholland, Hall, Deegan, Hook and Wheeler, who had stopped Saimes on the big fourth down play from the Gopher five in the first quarter, were singled out for praise.

"What can I say?" Daugherty offered in the silent State locker room. "They wanted it more than we did. Minnesota is a great team, hits very hard and is well-coached."

The Gophers were now tied with Ohio State for the conference lead and turned their attention to Iowa City.

•    •    •

Minnesota was ranked No. 3 in the nation when they went into Kinnick Stadium and completely dominated the explosive Hawkeyes thanks to a big margin in turnovers. Minnesota recovered three Iowa fumbles, picked off three passes and blocked one punt. The Gophers surrendered a safety in the opening moments and a touchdown on the game's last play, but managed to put 16 points on the scoreboard and took their record to 6-1, 5-0 in conference play.

Iowa came out with fire in their eyes and quarterback Matt Szykowny took the Hawks to the Gopher 14 on a nice 45-yard pass to end Felton Rogers. It was third-and-seven from the 11 when he tried to hit halfback Lonnie Rogers, but Gopher linebacker Bob Frisbee reached out and grabbed the throw for the interception. But he had nabbed the pass at his two and his impetus carried him into the end zone where he fell and Rogers dropped on top of him. It was ruled a safety.

Iowa couldn't move after receiving the free kick. Minnesota's next two possessions got it to the Hawkeye 35 and nine. On the latter possession, Tom Loechler hit his first collegiate field goal, a 26-yarder. Warmath played it somewhat close to the vest the rest of the half, keeping possession and staying near midfield. At the half, it was a baseball score of 3-2 in favor of Minnesota.

In the second half, Iowa came out fighting and drove to the Gopher five. But there, Tom Teigen once again proved that when he got a chance to play, he could put hits on people. Teigen clobbered fullback Bill Perkins as he went into the line and the ball popped loose and was recovered by Dick Enga.

Iowa forced a punt but Hawkeye Bernie Wyatt fumbled and Bobby Bell recovered giving Minnesota possession on the Hawkeye 45. The Gophers drove to the one and were stopped on fourth down. The Gophers received a personal foul for piling on Szykowny, moving the ball out to the 15. Szykowny tried another pass, but Teigen intercepted at the 34.

On third down, the Uniontown Connection struck again as Munsey got open at the three, took the Stephens' pass over his shoulder and stepped into the end zone. Loechler made the conversion and it was 10-2 with 12 minutes left to play.

The Gophers kept the Hawkeyes pinned in their end of the field. Enga broke through to block John Calhoun's punt from the 11 and John Campbell fell on it in the end zone, sealing the victory.

Iowa threatened again, but was stopped. The Hawkeyes finally hit on three consecutive passes inside of a minute, Cloyd Webb pulling one in a for 33 yards and a TD. Paul Krause kicked the PAT and the game ended with a 16-9 Gopher victory.

"We played a near-perfect game," Warmath told the media after the game. "We stopped their wide stuff very well."

The Gopher coach thought the fumbled punt by Wyatt was the turning point, adding that Iowa also suffered from the losses of Wilburn Hollis and Joe Williams, who were out with injuries.

"Our linebackers were great," said assistant Don Grammer, who added that he thought the Frisbee interception should have been ruled a touchback.

"Minnesota is a sound, sound football team. When you play a team like Minnesota you simply have to play sound football," said Hawkeye coach Jerry Burns, who was in his first year at the Iowa helm. "Mistakes. Mistakes."

In the meantime, the Gophers packed away Floyd of Rosedale for the return trip home and planned for the arrival of Purdue a week later. It was to be a game watched by a record Memorial Stadium crowd and it was such a bloodbath that the toll on Minnesota would have serious repercussions as the season drew to a close.

•　　•　　•

Murray Warmath and Purdue's Jack Mollenkopf liked each other a great deal, undoubtedly because they both loved to play a brand of football reminiscent of trench warfare. Football to them was a mean, rugged game, meant to be played with intensity. So when 67,081 people packed Memorial Stadium on Nov. 18, 1961, they saw a continuation of the brutal struggles between Warmath and Mollenkopf that dated back to the mid-Fifties and would continue on into the late Sixties. This probably was the most brutal game of all.

The Minneapolis Sunday Tribune had a sidebar story on the front page of the sports section after the game: "Trainer Stein Calls It Roughest Gopher Game Since 1941."

Long-time Gopher trainer Lloyd "Snapper" Stein, who was a Gopher player in the early 1930s and then became the team trainer after graduation where he remained for over 40 years, gave a historical perspective on the '61 Purdue clash.

"Back in 1941 when we played Washington, I remember we had five regulars on the bench with injuries at one time," Stein

182

recalled. "This game was just exactly like that. We have a lot of boys hurt."

The Gophers edged Purdue 10-7 to remain unbeaten in the Big Ten and among the nation's top teams, but paid a heavy price for the victory. Among the Gopher casualties that day were Dave Mulholland in University Hospital with a concussion; Tom Hall, bad knee; Judge Dickson, shoulder injury; Dick Enga, bad ankle; Jim Wheeler, bad ankle; Robin Tellor, hip bruise; Julian Hook, sprained knee; and Jack Perkovich, back injury.

The Gopher victory didn't follow the usual script. Heretofore, the Gophers had worn down and outlasted their opponents. But the Boilermakers were up to anything Minnesota would do and took the game down to the closing minutes only to come up short.

Minnesota controlled the first half and didn't allow Purdue any deeper than the Gopher 32-yard line. The Gophers dominated with eight first downs to two and 133 to 34 yards in total offense. The battle of the statistics was nearly reversed in the second half. A Purdue fumble and some questionable strategy late in the game enabled Minnesota to go into the following week's game against Wisconsin undefeated.

Minnesota's defense, especially the tackle play of Bell and Wheeler, kept Purdue deep in its territory during the first half. Minnesota finally scored in the second quarter. Jerry Pelletier fair caught a Ron DiGravio punt at his 38. Stephens ran for 16 yards around left end and Mulholland, who played one of his best games before being hurt, tore through right tackle and got 26 more.

From the Boilermaker 20, the Gophers could manage only three yards in three plays. Tom Loechler's 35-yard field goal kick barely cleared the crossbar.

Purdue penalties and a stubborn Gopher defense forced a Purdue punt on the next series from its two yard line. Pelletier returned it to the 27. The Boilermakers were offside on the kick, but Minnesota declined and took the good field position.

Mulholland got 12 yards on two carries and took a first down pass in the right flat from Stephens that went to the four.

Munsey was stopped for no gain. Stephens then took the snap and went around left end, deftly cut back in, broke a tackle by Ron Meyer at the goal line and went into the end zone for the score. Loechler made the kick and Minnesota led at halftime, 10-0.

With the end of the half, came the end of Minnesota's domination.

Quarterback Ron DiGravio and fullback Roy Walker marched the Boilermakers to the Gopher 24. Unable to advance further and facing fourth down, the Boilermakers exercised a bit of unorthodox strategy. They punted and the ball went into the end zone for a touchback. From the 20, the Gophers got enough yardage to punt out of trouble and keep Purdue back in its territory.

Purdue moved to the Gopher 20 where a fumble killed the drive. It was back-and-forth for several possessions until early in the fourth quarter. Fumbles were exchanged, the second one by Stephens gave Purdue the ball at the Boilermaker 40.

Reserve quarterback Gary Hogan threw to end Harold Wells for 53 yards. On fourth down and less than a foot Hogan snuck in for the touchdown. There was 5:10 remaining in the game.

After the kickoff, Stephens kept the Gophers (and the clock) moving with a 14-yard rollout. Minnesota finally punted with two minutes to play. Gopher fans watched the always-reliable defense stop Purdue on downs. The Gophers got possession and let the clock run out.

Both teams limped, crawled and dragged themselves off the field.

Even today, the players' memories of the game are vivid. Hook recounted how in the first half while playing at linebacker, he moved laterally in front of the Gopher bench to cut off a Purdue sweep.

"Purdue had three blockers leading the ballcarrier as I moved in," said Hook.

Known for his courage and willingness to take on anyone, Hook had thrown himself into the wall of Boilermaker blockers.

"I got clobbered so bad that I was dropped to my knees and bent backward as the blockers came over me," he remembered. "Some of our guys coming up from the secondary stacked up the play and I was down on the bottom of this immense pile, bent one-hundred- and-eighty degrees from my knees back.

"Warmath, who was especially wound up on the sidelines that day because of the incredible intensity of the game, started screaming, 'Hook's dead, Hook's dead, Hook's dead!' while I was lying under this pile of humanity."

Hook was not dead, but it was a wonder he wasn't.

In both locker rooms afterward, the discussion was centered around the incredible hitting.

Gopher captain Jack Mulvena said it was the most intense hitting he had seen in two years.

"Normally, we can wear teams out in the second half, but not Purdue," he observed.

Bell, Deegan, Jerry Jones—every Gopher—had a comment on the fierce contact in the game.

Purdue had nothing but praise for the Gopher defense and the equally murderous blocking and tackling by the Minnesota players.

"Minnesota deserves the top ranking in the country," Mollenkopf stated. "They are very difficult to defense and they put a tremendous rush on the passer."

As a side note to the roughness of the game, even the officials weren't immune. Joe Schneider, the game's field judge, collided with Stephens on one play and was carried from the field on a stretcher.

Two wonderfully-coached teams with a full appreciation of how football was meant to be played, went into their respective final games of the year aware that they had been through one of modern college football's roughest games.

Historians report that during World War I, the fighting at the Battle of Verdun in France was so fierce that citizens of London, hundreds of miles away, could hear the gunfire for weeks. On one November Saturday in 1961, the fighting at Memorial Stadium was so fierce that citizens probably heard the collision of helmets and pads all the way up Fourth Street in Dinkytown.

•　　•　　•

Minnesota had a chance to either share the Big Ten title with Ohio State or to win it outright if it beat Wisconsin and Michigan beat Ohio State.

But Minnesota, crippled with injuries sustained in the Purdue game and facing a superb Badger passing combination of Ron Miller-to-Pat Richter, came up three points short. On an unusually warm late November Saturday in Minneapolis, Miller passed for over 300 yards and Wisconsin capitalized on three big pass interceptions to leave Memorial Stadium with a 23-21 victory. The loss, coupled with Ohio State's 50-20 rout of Michigan in Ann Arbor, denied the Gophers a share of the Big Ten title.

The game appeared to be Minnesota's early after stopping Wisconsin's initial drive when Jim Bakken missed a 39-yard field goal attempt. On the next play from his 20 (placed there because of the touchback rule on a missed field goal), Stephens spotted a flanked Tom Hall uncovered near the 30 and hit him for an 80-yard touchdown. There was just 1:47 gone when Loechler kicked the conversion. The rest of the half, however, Minnesota was on the defensive.

With Jim Wheeler and Dick Enga out with injuries sustained in the Purdue game and Robin Teller and Bobby Bell playing only part-time (Tellor had also been hurt in the Purdue game, but dressed, whereas Bell cracked two ribs early in the Wisconsin game), the Gopher defense was a makeshift group.

Wisconsin kept Minnesota pinned down deep and then took a Jerry Jones punt and returned it to the Gopher 42. On second down from the 40, Miller found Richter at the 25 and laid a perfect pass into the lanky receiver's hands for the touchdown with 5:30 left in the first quarter. Bakken's extra point tied the score.

Miller kept taking the Badgers into Minnesota territory and giving Bakken chances to put three points on the board. In the first half alone, Bakken missed four field goals, including a 29-yard attempt which hit the crossbar with 15 seconds left in the half.

In the third quarter, Minnesota put together the early stages of a drive. It got to the Badger 39 on a Stephens' rollout, but a holding penalty brought the ball back to its 46. Stephens' throw on third down to Campbell was short and Wisconsin defensive back Jim Nettles picked it off. Nettles got a key block and went 60 yards for a touchdown. Bakken's extra point kick gave Wisconsin a 14-7 lead.

Minnesota got back in the game when Miller, under a fierce rush, threw an overhand lateral out in the right flat to fullback Jerry McKinney, who had yet to turn for the ball. It bounced off his back and the Gophers' Jones recovered at the Badger 39.

Stephens hit Munsey and Mulholland for 17 yards in passes. He then called a draw play to Jones who bounced off a couple of would-be tacklers and went 22 yards into the end zone. Stephens run for two points put Minnesota ahead 15-14. Four plays later, Wisconsin was back in the lead.

After two incomplete passes, Miller found Richter for a 39-yard gain. On the next play, Minnesota was called for defensive holding and from the Gopher 21, Miller threw to Richter, who reached up and over the shorter defender Jones and the Badgers' had their third touchdown. Miller's pass for the two points was no good, but Wisconsin led 20-15.

Minnesota couldn't get anything going and Wisconsin took possession on its 27. Again Miller went to the air and marched the Badgers to the Gopher seven. The defense held and forced Bakken to try his fifth field goal attempt. This one was good and it was 23-15 with less than four minutes to go in the game.

The Gophers roared back. Stephens hit Jim Cairns with a 47-yard pass that put the Gophers on the Wisconsin 25. Four plays later, Stephens found Al Fischer in the end zone for the TD. Minnesota had to go for two points and the tie. Stephens rolled right on a run-pass option but Bakken stopped Sandy at the one.

An on-side kick was recovered by Wisconsin and the Badgers ran out the clock.

The Gophers kept the locker room door shut for 40 minutes. It was morgue-like when the media entered.

"You're still the best team I've coached at Minnesota", a tearful Warmath told his silent locker room after the defeat.

"Miller had too much time to pass and killed us on third down plays," said the downhearted Gopher coach. "We were hurt with injuries, but that shouldn't detract from Wisconsin's win. They are a very fine team."

Stephens praised the Badger pass rush as the best he faced all year and Munsey muttered about how tough it was to cover Richter, who had six catches for 142 yards and two TDs.

Stephens, Hall, Dickson, Mulholland and company, removed their uniforms for what they assumed would be the last time. It was a wrong assumption.

# Twenty-Four

 From the moment the student managers put away the equipment on Sunday following the loss to Wisconsin, rumors started flying that maybe, just maybe, Ohio State, the Big Ten champion (and the outright champion thanks to the Minnesota loss to Wisconsin) would not be going to the Rose Bowl after all. If that were the case, the Gophers could possibly be in line to be the Big Ten representative in Pasadena.

"There was talk even before the final game that Ohio State's faculty might vote against going to the game if they were invited," Warmath recalled.

It's hard to imagine that the same school where Woody Hayes was the head coach that the faculty would dare to take such action. But they did, even if the vote was close.

On Nov. 28th, the Ohio State University Faculty Council voted 28-25 to turn down the invitation.

The Big Ten pact with the Pacific Coast Conference Schools was still in limbo. Starting in the late 1950s, several Big Ten schools, including Ohio State, were against post-season play. The Ohio State faculty was concerned, among other things, that under Hayes the Buckeyes were perceived as a "football school". Hayes, while possessed with his own rather remarkable style, was much like Warmath in that he expected more out of his players than just performance on the field. Like Warmath, Hayes turned out players who were, by and large, good students and quite successful after football.

"I don't want to see a schism result because of this," Hayes said in reacting to the vote. "What's important is that we honor the decision of the university. I think it's best we keep quiet and say nothing further. I respect the administration and the faculty although I question the intelligence of such a decision."

That was the diplomatic thing to say, but it probably was a good idea not to be within a 10-mile radius of Woodrow Wilson Hayes when he received word that his Buckeyes would not be going to the Rose Bowl.

Some 5,000 Ohio State students went to the streets to protest and stormed the faculty club and vandalized the main lobby.

In the meantime, the Senate Committee on Intercollegiate Athletics at Minnesota had unanimously approved going to the game if Minnesota was invited. On Dec. 1st, the Faculty Senate Committee, which had debated long and hard the previous year about the ethics of going to Pasadena and then finally voted to approve the trip, this time had a very noticeable change of heart. They overwhelmingly voted (108-33) to return. Perhaps the memory of the loss to Washington was just a little too vivid even for the most noble of academicians.

For a few days, everyone waited and wondered and then on Saturday, Dec. 2nd, the word came that for the first time in Big Ten history, there would be a repeat representative in the Rose Bowl.

The Gopher's opponent would be UCLA. The Bruins had a 7-3 record,. losing to Michigan, Ohio State and Washington. UCLA was coached by Bill Barnes, a Tennessee graduate who was a few years younger than Warmath. He had been on the UT varsity when Warmath was an assistant coach there in the mid-Thirties.

"Warmath was somebody I remember from the first time I came to Knoxville," Barnes said before the two ex-Volunteers squared off. "Back then you knew he was a man who knew the game of football."

"Bill was a man with a good football mind and I was not at all surprised to find him doing well as a coach," Warmath said.

On the surface, everyone in Minnesota was happy. The Golden Gophers were going back to the Rose Bowl. They had a chance to atone for the loss the previous year to Washington and it would offer a chance for further national exposure.

Many of the players, however, felt differently.

"A lot of us weren't thrilled about going out there, busting our asses in tough practices in that hot, smoggy air and then spending the rest of the time either in our hotel room or going on formal, planned sight-seeing trips," Bob Frisbee remembered.

In the team meeting called after the Gophers had been invited, there was a certain amount of dissension and discussion about the trip.

"It wasn't that we weren't appreciative of the chance to play in the Rose Bowl again," Frisbee added. "We just didn't want to go out there and do the same routine all over again. Many of us felt we got mentally stale and that was what contributed in large part to our losing to Washington."

"I couldn't believe the reaction by some of the guys," Stephens remembered. "I was mad as hell. I wanted to go back and prove we were a good team, one that deserved to be there. I was pissed at those guys who were reluctant to go back."

Sophomore tackle Carl Eller remembered standing up and telling the team that this was perhaps his only chance to go to the big show.

"Since I was a sophomore and wanted to go to the Rose Bowl more than anything in my life, I told the team that it might be my only chance. I pleaded with the guys not to turn down such an opportunity."

Warmath and his staff listened to the complaints and agreed that this time things would be a bit looser. They were—sort of.

Prior to arriving in Los Angeles on Dec. 18th, the Gophers did the usual conditioning practice in Minneapolis and had several people receive post-season honors. Stephens and Bell were named to many All-American teams and the Chicago

191

Tribune selected Sandy as the Big Ten's MVP. It was the second year in a row a Gopher received the honor, Tom Brown being the recipient the year before.

In LA, the routine was not much different than the year before except that Warmath gave the players more free time after practice. Everybody was more relaxed and better prepared and not so much in awe of the hoopla that surrounded the game.

Warmath played his cards close to the vest and did a fine job of peaking his team. He had to deal with the rumors he was going to leave Minnesota to take the head coaching job at Army where Earl Blaik's successor, Dale Hall, had been fired a few days earlier. Instead, he went about his business, preparing to win the Rose Bowl game which had been denied to him the year before.

•   •   •

For the two nights preceding the Rose Bowl, Warmath took his squad to a monastery run by the Order of Passionate Fathers. It was in the hills overlooking Los Angeles. Warmath wanted to isolate the team from the pre-game well-wishers and media pressure.

"Looking back, it was a smart move," said assistant coach Dick Larson. "One of the things that had happened the year before is that we were never mentally into the game. The mental outlook by the staff and players going into the 1962 game was much more focused than in 1961. Going to a retreat for a few days gave us a chance to get ready."

It was more than just the retreat. The entire approach to the Rose Bowl paid off in a 21-3 Gopher victory.

The Bruins took the opening kickoff and using the single-wing running of tailback Kermit Alexander and wingback Bobby Smith, drove to the Minnesota 24.

"It was important that we not get in a hole early like we did the previous year," Tom Hall said after the game. "When we forced the UCLA field goal, we got some breathing room."

The field goal was the result of a solid defensive play when Dave Mulholland and Robin Tellor broke through and tossed Smith for a six-yard loss. The field goal was good and the Uclans enjoyed their first and only lead of the day.

Minnesota's opportunistic defense got the Gophers moving. Late in the first quarter, Bob Deegan smacked Bruins' running back Almose Thompson, the ball popped loose and Dickson fell on it at the Bruin six. Three plays later, Stephens went into the end zone from the two and Loechler added the extra kick.

Minnesota took a 14-3 lead in the second quarter. The Bruins were stopped by the Gophers' second unit after taking the kickoff and were forced to punt. Minnesota took possession at its 25. Dickson and Munsey did some nifty running during a 75-yard march. It was Munsey from the three for the TD. Loechler followed with the extra point kick.

Clearly, Minnesota was winning the battle along the line of scrimmage as the first half ended. That domination continued in the second half. However, Minnesota's offense sputtered a couple of times in the third quarter. First, Mulholland fumbled a punt at his own 39. UCLA looked as if they might take advantage of the break, but returned the favor by coughing up the ball at the Minnesota six.

The Gophers got a couple of first downs, then punted. The defense held. UCLA had to punt as the quarter ended, so Minnesota took possession at the start of the fourth quarter with the ball at its 16. From the Gopher 16, Stephens did a masterful job of using up the clock. He ate up 11 minutes, calling nothing but running plays.

"UCLA was stopping the wide stuff, but our interior line was blowing them off the ball and we moved it pretty easily up the middle," Stephens later recounted.

From the two, Stephens scored the touchdown and Loechler kicked the point after touchdown.

Not just Warmath, but all the coaches, were carried off the field on the shoulders of the players as the game ended. It was a gesture clearly intended to let everyone know how much the players appreciated the excellent effort Warmath and his staff had made over the past two seasons.

Warmath was jubilant, for the monkey was off his back from the year before.

"We had a big advantage in ball possession (66 plays to 42) and except for the fumbled punt, our mistakes were never at a critical point of the game or in our territory," he said over the noise of the happy Minnesota locker room. "In the end, we just physically whipped them."

"I thought our conditioning paid off in the second half," Tom King offered. "We seemed noticeably stronger than UCLA as the game moved along."

Stephens, named the game's most valuable player, had made 7 of 11 passes for 75 yards, but really used the great up-front blocking to put together the Minnesota scores, especially the second and third touchdowns.

"The line play, both offensively and defensively, was great," he said in summarizing his last game as a Golden Gopher.

Captain Jack Mulvena said it was a lot easier in Rose Bowl II than in Rose Bowl I.

"We just knew what to expect this time," Mulvena added.

UCLA coach Barnes made no excuses.

"Minnesota is just too strong. Stephens ran the offense very well and Dickson, Mulholland and Munsey hurt us with their solid running."

Foster Anderson, the fine Bruin tackle, added that the Gopher line was very quick and singled out Eller, adding he was surprised how good the Gopher tackle was for being only a sophomore.

It was a happy group of Gophers that left the Rose Bowl late that New Year's afternoon. Most of the players stayed in Los

Angeles for a few days of relaxation by the hotel pool or at Santa Anita race track. Murray and Mary Louise Warmath slipped off to Palm Springs to spend some time with old friend Don Knutson.

Two of the finest consecutive years in Gopher football history were over. The stormy days of only a few years before had passed from Murray Warmath's life.

# Twenty-Five

Minnesota faced questions—the same questions it faced a year earlier—could it fill the holes caused by graduation? Naturally, the biggest loss was Sandy Stephens.

In addition, Tom Hall, Jack Mulvena, Robin Tellor, Bob Frisbee, Judge Dickson, Dave Mulholland, Jim Wheeler, Bob Deegan and Tom King were gone along with reserves Tom Loechler, Bob McNeil, Jack Park, Ted Rude and Steve Kereakos.

"I felt that the '62 team was as talented as the '60 and '61 squads," Julian Hook said. Hook was among a good group of returning players who had seen extensive playing time the previous two years. Along with Bobby Bell, John Campbell, Bill Munsey and Jim Cairns, the Gophers also had some talented players returning such as Jerry Jones, Bob Prawdzik, Carl Eller, Dick Enga (that year's captain), Paul Benson and Jerry Pelletier.

The key was Stephens' replacement at quarterback. Warmath turned to Duane Blaska, a senior from Anoka who had played in Stephen's shadow the previous two seasons.

"We were confident in Blaska's talent," Warmath recalled. "The question was how well he would handle the pressure."

Blaska would do well, but the opener was a tough and frustrating debut.

The Missouri Tigers under Dan Devine were the Minnesota opening opponents on Sept. 29th.

Minnesota blew two first-half scoring chances and another late in the game to leave Memorial Stadium that day with a 0-0 tie.

In the first quarter, Gopher linebacker Paul Benson fell on a Tiger fumble at the Missouri 21. Jerry Jones and Bill Munsey got the ball to the three. But a fourth down dive by Munsey was stopped at the two.

In the second quarter, Blaska engineered a long drive from the 11 by hitting Cairns on a 30-yard pass and using the hard-nosed running of sophomore reserve fullback Jay Sharp. On third-and-goal from the six, Blaska chose to run options twice. The first to the right got the ball to the one. Then Missouri defensive back Jay Johnson stopped the Gopher quarterback at the line of scrimmage on fourth down.

Minnesota took the second-half kickoff and got as deep as the Tiger 44 before being forced to punt. Missouri, starting at its 15, put together its only drive of the day, but a 36-yard field goal attempt was no good. Missouri drove again in the fourth quarter, but was forced to punt.

Late in the game, Munsey picked off a halfback option toss by John Roland at the Gopher 26. Blaska completed three passes for 37 yards, but with less than a minute to play, another pass was intercepted by Vince Turner at the three.

"Well, we're still unbeaten and the experience helped", Warmath said optimistically afterward. "We thought about a field goal on the last series but the interception on third down nixed that."

"It was an excellent defensive game and I was very pleased with our stopping Minnesota twice inside the five," Devine said. "Bobby Bell was magnificent for the Gophers. We couldn't handle him."

The Gophers looked ahead to Navy.

•　　•　　•

The University of Minnesota's first-ever clash with a service academy team drew a capacity crowd of 64,364 to Memorial Stadium the next week and they saw the Gophers dominate the Midshipmen.

The Gophers took the opening kickoff and went 72 yards in 13 plays with Jerry Jones scoring from the three. That was all the scoring in the first half. Minnesota's defense stifled the Navy offense. The Middies got only one first down that wasn't the result of a penalty and had minus seven yards rushing.

In the second half, Minnesota struck quickly and got the ball to the Navy 29. Blaska then connected with Cairns at the 25. Campbell threw a key block and Cairns deked one Navy defender and went into the end zone.

With 1:06 left to play in the fourth quarter and the ball at the Navy four, reserve quarterback Bob Sadek pitched out to Pelletier sweeping to his left. Pelletier got through two defenders to score, capping a 51-yard march. Mike Reid kicked his third consecutive extra point of the day giving the Gophers a 21-0 victory and had their second consecutive shutout.

"That's the hardest pass rush I have ever seen in college football," Navy coach Wayne Hardin said. "Our kids were just overwhelmed."

Warmath praised several players, but especially Bell and Eller at the tackles and Blaska who hit six of 12 passes.

"Eller never looked better," he added.

For the third week in a row, the Gophers were at home, this time against a fine Northwestern team which had routed Illinois 45-0 a week earlier. Minnesota's unscored on defense was receiving widespread praise, but by the time the game was over, the Gophers had given up 34 points.

The Wildcats had a talented sophomore quarterback named Tom Myers. Both teams filled the air with passes and tallied 45 points in the game's final 16 minutes.

Northwestern scored first, although Minnesota dominated the first half. The Gophers took over at the Wildcat 14 following a bad snap from center on a first-quarter punt attempt. Minnesota got only three yards on three plays and Cairns missed a field goal attempt. Northwestern couldn't move and the Gophers got the ball back and moved to the 24. A fourth down pass play from Blaska to John Campbell was a yard short of the first down.

Then Myers went to the air and marched Northwestern from its 13 with four long passes. From the Gopher 10 he hit end Gary Crum, who had split the defense at the goal line for the first touchdown. Dick Uhlir made the PAT.

Minnesota took the kickoff and marched 61 yards in 11 plays with Blaska hitting Jones on a running pass play good for eight yards and the touchdown. Cairns kicked the point after to tie the score.

The Gophers got another break on the next possession and turned it into their only lead of the day. Myers made an errant pitch on a lateral to halfback Larry Benz and Bell pounced on the fumble at the Northwestern 19. On third down from the 17, Jones blasted over right guard for the touchdown. Cairns hit the point after and the Gophers took a 14-7 lead into the locker room at halftime.

In the third quarter, Myers came out throwing again and marched the Wildcats 80 yards in 12 plays. Northwestern got the ball after a Gopher drive was thwarted. A Blaska throw into the end zone, which was intended for end Bob Prawdzik, was too high and intercepted by Charles Brainerd. From the 20, Northwestern began its march. Key plays in the drive were a twisting 35-yard run by halfback Willie Stinson and a critically- important pass interference call against Cairns on a crucial fourth down play deep in Minnesota territory.

Myers throw from the Minnesota four bounced out of the hands of halfback Paul Flatley and toward end Chuck Logan, who was just inside the end zone. Cairns hit Logan just before the ball got to Logan. Instead of turning over the ball on the four, Northwestern got another chance. Three plays later from the one, fullback Steve Murphy hurdled the line and scored. Ara Parseghian decided to go for the two points and Myers found Logan alone in the end zone to make the score 15-14 in favor of Northwestern.

Northwestern scored again early in the fourth quarter when a Minnesota drive got nowhere. A 19-yard punt return by Roland Wahl gave the Wildcats good field possession at the Minnesota 46. Several plays later from the nine, Myers hit Murphy for the score and Uhlir made the conversion kick to increase Northwestern's lead to 22-14.

The Gophers rallied with eight minutes left, going 65 yards in two plays to score. A 12-yard pass from Sadek to reserve end Myron Rognlie set up Sharp who went 53 yards for the touchdown on a draw-trap play. Sadek hit the other reserve end, Ray Zitzloff, for the two-point conversion. The game was tied with 5:09 left to play.

It was all Northwestern the rest of the way. On the second play after the kickoff, Myers faded back and hit Stinson in the flat and the Wildcat speedster went down the sideline for a 65-yard scoring play. The two-point pass attempt failed.

Minnesota couldn't move and Northwestern got some insurance when Myers scored on a three-yard run. The final was 34-22.

In the Gopher locker room, everyone agreed that the interference call against Cairns was the turning point.

"We were ahead 14-7 at the time," Warmath said. "Had we stopped them, it might have sealed the game for us. They gave Myers very good protection on the pass plays".

Myers completed 16 for 25 for 261 yards.

"Minnesota has that tremendous pass rush, but our line did a great job of protecting Tom," Parseghian said. He waved one of the game balls under the nose of Minneapolis Tribune reporter Bill McGrane. "I've waited two years for this ball!"

Minnesota was 1-1-1 and Warmath knew the team had to make a move quickly if it hoped to contend.

•  •  •

That move came the next weekend when the Gophers hosted Illinois for homecoming. A crowd of 59,427 witnessed a lethargic Gopher team prevail because they had more talent. It took two long scoring marches in the final quarter to assure victory. That, coupled with a bending, but not breaking defense that thwarted Illini drives that went to the Minnesota 15, 37, 9, 10 and 8, was the difference. Added to the Gopher arsenal that day was the debut of a transfer from Hibbing Junior College, Collin Versich, who emerged as a fine placekicker. The result was a Minnesota 17-0 victory.

There was no scoring the first quarter. Illinois threatened, but missed a field-goal attempt when the snap from center was bad. In the second quarter, Munsey and sophomore back Bill McMillan each rushed for a total of 24 yards. Blaska scored on a short keeper and Versich kicked the extra point for a 7-0 lead.

In the fourth quarter, Blaska orchestrated a nice drive, combining the pass and run. Two completions to Fischer and Zitzloff got the Gophers to the Illini 10 where Versich kicked a 17-yard field goal.

Illinois called on the arm of quarterback Mike Taliaferro, to move to the Gopher eight. But Munsey picked off a pass to end the threat. Blaska consumed time in an 11-play march which was highlighted by his own 25-yard fake pitch keeper and a scoring pass to Rognlie with just 42 seconds to play.

The kick was good and the Gophers were 2-1-1 overall and 1-1 in Big Ten play.

"We were flat, not sharp," Warmath said.

"We didn't seem to play very inspired football," Munsey added.

"Blaska was great," Julian Hook pointed out. "He kept us in the game."

It was noted out that Versich, a late transfer to Minnesota, didn't show up for practice until mid-September and languished deep on the reserve chart. In fact, he had to talk his way past the

201

guards at the stadium before the game since his name wasn't on the player list.

Pete Elliott said afterward that his team was young and Minnesota was mature, well-coached and experienced.

Still, Warmath knew that he would have to get a better performance the following Saturday because his team was taking on Pete's brother's team, the University of Michigan in Ann Arbor. He got it.

"A magnificent Minnesota defense smashed the Wolverines of Michigan into almost complete impotency for a decisive 17-0 Little Brown Jug victory Saturday.

"Murray Warmath's pursuit tackling was so tremendous against inept Michigan blocking that unprotected ball carriers took their lives in their own hands while being socked sprawling on the sunny gridiron to this telltale tune:

"Michigan showed a net minus of 46 yards on 37 rushes."

The Minneapolis Star's Dick Gordon opening paragraphs in the Sunday paper report of the annual Gopher-Wolverine clash said it all. The Gopher defense, in fact the entire team, was really starting to jell and Michigan felt their full wrath.

More than 65,000 were on hand as Minnesota came to town for the Wolverines' homecoming. The Gophers dominated from the opening kickoff despite being baffled by some trick option and halfback pass plays by Michigan quarterback Frosty Evashevski, the son of Forrest Evashevski. But that ploy lasted for only a short time and the Golden Gopher defense soon had things going their way.

Versich kicked a 14-yard field goal which was the result of a bad punt snap by the Wolverines that Minnesota recovered at the Michigan 18. With two minutes left in the half, Hook intercepted an Evashevski pass and returned it 10 yards to the Wolverines' 43. Jones got 11 yards and then 15 yards were added on for a personal foul. Two plays later, Blaska tossed to Munsey, who went to the six and then he then found John Campbell deep

202

in the end zone for the touchdown pass. Versich's extra point kick was good.

The Gophers padded their lead in the third quarter going 88 yards in just six plays to score. Jones got 19 yards on three carries. Cairns went around end for 10. On a second down play, Blaska threw to Cairns at the Michigan 48. The 165-pound scatback danced into the end zone. The Gophers were ahead 17-0 following the successful point-after kick by Versich. The rest of the game was a back-and-forth exercise by both teams, featuring fumbles and penalties, but no scoring.

"Cairns' run after the pass was the best run anybody has made for us all year," Warmath said following his team's fourth shutout in five games. "But, we had too many fumbles and too many dropped passes."

Hook said the defense, which besides limiting the Wolverine offense to the minus yards rushing and giving up just 90 through the air on 29 passes, played the best game of the year.

Pete Elliott, asked to look ahead to the following weekend when Minnesota would return to the State of Michigan to play Michigan State, wouldn't pick a winner. The Spartans were loaded again and Warmath took his team into East Lansing as a clear underdog. When he came out, there was no question that his team was one of the finest defensive squads in post-World War II Big Ten history.

# Twenty-Six

In the Minnesota locker room after the Michigan State game, assistant coach Bob Bossons was looking for a newspaper photographer to take a picture of the celebration following the upset of the Spartans. Bossons wanted to counter the photo which had appeared five years earlier, the last time Minnesota played in East Lansing. That was 1957. Minnesota had been a pre-season favorite—along with Michigan State—for the Big Ten and national championship. The roof had fallen in a month earlier when Illinois knocked off Minnesota and the Gophers never recovered.

That first photo had shown a dejected Warmath, head down, sitting on a bench in the visitors' locker room following the 42-13 drubbing by the Spartans. The caption read "When a fella' needs a friend".

On Nov. 3, 1962, it was the Spartans who were looking for friends. That's because Warmath's team had just manhandled Michigan State.

The latest photograph showed a beaming Warmath surrounded by players and assistant coach Butch Nash. It was little wonder they were so happy. They had just come off a playing field where they had demonstrated again they were among the best teams in the country.

The 28-7 rout of Michigan State was not indicative of the game. Gordon said in his Tribune report the following day that Minnesota outplayed "the favored Spartans by twice the margin."

Gordon wrote it was a drizzly Saturday in East Lansing, one which saw the 64,000-plus MSU fans finally "mingle their tears with the raindrops."

The Spartans featured the nation's top rushing offense. That day, however, they managed only 30 yards rushing.

Minnesota built a 13-7 halftime lead and they did it with a mix of Warmath's offensive ingenuity consisting of both a balanced and an unbalanced line. The first quarter was scoreless as the Gophers staved off a couple of Spartan threats. The first quarter ended with Michigan State unable to move and punting to Minnesota.

Warmath used his second unit and reserves to start the second quarter, but stayed with Blaska at quarterback. On fourth and 11 at the Michigan State 30, Blaska connected with Cairns at the five. Jerry Jones went in on the next play and Versich made the conversion.

It was here that the Gophers really took command of the game. Bell, Jones and Perkovich smacked the Spartans and smacked then hard. State could not move. They had to punt. Cairns gave another fine open-field running demonstration. He took the Lou Bobich kick in full stride at his own 40 and dippsy-doodled his way down the field. Campbell splattered Bobich on the curl-back block. Cairns faked-out George Saimes, then went easily into the end zone. Versich's point after attempt was blocked.

State scored its only TD on the next possession when Ron Rubick took the kickoff to the Gopher 26. The Spartans got to the three and on fourth down, Rubick got good blocking to score the touchdown. The PAT was good and the halftime score was 13-7.

In the third quarter, Minnesota had a third-and-eight at the State 46. Blaska rolled out and threw to Campbell deep down field. The pass bounced off Campbell's outstretched hands into the grasp of Munsey who was standing alone at the five. Munsey coasted in for the touchdown. Versich missed the conversion. A couple of series later, the points came back when Cairns and Enga nailed Charles Migyanka, a State quarterback, in the end for a safety to make it 21-7.

In the fourth quarter, the Gophers added to their lead when Jay Sharp scored on a one-yard plunge.

"I can't remember when one of our teams was so completely dominated," State coach Duffy Daughterty reflected afterward. "I never thought I'd see our offense stopped like that (30 yards rushing and 56 passing)."

"I thought we were ready for this one," he added. "We had a great week of practice I felt, but give Minnesota credit. They richly deserved to win."

"We kept hearing all week how State was going to punish us for the upset last year when they were ranked first in the country," Jones said. "All we heard was how they were going to kill us. We don't frighten very easily. The score told the story."

Jones had played an exceptional game and was carried off the field by his teammates.

Assistant coach Don Grammer said the Gophers won because "we punished them physically and we were more mobile than they were."

•　　•　　•

The next week the Gophers got back to whitewashing their opponent and climbed into a three-way tie for the Big Ten lead. Iowa came to town and once again the Gopher defense was magnificent in a 10-0 victory. In seven games, Minnesota had allowed only 41 points, the best in the country.

The game against the Hawkeyes was extremely hard-hitting, yet clean. Only one penalty was called.

Minnesota had a tough fight to earn the victory and led only 3-0 entering the final quarter. The three points came on a 27-yard Versich field goal in the second quarter. In the first quarter, Iowa threatened after recovering a Jones fumble at the Gopher 45. Minnesota's defense, playing without Campbell and Eller who were hurt early in the game, held off the Hawkeyes. Gopher safety Paul Ramseth jarred the ball loose from Lonnie Rogers and Cairns fell on the pigskin at the one to end the threat.

Again Iowa moved deep into Gopher territory, but a hard tackle by Hook popped the ball loose and Ramseth recovered at the 14.

Versich made a 24-yard field goal at the end of the next possession. The Gophers got into position for the successful field goal attempt on a drive featuring flat passes to Munsey and McMillan and the running of fullback and captain Enga.

In the third quarter, Minnesota stopped Iowa at the Gopher 34 on a fourth down play, but couldn't get any kind of drive going. Iowa took over only to fumble again. Minnesota's reserve guard Willie Costanza fell on the ball at the Iowa 35, but again Minnesota couldn't capitalize.

In the fourth quarter, Ramseth returned a punt to the Iowa 44. Munsey, McMillan and Bill Crockett worked with Blaska to get to the Iowa eight. On fourth down-and-four, Blaska rolled left and faked the pitch, broke a tackle at the two and fell over the goal line. Versich made the kick with 14 minutes left in the game.

Iowa marched for a short time, but Paul Benson ended the Hawkeyes last threat by picking off a Matt Szykowny pass.

Warmath attributed the victory to good depth, citing that Minnesota seemed stronger toward the end of the game and singled out Ramseth and end Bob Prawdzik for their fine play.

Jerry Burns said fumbles stopped Iowa. "We had our kids convinced that we could move against the Gophers and we did (a season-high 122 yards rushing, the best of the year by anyone against the stout Gopher defense). But we killed ourselves and you can't do that and expect to win against a team like that."

•    •    •

To quote Yogi Berra, "it was déja vu all over again." In other words, another tight, bloody Minnesota-Purdue battle that featured rock-em, sock-em, hard-nosed football. It required a Gopher quarterback to overcome 14 incomplete passes before hitting on the throw that would win the game.

As usual, the Boilermakers and Gophers gave no quarter with Purdue taking a 6-0 lead at halftime thanks to two field goals by Skip Ohl.

Minnesota kicked off to start the game and Purdue went 62 yards in 14 plays to the eight where the Gopher defense stiffened and Ohl kicked a 25-yard field goal attempt. Minnesota drove inside the Boilermaker 30, but Versich missed a 35-yard attempt.

In the second quarter, Munsey fumbled and Purdue cashed in on another Ohl field goal, this one a 37-yarder.

It was evident that the Purdue line was more than a match for Minnesota's forward wall. However, Minnesota's staying power and greater depth began to show itself in the second half.

Twice the Gophers drove inside the Purdue 40, but came away empty. In the same interval, Purdue got inside Minnesota territory only once.

Early in the fourth quarter, the Gophers reached the Boilermakers' 29 where Blaska, suffering from a poor day of throwing, made his first completion when he drifted back to his left on third and eight and passed up the middle to Zitzloff. The end from Wayzata split two Purdue defenders, Tom Bloom and Ron Meyer, at the two and stepped into the end zone. Versich hit the conversion with 10:23 left in the game.

Charles King returned the kickoff to the Purdue 41 where Roy Walker, a bulldozer fullback, kept powering his way into the Minnesota line. Purdue got to the Gopher 29, but Bell showed his All-American talent when he stopped Walker for no gain on third-and-two. Then Bell and Campbell nailed quarterback Gary Hogan for just a one yard gain. The Gophers took over and kept the ball on the ground to consume time and then punted. The Boilermakers took it over at their 12, advanced to their 41, but had to give up the ball when Hogan missed a fourth down pass attempt. Minnesota took over and ran down the clock.

In the Minnesota locker room, credit was given to Gopher assistant coach Dick Larson, who called the winning touchdown pass from the press box.

"Zitzloff kept telling me that play was open and he was right," Blaska added. "The Purdue linebackers and corners kept playing further and further out, so it left the middle open."

"Bobby Bell never played a better game, and he's played some great ones," Warmath pointed out. "He made at least four big defensive plays, including the stopping of Hogan on fourth down at our 28 in the fourth quarter."

In the meantime, the Gophers looked ahead to the trip to Madison for the season finale and the Big Ten Championship on the line. For Minnesota, it would be a terribly sad...and very controversial...end to three great years in Golden Gopher football history.

# Twenty-Seven

 Rarely in the history of modern college football has an official's call been so universally disputed and the outcome so tainted as was the case on Nov. 24, 1962 in Madison, Wis.

Minnesota and Wisconsin came into the game tied for the Big Ten lead with 5-1 records. Northwestern had been beaten by both the Badgers and Michigan State, lost its No. 1 ranking and any chance for a conference title. It came down to the battle for Paul Bunyan's axe.

As in past years, the Badgers had an excellent passing attack. Pat Richter was back at end and a new quarterback, Ron VanderKelen, was at the helm replacing the very talented Ron Miller who had graduated. While the Gophers' lone Big Ten loss had been to Northwestern, Wisconsin had fallen to Ohio State four games earlier 14-0.

A record-setting crowd of 65,514 was on hand on an overcast day at Camp Randall Stadium. What they witnessed was a very close game, marked by highly-disputed officiating. Minnesota opened the scoring when Blaska completed three passes to Zitzloff, Crockett and Cairns for 59 yards. The throw to Cairns came with the second quarter just 10 seconds old. Blaska found Cairns out in the right flat and the shifty Gopher back used a nice curl-back block by Munsey on defender John Fabry, then made a move on Jim Nettles and went into the end zone for the score. Versich missed the PAT.

The Minnesota offense would eventually outrush Wisconsin, 223 to 83 yards. It was a virtual standoff in passing with Wisconsin having a slight edge, 136 to 130. The Gophers would be penalized in the game a total of 14 times compared to the Badgers eight.

After the Gophers scored, Wisconsin came right back with halfback Lou Holland taking the kickoff to his 35. VanderKelen went to the air and moved Wisconsin 65 yards in eight plays for the TD. Key plays were a draw by fullback Ralph Kurek for 11 yards and the touchdown pass to reserve end Ron Leafblad. Gary Kroner kicked the conversion and the Badgers led 7-6.

Minnesota was denied a third quarter touchdown when Blaska hit Munsey on a short pass of about 10 yards. While fighting to get into the end zone against a swarm of Badger tacklers, Munsey was illegally assisted by a Bell, Eller and even Blaska, all of whom came to his aid and tried pushing him in for the score. Minnesota had driven to the four, got two yards on a bench penalty against Wisconsin, but was in turn penalized for the Munsey pushing incident and settled for a 22-yard field goal by Versich to take a 9-7 lead.

The Gophers got two breaks, but failed to capitalize. First, Julian Hook recovered a Kroner fumble at the Minnesota 15. Then two series later at the Wisconsin 36, Crockett fell on a Badger fumble of a Gopher punt. Then Wisconsin's Billy Smith picked off a Blaska throw.

In the fourth quarter, Minnesota punted into the end zone with less than four minutes left. Wisconsin drove to the Gopher 43 where the play of the game and one of the most historical of this long rivalry, occurred.

With 2:30 left, VanderKelen dropped back to throw to Richter. Bobby Bell made a great rush and hit the Wisconsin quarterback as he tried to release the ball. Bell's rush was so complete that he partially batted the ball as he hit Vanderkelen. The ball fluttered like a wounded duck and Bell crashed down on top of VanderKelen who was falling back from the impact of the hit. Gopher linebacker Jack Perkovich was at his 37 and let the end-over-end throw settle gently into his arms. He took it back to his 42 and the Gophers started celebrating what appeared to be the interception that had sealed a Big Ten championship.

But back behind the sprawled Bell and VanderKelen, a flag lay on the ground, thrown by referee Bob Jones who called "roughing the passer" on Bell. Wisconsin was granted possession and a 15-yard penalty. Warmath was irate.

"Another official—I can't remember which one—was walking down the sideline in front of our bench and I reached out and pulled at his sleeve and asked what the call was for," Warmath remembered. "He immediately snarled 'you can't touch me like that' and threw his flag saying I was guilty of unsportsmanlike conduct. They tacked on another 15 yards."

The Minnesota bench was going crazy. Wisconsin got the ball at the 13. Holland got eight, then VanderKelen three to the two yard line. From there, Kurek scored. Kroner kicked the point after and Wisconsin was ahead 14-9.

Minnesota, however, didn't die and the officials, seemingly feeling guilty, made some calls to try to even things up. They called three consecutive major penalties on the Badgers—two for pass interference and one for piling on.

Suddenly, Minnesota had the ball at the Badger 14 with 70 seconds left. On first down, Blaska threw into the end zone for Munsey, but Jim Nettles picked it off. Even then, the Gophers didn't quit. They forced a Wisconsin punt, got the ball back, but on the last play of the game, Nettles again made a great play and knocked down a Blaska throw to Crockett at the Wisconsin 15.

Minnesota was stunned and enraged.

Minnesota athletic director Ike Armstrong and Big Ten commissioner Bill Reed came down and escorted an angry Warmath to the locker room.

Hook stormed through the throng on the field, and in a fit of anger, took his helmet and hit one of the officials, now fleeing for his life from the infuriated Gopher team and its fans.

"Sid Hartman, who was mad as hell about the whole thing and had seen it from the press box, said in the locker room later not to worry, he'd report it was not me, it was a fan," Hook said.

"There were rumors I might be suspended from school for my outburst."

The post-game comments were reflective of Warmath's philosophy of always playing the gentleman and never detracting from the other teams efforts. Still, the Gopher coach could not fully contain himself this one time.

"We were the better team today, no doubt about it. We had Wisconsin shut down and outplayed them physically and Duane Blaska was great at quarterback."

Other players were flabbergasted over the events of the day. To a man they cited blown calls by the officials and the fact they had outfought the Badgers, although they said Wisconsin was a tough, well-coached team.

Earlier, at the conclusion of the game, the officials tried to hide out in their locker room. Several Gopher players, led by Carl Eller, were outside banging on their door.

"I remember being struck by the fact the game seemed to be an unnatural order of things," Eller reflected. "It was this unfolding of events that now seem totally bizarre."

It was Warmath, however, who directly confronted the officials.

"I sorta' slinked around outside their locker room door after things initially quieted down," Warmath remembered. "After a few minutes, one of the members of the sideline 'chain gang' came to the door and pounded on it.

"The door was locked and from inside I heard someone call out, 'who is it?, who is it? The 'chain gang' guy identified himself and said he wanted to come in and change into his street clothes."

From inside, came the click as the door was unbolted. The door gradually opened and a pair of eyes suspiciously peered out into the hallway. The chain gang official started to step into the locker room.

Warmath crashed past him and into the locker room.

213

"I grabbed the official who had opened the door by the throat and pushed him up against the wall," Warmath remembered. "The rest of the officiating crew suddenly were quiet and sat down on the benches in front of their lockers. I let go of the guy I had by the throat. I then went around individually to every one of 'em."

"Most of them wouldn't look me in the eye. I went around pointing at each of them and telling them what I thought. They just sat there and silently listened to my tirade."

Warmath let loose.

"I told those guys that they had just stolen the Big Ten championship from the finest group of young men I had ever known and I would never forgive them for the fact they had been so incompetent and so unfair."

Warmath maintained his life-long policy of making sure disputes remained private.

"I told them that I would not say anything to the newspaper or broadcast reporters about my confrontation with them and that what I had to say was strictly between us."

It is only now that Warmath has been public about the confrontation.

•    •    •

More than a quarter of a century later, the memories of the game are painfully vivid for Gopher players.

"There was no way in hell that I roughed VanderKelen," Bell said years later. "I hit him so early in the process that the ball barely got beyond the line of scrimmage and he was obviously throwing for Richter who was well down the field."

Nearly 30 years later, Bell recounted a somewhat humorous story. Named to every All-America team that year and winner of the Outland Trophy as the top interior college lineman, Bell spent a couple of weeks in December doing media junkets associated with the All-America teams. The first weekend of

214

December always is when the Army-Navy game is held in Philadelphia. Bell and other All-Americans were invited to the game and were introduced before kickoff.

"President Kennedy came out on the field," Bell said. "We were lined up in a row at the center of the field and were being introduced to the crowd and television audience over the public address system."

In the office of his restaurant in downtown Kansas City, Bell rose from behind his desk and walked over to a corner and picked up a large, framed black and white photo. In the photo, he is shown standing in the line of the 1962 All-Americans and shaking JFK's hand.

"Right there, Kennedy was talking to me. One of his aides had introduced me to him and his immediate response was 'Bobby Bell! You're the one who got that really bad roughing call against you a couple of weeks ago in that big game against Wisconsin, right?'"

Bell pointed to the player standing next to him who has a rather incredulous look on his face. "That guy next to me is Pat Richter."

The call was so bad even the President of the United States was aware of it.

Thirty years later, Warmath is more vitriolic in his reflections on the 1962 Minnesota-Wisconsin battle.

"I can't help but think there was something fishy about the officiating. It was almost as if the game was rigged. I watched films for years afterward and was amazed at how ineptly the game was handled."

A wry smile crosses his face.

"I'll tell ya' something. It's just been within the past year or two that I finally haven't awakened in the middle of every night of every week and started thinking about that goddamn game."

# Twenty-Eight

Following the 1962 season, Warmath and his staff faced the most significant rebuilding period since the conclusion of the 1957 season. Gone were Bell, Hook, Munsey, Jones, Blaska, Benson, Cairns, Perkovich, Enga, Campbell, Prawdzik and Fischer along with reserves Dave Lothner, Jim Zak, Gary Colberg, Tim Cashman and Don Miller.

Carl Eller was the only returning starter, although there were players coming back who had seen extensive duty during the 1962 campaign as reserves. In 1962, Blaska had done a good job replacing Sandy Stephens. The challenge in '63 was to again take an inexperienced quarterback and develop him. John Hankinson, Bob Sadek and Larry Peterson were the players fighting for the starting job, but it got paired down to two when Hankinson broke his collarbone in pre-season practice and was lost for the year. Sadek got the nod over Peterson.

The Gophers opened against Nebraska and its excellent coach Bob Devaney, who in his inaugural year of 1962 led the Cornhuskers to a 9-2 record. The week before coming to Minneapolis for the 1963 Gopher opener, Devaney's squad whipped South Dakota State 58-7. A little more than 61,000 were on hand at Memorial Stadium for the Nebraska game.

Minnesota scored in the first quarter when Sadek hit Jerry Pelletier on a 44-yard pass to the two. Sadek made two consecutive sneaks to score. Mike Reid's conversion kick was good.

Dennis Claridge, a Robbinsdale graduate, who had played with Julian Hook and chose Lincoln over Minneapolis, was the excellent all-around Nebraska quarterback. He punted to the Gopher two. Nebraska held and Stan Skjei kicking from his end zone got the ball out to the Minnesota 36. Nebraska drove for a touchdown, the big plays being a 14-yard run by Bruce Smith and an eight-yard touchdown run by Claridge. The conversion tied the game.

Claridge hit another punt, this one in the second quarter, which put Minnesota in poor field position. He boomed one 70 yards to the Minnesota 19.

In the second half, the defensive momentum swung to Nebraska. Minnesota got only 88 yards in total offense in the half. In the fourth quarter, Claridge connected with sophomore end Tony Jeter on a 65-yard TD pass. The kick was good and the game ended with Nebraska the 14-7 victor.

"It was the Nebraska kicking game that kept us in poor position a good share of the game," Warmath commented.

Pelletier praised Nebraska's ball control.

"It was the kind of tough game we expected," Devaney added. "As usual, Minnesota played well."

The following week, Minnesota hosted Army, the second year in a row it had played a service academy team. Under Paul Dietzel, who had coached some excellent teams at LSU, the Cadets were predicted to be a strong team in the East, but no match for a Big Ten squad. Minnesota was a 24-8 winner.

It was 80 degrees the first Saturday in October and more than 60,000 were in attendance as Minnesota got 17 points in just under 10 minutes of the first half. Reid opened the scoring in the first quarter with a field goal. The Cadets then lost a fumble on the next possession. The Gophers worked it to the Army three where Reid's line buck got it in for the touchdown. He scored his tenth point of the game with the ensuing extra point kick.

Willie Costanza intercepted a Carl Stichweh pass at the Army 42 to set up a Sadek touchdown a few plays later. Reid made the conversion for a 17-0 lead.

The third quarter was less than five minutes old when Jay Sharp scored from the Army seven, thanks to a Stichweh fumble at the 10. Reid's conversion was his 11th point of the day.

Army scored late in the game from the shotgun formation. Stichweh moved Army inside the Minnesota five and Ken Waldrop scored off tackle. Flanker John Seymour caught the two-point throw.

"Army's seven turnovers helped our cause a great deal," Warmath pointed out, "and Sadek did a nice job of calling plays and passing (9 of 15)."

"Minnesota outmuscled us in the line," Dietzel added.

The following week, the Gophers traveled to Evanston for a nationally-televised game against Northwestern. The 45,000 at Dyche Stadium, along with the TV audience, were well-entertained.

The game was a defensive struggle with neither team scoring until late in the game. In the first half, Eller led a solid defense that held the 'Cats to just two first downs and sacked quarterback Tom Myers three times and intercepted three passes.

In the fourth quarter, the Wildcats struck first when Myers passed to Mike Buckner for a 54-yard touchdown. The point after was good.

Larry Peterson, subbing for Sadek, took the Gophers on a 75- yard march on the succeeding possession. Behind key blocks by Reid and center Frank Marchlewski, sophomore back Al Harris took a pitchout and streaked 20 yards into the end zone. Peterson then rolled right into the end zone and got the two points for an 8-7 Gopher lead.

On the next kickoff, Gopher Larry Hartse roughed returner Willie Stinson giving Northwestern good field possession near midfield. Myers passed to Chuck Logan and Gary Crum and then threw one to Stinson for 25 yards and the touchdown. The two-point pass play to Buckner was good and Northwestern held on for a 15-8 victory.

218

"The two long passes by Myers were the difference," Warmath said. "We had really rushed Myers well in the first half, but we couldn't score. We made too many young team mistakes."

Captain Milt Sunde said the Wildcats adjusted in the second half to the Minnesota defense and the Gopher pass rush was not nearly as effective.

"Minnesota did an awfully good job in the first half on Tom," Ara Parseghian added. "He was under a lot of pressure and people expect too much out of him, but he came back when it counted."

It was back to Illinois the next Saturday. Fumbles cursed Minnesota and it cost the Gophers as Illinois recovered four of five and posted a 16-7 victory.

Aided by an interference call in the first quarter, Illinois got to the Minnesota seven where Mike Taliafero hit end Gary Schumacher for a touchdown. The PAT attempt was no good. Late in the second quarter, Paul Ramseth fumbled an attempted fair catch and Illinois recovered. The Illini turned the mistake into a Jim Plankenhorn field goal with nine seconds left.

In the third period, Minnesota drove 58 yards, primarily on the arm of Sadek, who hit Myron Rognlie on a third down pass to the Illinois 29. He then threw to Pelletier at the 11. Pelletier scored a few plays later from the six, but the two point conversion attempt was no good.

The teams went back and forth for several drives before Pelletier mishandled a punt midway in the fourth quarter and Illinois recovered at the nine. Reserve quarterback Fred Custardo shook two tackles while scoring the first play. The PAT was good and the final score was 16-6.

"I'm amazed we didn't lose by more given the number of turnovers we had," Warmath muttered after the game.

"Nobody's outclassed us, we just beat ourselves," added end Dan Drexler.

Everybody on the Minnesota team praised an Illini middle linebacker named Dick Butkus. The hard-nosed junior was a major reason the 1963 Illinois team became Big Ten and Rose Bowl champions.

The Gophers returned to Minneapolis and hosted Michigan. For the fourth year in a row, the Gophers beat the Wolverines. This time the score was 6-0. The game came down to key mistakes, three big defensive stands by Minnesota and the punting of Stan Skjei.

Early in the second quarter, Pelletier scored on a six-yard scamper. His TD run finished off a 41-yard, 10-play drive that started in the first quarter. Minnesota got the ball following a short Michigan punt. The big play was a fourth-and-two at the 33 when sophomore halfback Fred Farthing swept end for four yards and the first down. Reid was wide with the point after attempt.

Twice more in the first half the Gophers drove into Michigan territory, to the 17 and 10 yard lines, but came away empty.

In the third quarter, the Wolverines drove 64 yards to the seven, but on fourth-down quarterback Bob Timberlake fumbled at the seven and Skjei recovered. Minnesota got to its 31. On fourth down and into a strong wind, Skjei punted for 50 yards to the Michigan 19.

Twice in the fourth quarter, big defensive plays aided the Gophers. At the Minnesota 23, a fourth-down Wolverine pass was short and late in the game, Eller sacked Timberlake who fumbled and Costanza recovered. The Gophers then ran out the clock.

Warmath, always appreciative of a good kicking game, praised Skjei's punting. The Appleton, Minn. junior averaged 41 yards on seven kicks.

"Eller saved us with his play," the Gopher coach said. "With 10 fumbles in the game, it wasn't a very well-played affair."

Bump Elliott agreed with Warmath, citing Eller's play, symbolic of a superb Minnesota pass rush.

Minnesota played sloppy football against Michigan and won. Minnesota played sloppy football against Indiana and lost. A very subpar Hoosier team came to Minneapolis and got only their second Big Ten victory since 1959.

Turnovers killed Minnesota as they lost six fumbles and threw three interceptions. In the first quarter, Minnesota marched to the Indiana 18 and the 30 without scoring. Later, Skjei fumbled at midfield. Indiana got the ball and drove for the score. Tom Nowatzke, a fine fullback who would rush for 138 yards, broke loose for 32 yards to the Minnesota five and substitute halfback Don Dilly scored on the next play. Nowatzke made the extra point kick.

The next score wasn't until the third quarter when Indiana went 65 yards in just six plays, a 35-yard run by Dilly to the seven being the big play. Quarterback Rich Bader took it in from the one a few plays later. The PAT was good. Minnesota came back and drove 62 yards in 12 plays for its touchdown with Sadek taking it over from the two. The conversion kick was no good.

Later in the third quarter, Pelletier lost the ball on a fumble at the Minnesota 29. Dilly scored on the first play from scrimmage. Nowatzke hit the conversion to make the score 21-6. Nowatzke added a 42-yard field goal in the fourth quarter. Minnesota got as far as the Hoosier 26, but Indiana intercepted a pass to secure the 24-6 victory.

"Everything that could go wrong, did," Warmath lamented. "We were bad in all departments."

Things didn't improve at Iowa the next week where Jerry Burns won his only game ever against Warmath. The Hawkeyes' sophomore quarterback Gary Snook threw three touchdown passes in a 27-13 trouncing of the Gophers.

Minnesota scored first when Sadek hit Kraig Lofquist for a 10-yard touchdown pass after Sunde and Larry Hartse jarred the ball loose from Snook at the 13 and Aaron Brown recovered. Later in the quarter, Paul Krause intercepted a Sadek throw at the Minnesota 18 and took it to the 12. From the eight, Snook hit end Cloyd Webb for the touchdown as the second quarter started. Later in the quarter, Krause caught several key passes, including a 26-yard leaping grab in the end zone. The catch capped an 80-yard drive. Iowa led at halftime 14-7.

In the second half, a 46-yard pass to Webb gave Iowa a 21-7 lead. Iowa's John Sherman intercepted a Sadek pass at the Minnesota 30 and returned it for the score. Behind 27-7, Minnesota drove 52 yards in five plays with Sadek connecting with end Kent Kramer for the score from the 10. The conversion attempt was no good.

"Neither team could run, we couldn't pass, they could, so they won," was the simple summary by Warmath. "They had an interception at the start of the second half that hurt us and we kept making mistakes."

Jerry Burns cited linemen Mike Reilly and Wally Hilgenberg for their fine play, pointed out Krause and Webb's big catches and said Snook played great.

"It's nice to finally beat Minnesota after three losses."

Minnesota dominated the next weekend...and lost neverthess.

It was the first Minnesota-Purdue game in West Lafayette since 1959.

In the first quarter, Reid kicked a 33-yard field goal. The following kickoff was taken by Purdue's Gordon Teter at the 12 and he went 88 yards for the score. Gary Hogan kicked the point after.

Larry Peterson's fumble set up the next Boilermaker score. Ron DeGravio snuck into the end zone.

In the second quarter, Minnesota came back and went 78 yards in nine plays for a touchdown. The big plays were a run of 29 yards by Gopher halfback Dick Harren, pass receptions by Harren and Lofquist, and Reid's run on a draw play for 12 yards.

Sadek snuck in for the touchdown and then passed to Harren for the two points to narrow Purdue's lead to 14-11.

In the third quarter, linebacker Joe Pung intercepted a Hogan throw at the Purdue 48 and took it to the 31. But Minnesota couldn't move the ball and Reid's field goal attempt from the 35 failed. In the fourth quarter, Deryl Ramey missed two field goal attempts from the 19 and 30.

Late in the fourth quarter, the game came down to a good punt return, an exhausted pass receiver and a missed field goal.

First, Pelletier took a punt at the Gopher seven and ran it out to the 31. On second down, Sadek hit Brown over the middle at the Purdue 42. The big Port Arthur, Texas sophomore took off for the goal line, broke through two tacklers and looked as if he would score the go-ahead touchdown. But a fleet Jim Morel closed fast on Brown, who was slowing down and got him at the Boilermaker 11.

Minnesota got to the two. On fourth down Reid's field goal attempt was wide.

The game ended and it was a disconsolate group of Gophers who went into the locker room.

"This was the best we've played all year," Eller said. "We didn't take advantage of the opportunities."

"It was finally nice to have the breaks go our way," Jack Mollenkopf added. "Teter's run and the mistakes by Minnesota got us our win."

The Gophers went home for the season finale against Wisconsin. They were out for revenge after the nightmare in Madison at the end of the 1962 season and looked forward to the following Saturday. They would get their revenge, but a national tragedy would make them wait an extra five days.

•　　•　　•

"I was getting a haircut at a campus barbershop when the news came," Warmath remembered.

President Kennedy has been assassinated in Dallas, Texas at 12:30 p.m. on Friday, Nov. 22, 1963.

Along with everyone else, Warmath was shocked and immediately left and returned to his office in Cooke Hall. Wisconsin had arrived earlier in the day for the game. Like virtually all institutions and sports establishments around the country, officials from the two schools debated what to do. Finally, it was decided to postpone the game until Thanksgiving.

"We fully realize that this grievous situation calls for a postponement," Warmath told the sports writers.

"All of us on the team are stunned by the President's death," Sunde added.

On Nov. 28th, five days after the originally scheduled game, Minnesota and Wisconsin met in 34 degree weather before 50,000 fans. The game started at 10:30 in the morning because it was Thanksgiving and people wanted to spend time with family and friends later that day. For Warmath, it was sweet revenge and in light of the 1962 game, it was nice to make the Badgers the "turkey" for the day.

The game came down to magnificent defensive play, especially by Eller, who was married the night before and was playing before his mother for the first time as a Gopher. He secured his first team All-America status that day.

In the first quarter, Minnesota took possession at the Badger 44 and Reid, a native of Spring Valley, Wis., scored from the three and kicked the extra point. Wisconsin threatened, but a sack by Eller of quarterback Harold Brandt at the 23 forced a 40-yard field goal attempt by the Badgers which was no good.

The turning point in the game came late in the second quarter. Wisconsin marched 73 yards in 13 plays and aided by an interference call on Minnesota defensive back Paul Ramseth, was at the one yard line with 33 seconds left.

Four times the Badgers hit the line and four times the Minnesota defenders rose up and threw them back. First it was

Joe Pung stopping fullback Ralph Kurek. Then it was Eller, in three terrific defense plays, stopping Brandt three times for no gain. Minnesota went off the field with a psychological lift.

Late in the third quarter, Reid scored again on a two-yard plunge and kicked the point after. The play that got them there was a 35-yard pass from Sadek to Harren.

On the ensuing kickoff, Badger Ralph Farmer fumbled and Rognlie recovered. Minnesota couldn't capitalize on the turnover. Wisconsin couldn't move the ball either, their deepest penetration being to the Gopher 44 in the fourth quarter. There, Brown deflected a pass which fellow-end Bob Bruggers intercepted.

The Gophers won 14-0.

The Gophers were jubilant and Warmath took delight in the victory given the circumstances surrounding the 1962 game. He cited Minnesota's well-balanced offensive game, only one turnover, two interceptions of Brandt and Eller's play as the keys to the victory. It was a nice way for the big tackle from Winston-Salem, N.C. to end his career as a Gopher. He would continue as a local athletic hero with the Minnesota Vikings.

The victory was also a nice way for Warmath to conclude his 10th season as the University of Minnesota football coach.

# Twenty-Nine

 Following the 1963 season, Minnesota's staff completed another fine recruiting effort and landed a group of high school seniors whose talents would come to fruition a few years later. They included John Williams from Ohio, Tom Sakal, Gordie Condo and Hubie Bryant from Pennsylvania, McKinley Boston ( the current U of M athletic director), Ed Duren and Charlie Sanders from North Carolina, Curt Wilson from Oklahoma and Dave Baldridge, Wayne King and Dick Peterson from Minnesota.

Of this group, the recruiting battle for John Williams was the most intense. A nationally touted high school fullback from Libbey High School in Toledo, Williams was pursued by many schools and it appeared Ohio State had the inside track.

"Don Grammer, the Minnesota assistant, had contacted me and talked me into visiting Minneapolis," Williams recounted. "I remember meeting Murray for the first time. He was sitting in his office throwing darts at a board with a picture of a football official on it. He looked up and commented he didn't realize I was big as I was."

Williams got positive feedback from black players, who had played for Warmath. Dickson, Stephens, Bell, Eller, etc. convinced him to attend Minnesota.

"When I told Woody Hayes I wasn't coming to Minnesota he was furious and called me 'a lying bastard' for supposedly making him think I wanted to play at Ohio State."

Minnesota opened the 1964 season at home again to Nebraska.

A national television audience and 50,000 at Memorial Stadium watched another Gopher-Cornhusker clash go down to the final minutes.

Minnesota scored first when John Hankinson marched the Gophers 65 yards in 14 plays and tossed an eight-yard touchdown pass to Aaron Brown. Mike Reid kicked the point after. Later in the quarter, Ray Whitlow of Minnesota fumbled a punt and Larry Kramer recovered for the Cornhuskers at the Minnesota 17. Nebraska moved to the one where, on fourth down, quarterback Fred Duda snuck in for the TD. Bob Bruggers blocked the conversion attempt.

In the second quarter, Brown caught an 18-yard pass for the Gophers, but lost the ball when he fumbled at the Nebraska 32. Nebraska mixed up running and passing plays with Kent McGloughan scoring on a 10-yard run. The point after attempt was wide and it was 12-7 at halftime.

In the third quarter, Minnesota moved into Nebraska territory and Hankinson scored from the Cornhusker 32. Reid kicked the point after and Minnesota led 14-12. Nebraska came back and got to the Gopher 10, but on a fourth down play Joe Pung and Fred Nord stopped Bruce Smith.

Nebraska lost the ball again in the fourth quarter when Harry Wilson fumbled at midfield. Minnesota reached the 12, but on fourth-and-three Reid missed a field goal attempt.

Nebraska was stopped and punted. Whitlow fielded it at the Gopher 28, handed off to Bill Crockett who, with a critical block at the Nebraska 30 from Reid, went all the way for the touchdown. The conversion was good and Minnesota led by nine points.

But Nebraska wasn't finished. The kickoff was accidently squibbed and Minnesota was called for touching the ball before it went 10 yards. From the Minnesota 45, Duda missed on two consecutive throws before hitting Frank Solich for the score. The point after was good, cutting the Minnesota lead to 21-19.

Minnesota couldn't move after taking the kickoff and Skjei got off only a 19-yard punt into a 30 mile-per-hour wind.

On a critical fourth-and-13, Duda hit Freeman White for a first down. Nebraska got to the Minnesota 18 on a screen pass to Bobby Hohn. Duda tried to hit McGloughan in the end zone. It looked like Reid might have an interception. Instead, the ball skipped threw his hands, glanced off his helmet, and then to McGloughan, who grabbed it for the score. Minnesota couldn't sustain anything after that and lost the season opener 26-21.

"It's a good thing we had Crockett or we would have been beaten worse," Warmath said. "Just too many lapses in key areas."

Hankinson felt the missed 19-yard field goal and the wind disadvantage in the fourth quarter were critical.

Bob Devaney called his team's comeback courageous. Cornhusker Larry Kramer, himself a native of Austin, Minn., felt the Gophers were an improved team over 1963.

Warmath ventured west to Berkeley the next week to play the California Bears and Craig Morton. In 82-degree weather, Minnesota prevailed 26-20 , but had to hang on to do it.

Minnesota scored in the first quarter when Hankinson connected with Kent Kramer for a 29-yard touchdown pass just 3:16 into the game. Reid missed the conversion.

A couple of series later, Gopher middle guard Brian Callahan hit Morton, who fumbled and Kramer fell on the ball at the Bears' 20. Minnesota couldn't move and Reid connected on a 33-yard field goal to make it 9-0.

Reid followed with another field goal in the second quarter, this one for 19 yards.

Morton came out throwing in the third quarter and on a 71-yard drive (65 throught the air), got to the two where Tom Blanchfield scored. The conversion was good to make it 12-7.

Minnesota answered with an 80-yard drive climaxed by Hankinson rolling out and passing to Brown in the end zone for the score. The kick made it 19-7. Cal came right back and an eight-yard Morton-to-Jerry Bradley touchdown pass, but a wide extra point attempt still left Minnesota ahead 19-13.

Minnesota fumbled twice in the fourth quarter and it almost cost the Gophers the game. At the same time, Cal gambled late in the game and it may have deprived it of a victory. With the ball at the Cal 27 on fourth down, Morton overthrew end Jack Schwab and Minnesota took over. In five plays, the Gophers scored with Reid going in from the one. The kick was good and Minnesota led 26-13 with 2:32 left in the game.

The Bears stormed back. The kickoff was returned to the 47 of California. Skjei then interfered with Schwab in the end zone, so the ball was placed at the Gopher one. Blanchfield dove over for the touchdown and a two-point play was successful.

An onside kick bounced off Minnesota's Gale Gillingham and Cal recovered at the Minnesota 32. With just seconds left, the ball was advanced to the Minnesota 20, but two passes by Morton, first for Bradley, then for Schwab, were overthrown. The gun sounded with the Gophers a 26-21 winner.

"We deserved to win and when that's the case, it kills you to give away a game," Warmath added. He cited Crockett for excellent two-way play and called both Morton and Hankinson fine collegiate passers. Hankinson completed nine of 13 passes for 145 yards and two touchdowns while Morton was 17 of 29 for 259 yards and one TD.

Ray Willsey, the Cal coach, said "Minnesota knocked us around all day. We played lousy defense. We passed well, but circus football doesn't win you many games."

●     ●     ●

Hankinson continued to go to the air the next week against Northwestern. The junior quarterback combined passing and running to account for 239 yards in total offense. The result was the first win in three years over the Wildcats, who were coached by Alex Agase after Ara Parseghian moved to Notre Dame.

The first quarter at Memorial Stadium was a back-and-forth affair with neither team threatening to score. In the second quarter, Hankinson threw from the Gopher 29 to Kramer at the Wildcats' 46 and the junior end went to the six. On the next play, Reid smashed through on a right tackle trap and scored. He then hit the point after.

Minnesota scored again six minutes later. After stopping Northwestern at midfield and taking over at their 10 following a punt, the Gophers marched 90 yards for a touchdown. Most of those yards came on two pass plays. On the second play of the series from the 11, Hankinson hit Whitlow on a 50-yard throw. Then from the 39, he connected with Crockett to the eight. Hankinson followed with a rollout into the end zone and the PAT was good to give Minnesota a 14-0 advantage.

Northwestern got a last second touchdown before the half when Dave Milam, filling in for the injured Tom Myers, passed to end Dick Smith on a 38-yard play. Smith darted between Skjei and Glen Wirtanen into the end zone. The two-point pass attempt was overthrown.

Milam and Smith connected again in the third quarter, this time for 26 yards and a touchdown to finish a 59-yard drive. Another two-point attempt failed. Minnesota came back in the fourth quarter and Hankinson directed a 76-yard drive, scoring from the one. The kick was good. A late TD by Northwestern was too little, too late and Minnesota won 21-18.

Hankinson had not thrown an interception in three games and he had accounted for 67 percent of the Minnesota total offense in the victory.

"I got great protection and the receivers did a fine job of getting open," the Edina native said at the post-game press conference.

Warmath praised Nord, Lofquist, Reid and Costanza for their defensive play. He then went off to prepare for the arrival of Dick Butkus and a fine Illinois team, which was defending conference champion.

On a beautiful Indian summer day, 60,000 fans were on hand for the homecoming battle with the Illini. The only thing that was beautiful that day was the weather. Illinois completely manhandled the Gophers.

The injured Crockett didn't play. Hankinson suffered a concussion in the first quarter and didn't return. Fred Farthing, Glen Wirtanen and Brian Callahan joined Hankinson for overnight stays at University Hospital.

Illinois totally shut down the Gopher offense. Minnesota got just 195 yards, 133 through the air and had only 62 on the ground in 30 rushing attempts. The Gophers lost four fumbles and substitute quarterback Larry Peterson, hounded all day, hit on only nine of 22 passes and was intercepted five times.

Illinois scored late in the first quarter after Butkus clobbered Reid and forced a fumble which the Illini recovered at the Gopher 35. Seven plays later, Jim Grabowski went in from the two. Fred Custardo made the conversion kick. Nearly 15 minutes later, Dave Mueller intercepted a Peterson throw at the Minnesota 38 and several plays later, Custardo tossed a four-yard TD pass to Bob Trumpy. The extra point was good and Illinois won 14-0.

That was all the scoring needed by the Illini as their defense never allowed Minnesota to mount any kind of offense.

"Too many mistakes with fumbles and interceptions and too many hurt people to beat a fine team like Illinois," Warmath summed up afterward.

It was on to Ann Arbor the following week.

In the traditional meeting for the Jug, it was Michigan's early scoring followed by a desperate Gopher rally that was the focal point of the game.

Michigan scored the first four times. It started in the first quarter when Michigan went 54 yards in 11 plays. Fullback Mel Anthony plunged from the one for the TD. The conversion was good. In the second quarter, Wolverine quarterback Bob Timberlake kicked a 29-yard field goal attempt.

Michigan scored twice in the third quarter. A Minnesota punt snap sailed over kicker Bruce Van De Walker's head into the end zone for a safety. The Minnesota free kick followed and Michigan marched from its 49 to score the touchdown in 12 plays with Timberlake sneaking in from the one. He then kicked the point after touchdown.

Minnesota, which had looked dead, suddenly came to life. It was the Hankinson-to-Kramer combination once again, this time for an 11-yard score to cap an 11-play drive that started at the Minnesota 20. The two-point attempt was not good.

Michigan looked as if they were going to score again very early in the fourth quarter. The Wolverines got to the Gopher nine where Timberlake threw a square-out pass to his left. Gopher Kraig Lofquist stepped in front of the pass and took it 91 yards for the touchdown. In the process, he bowled over Timberlake at the Wolverines' 40. Again, the two-point attempt was no good. Michigan was in front 19-12.

On the next series, Minnesota held and Michigan had a terrible punt of only 14 yards to midfield from where Minnesota started another drive. With fourth-and-goal from the three, Lofquist went on an off-tackle slant to the left and was immediately hit. In a desperate move to make something happen, he lateraled to Aaron Brown who circled to his right. But Wolverines defensive back Dick Volk came bolting through and stopped the Gopher end for a loss at the seven.

After the game, Hankinson reflected that he perhaps called the wrong play on the Lofquist run and instead should have looked at the run-pass option. Warmath added that it was only in the last 20 minutes that the Gophers played well. Bump Elliott said it was nice to have the Little Brown Jug back after not seeing it since 1959. The Gophers knew they needed a victory. It came the next week in Bloomington, Ind.

•     •     •

The contest against the Hoosiers came down to a tough Minnesota defense, which gave the offensive unit enough time to put points on the board.

The first half was scoreless. Midway through the third quarter, the Gophers marched to the Indiana seven where Hankinson passed to sophomore split end Ken Last for the touchdown. Reid followed with a successful conversion attempt for a 7-0 lead.

Early in the fourth quarter, Minnesota took possession at the Hoosier 39 and in eight plays went in for its second touchdown. Reid scored from just inside the one yard line. He made the conversion for a 14-0 lead. Indiana couldn't get anything going and punted to Minnesota. The Gophers were likewise stymied and Van De Walker's punt rolled to the Hoosier three where Skjei downed the ball.

The Gophers looked liked they had things well under control when a few plays later Lofquist intercepted a Rich Bader pass at the Gopher 30. However, the favor was returned when Hankinson was intercepted at the Indiana three. Just as quickly, sophomore linebacker Tim Wheeler intercepted a Bader pass at the Indiana 38 and returned it to the one. From there, Fred Fathing carried it in. Reid kicked the conversion and that was the game as Minnesota shut out Indiana 21-0.

"Wheeler's interception and great punting were the keys to the win," a happy Warmath told the news corps afterward. "I was very pleased with Hankinson's play."

The junior Gopher quarterback had connected on 11 of 24 passes for 149 yards and the one TD throw to Last.

"Obviously, our defense played very well," Warmath added.

Murray's former Tennessee teammate Phil Dickens in the loser's locker room, cited the same defense and singled out Brian Callahan's play at middle guard.

"Clearly, if you watched Minnesota against both Nebraska and Michigan, two excellent teams, you know that the Gophers are a very fine team even when they don't win," the ex-Volunteer said.

It was back to Minneapolis and another classic 1960s-style Minnesota-Iowa battle.

A crowd of 63,350 settled in for the slugfest and waited until the late moments of the first quarter before seeing the first score.

Iowa had driven to the Gopher 35, missed a field goal, but then picked off a Hankinson pass at the 40. Two plays later, Iowa quarterback Gary Snook, who the previous year had torn apart the Minnesota defense with his passing in the victory at Iowa City, found Karl Noonan at the Minnesota seven and the Iowa receiver went in for the score. The conversion was good.

The Gophers came right back and looked as if they were going to tie the game, but Hankinson fumbled at the Hawkeye seven. Gale Gillingham stopped Snook a few plays later and the Hawkeyes had to punt. Minnesota took over at its 27 with 1:17 left in the half.

At first it appeared the Gophers had been stopped. They punted from their 45, but Van De Walker was roughed and Minnesota kept possession with 31 seconds remaining. Hankinson lofted a pass for Kramer, which looked at first as if it might be intercepted. But, the big, rangy end grabbed it at the seven and went in for the score. Reid made the conversion to tie the game at halftime.

Things got somewhat zany in the second half. First the Hawkeyes' Ivory McDowell intercepted a Hankinson throw at the Minnesota 31 and returned it to the 22. The Hawks advanced to the two. On third down, an Iowa run lost one. Then Skjei, Costanza and tackle Jim Fulgham dropped halfback Craig Nourse for another one-yard loss at the four and Minnesota took over.

Play went back-and-forth a while until late in the third quarter when Skjei intercepted Snook at midfield and took it down to the 10. Farthing carried three straight plays and scored.

Reid made the extra point for a 14-7 lead.

In the fourth quarter, Iowa came back on the arm of Snook and went to the Minnesota 27 on a Noonan reception of 56 yards. Still, Minnesota was undaunted and the defense rose up, bent a bit, but prevailed. First, Costanza, Joe Pung and Bob Bruggers sacked Snook for a loss at the 37. Iowa got 12 of those yards back, but that was followed by an Aaron Brown, Jerry Newsom-led charge which caused a Snook fumble that Fulgham fell on at the Minnesota 43.

Minnesota couldn't mount a drive and its punt went to the Hawkeye 21. There was just 2:03 left when Snook hit Nourse on a crossing pattern at the Gopher 34 and the Iowa halfback went all the way for the score to pull the Hawkeyes within one point of Minnesota. Iowa coach Jerry Burns went for the win. On the pass play, Brown and Callahan hit Snook as he threw and the ball overshot Noonan. There was 1:49 left when the Hawkeyes tried the onside kick.

Minnesota center and linebacker Chuck Killian bobbled the bouncing kick at the 38, Gopher players scrambled after the ball before it was shoved out of bounds at the Minnesota 33. Iowa screamed bloody murder, but the officials said it was legal and the Gophers ran out the clock for a 14-13 victory.

"We always drill against the two-point play and it certainly paid off today," Warmath said. "I'm delighted, especially in light of the fact the Iowa passing game was so strong."

"Snook is really tough," said Minnesota's Lofquist and teammate Pung called the Iowa quarterback "great against the pass rush."

Burns said the game really came down to the two-point conversion that didn't work and the roughing-the-kicker call on his team in the waning moments of the second quarter which gave the Gophers life and an eventual touchdown to tie the game.

•    •    •

Bob Griese already was in the national spotlight although 1964 only was the Purdue quarterback's sophomore year.

When he brought his team to Minneapolis the following week, Griese already had established himself in the tradition of fine Purdue quarterbacks such as Len Dawson, Bernie Allen and

Ron DeGravio. However, Hankinson proved to be as much a star as Griese.

A cold wind was howling through more than 50,000 chilly fans at Memorial Stadium at kickoff time.

In the second quarter, Gopher linebacker Newsom intercepted a Griese throw at the Minnesota 38 and took it back 31 yards to the Boilermaker 31. Two plays later, Hankinson found Last curling in at the Purdue three between defenders George Catavolus and Tom Kuzniewski. Hankinson drilled a pass to his lanky receiver who stepped into the end zone. Reid made the point after touchdown.

It stayed at 7-0 until late in the third quarter. Purdue drove 67 yards in five plays. Two of Griese's throws were on target, but both finished with questionable fumbles that the officials called completed passes. From the one, Randy Minnier scored, the kick was good and it was a tie game.

As the fourth quarter got underway, Ray Whitlow took the kickoff and went to the Gopher 27. Then in two plays, Hankinson's passing put Minnesota ahead. A pass to Last moved the Gophers to the Purdue 43 and from there Hankinson hit Kramer at the 30 and the Gopher end went the rest of the way into the end zone. Reid kicked the point after.

Purdue reached the Minnesota 23 before being stopped. Later, Reid intercepted a pass at the Gopher 46 and Minnesota had pulled off a mild upset 14-7.

Warmath praised both Last and Kramer, calling their play "as good as we've had from a pair of ends in a long time."

Kramer returned the compliment and praised Warmath for designing some great pass plays.

"Our defensive backs are as good as any in the country right now," Warmath commented. "They did a great job on pass defense today."

The Gopher coached singled out Hankinson who completed 15 of 29 passes for 159 yards and the two Minnesota touchdowns.

"Minnesota had a nice, well-executed passing game," said Purdue's Jack Mollenkopf. "We didn't seem to be inspired and acted as if we didn't want the game enough."

With a 4-2 Big Ten record, it appeared the Gophers could finish in a tie for second place.

The weather turned worse as the season concluded in Madison for the annual showdown against Wisconsin. It was just 10 degrees and the game was all Wisconsin.

Hankinson couldn't connect on his passes and wound up completing only 8 for 31. Wisconsin amassed 418 yards in offense led by fullback Ron Smith, who ran for 160 yards in 22 carries.

It was a simple, straightforward football game.

Ralph Kurek scored in the first quarter for the Badgers on a one-yard plunge. Lofquist was injured during that drive and never returned.

In the second quarter, Minnesota took possession at the Badger 44 after keeping Wisconsin contained deep in its end of the field. On the first play, Hankinson ran a keeper, was hit at the 33, then pitched out to Farthing who went the rest of the way for the touchdown. Reid's kick made it 7-7.

The last score came in the fourth quarter when Smith took a pitchout at the Minnesota 48 and streaked all the way for the score. The game ended with Wisconsin a 14-7 winner.

Warmath, always objective in his post-game comments and sincere in his praise of that day's opponent, called Wisconsin the better team and stated matter-of-factly that his squad simply couldn't pass.

The Gophers were 5-4 for the year and 4-3 in conference play.

# Thirty

 Hankinson was the core of the 1965 team and with returning veterans Aaron Brown, Ken Last, Kent Kramer, Bob Bruggers, Tim Wheeler and Jerry Newsom, it appeared to be a team with a chance to do well, especially when it opened the season and tied one of the country's top squads.

That year was the start of a 10-game schedule for the Big Ten schools. Minnesota faced not only that challenge, but also opened on a Friday night in Los Angeles at the Coliseum against Southern California. USC was led by halfback Mike Garrett, who would go on to win the 1965 Heisman Award. Garrett and Hankinson ignited the Coliseum that night.

The game was scoreless until early in the second quarter. Starting late in the first quarter from their own 20, the Trojans went 80 yards in 11 plays for the game's first score. Garrett took a pitchout and went the final seven yards. Rod Sherman made the point after.

A couple of series later Bruggers intercepted a pass and returned it to the Trojans' 38. Hankinson passed to end John Rajala at the one and then Hankinson scored on a sneak.

Sophomore flanker Hubie Bryant was stopped short on a two-point conversion run. Minnesota scored again late in the half, going 66 yards in seven plays. Hankinson passed 16 yards to Kramer for the TD and the kick was good for 13-7 Minnesota lead with 58 seconds left in the half.

Southern Cal returned the kickoff to its 33. With 53 seconds to go, the Trojans connected on a short pass to their 38. Then Troy Winslow threw long, but there was an interference call on Gopher defensive back Stew Maples. Suddenly, the Trojans were at the Minnesota 28. A couple of plays later, Winslow hit Garrett on a crossing pattern at the six. He faked out Brown, who had fallen back into coverage from his defensive end position, and went into the end zone. The conversion kick was good to make it 14-13 for USC.

In the third period, Winslow fumbled and Tom Sakal recovered for Minnesota at the Trojan 31. A motion penalty called back a 17-yard pass play to Ray Whitlow. From the 26, Hankinson threw to Rajala at the nine. On the next play, behind a block from guard Randy Staten, Hankinson kept the ball and went in for the score. Deryl Ramey made the point after for a 20-14 Minnesota lead.

The Trojans tied the game early in the fourth quarter, marching 70 yards in 15 plays with Garrett gaining most of the yardage on runs and short pass receptions. Winslow snuck in for the score from the one. However, Sherman's point after attempt was wide and the game was tied at 20-20.

Both teams threatened later. Minnesota got to the 23 of USC, but was stopped on fourth and one. The Trojans came back and got to the Gopher 31. On fourth down, Tim Rossovich was wide with a field goal attempt with 23 seconds remaining.

Warmath called Garrett and USC "great", then mumbled about the interference call on Maples late in the first half.

"It would have been a 40-yard field goal attempt for us late and those are pretty rare. The attempt for the first down seemed the right call," the Gopher coach explained.

John McKay, the Trojans' mentor said his defensive line play was "miserable. We didn't put any pressure on Hankinson."

The Gopher quarterback was 17 of 29 for 103 yards and two touchdowns. He ran for the third score.

The next week another Pacific Coast team played Minnesota. It was almost as close as the USC game, but the Gophers lost 14-13. The loss to Washington State was because of fumbles. There were seven by the Gophers and they lost all of them.

Minnesota struck first when it put together a 48-yard drive in 10 plays. Fullback Joe Holmberg scored from the one. Ramey made the kick. In the third quarter, Minnesota got another score on a 61-yard march in 10 plays with halfback Dave Colburn going around end for the final nine yards and the touchdown. The point after was good, but a motion call on the Gophers was assessed and Ramey missed the second attempt. That, along with the fumbles, proved costly.

Late in the third quarter, State scored when fullback Larry Eilmers went in from the three to cap a 72-yard drive which took 15 plays. Willie Gaskins hit his first-ever conversion attempt.

In the fourth quarter, both teams traded fumbles. Late in the game, Colburn fumbled and Washington State recovered at the Gopher 15.

State got to the Minnesota one, was set back by a motion penalty and then on fourth down and less than a yard, Cougar quarterback Tom Roth snuck in for the TD. The point after was good to clinch the victory.

Warmath was stunned.

"We were awful. I am not pleased with any aspect of our game," he groaned.

His one compliment was to Brown, who had his jaw broken early in the game but continued to play. He called his fine end "very courageous".

Bert Clark, the Washington State coach, had a simple explanation. "Fumbles were the difference."

Things didn't get any better the next week.

Missouri came to Minneapolis and Dan Devine's Tigers unleashed quarterback Gary Lane as a runner and left town with a 17-6 victory.

The Tigers first score came in the second quarter when Lane went 11 yards on an option play. Then two series later, Lane scrambled on a broken pass play and went in for the touchdown from the 20 aided by a Francis Peay block. The conversion was good to give Missouri a 14-0 lead.

240

In the third quarter, a poor Missouri punt gave Minnesota the ball at the Tiger 42. Eventually, the Gophers faced fourth-and-goal from the seven. Hankinson hit halfback Dick Peterson at the goal line for the touchdown. The two point attempt was no-good.

On the subsequent drive, Missouri took it from their 20 to the Minnesota 11 in 11 plays. Stopped there, the Tigers turned to Bill Bates who made a 28-yard field goal. There was no further scoring as Missouri controlled the ball. Lane had gained 179 yards on 13 carries and Missouri had run 86 plays to just 55 for the Gophers.

"Missouri got 324 yards rushing, which is about as bad as I can remember one of our teams playing defensively," Warmath snapped afterward. "That Roland (John) was as fine a defensive back as I've seen in some time."

The Missouri defender was instrumental in stopping Minnesota. He led the Tiger defensive effort which intercepted two Hankinson passes and limited the Minnesota quarterback to 16 of 34 and 142 yards.

The Big Ten season opened the next week at Memorial Stadium as Indiana came to town and the Gophers needed to win badly.

The Hoosiers obliged.

Sophomore Curt Wilson returned the opening kickoff 52 yards to the Indiana 46. Several plays later, Holmberg took it in from the one. The kick by Ramey was good and the Gophers were ahead with 12 minutes left in the opening quarter. Minnesota scored late in the quarter on an 11-yard pass from Hankinson to Colburn.

Indiana intercepted a Hankinson pass early in the second quarter and John Ginter scored from the one, but the point after was no good. Minnesota came back and scored twice. A 65-yard drive in 13 plays was capped off when Whitlow took a six-yard throw from Hankinson for the touchdown. Then Sakal intercepted Gary Tofil at the Indiana 38 and returned it to the 12. A couple of plays later, Holmberg went five yards for the score and it was 21-6.

In the third quarter, Sakal intercepted another Hoosier pass, this time at the Indiana 40. Hankinson hit Last for 11 and then found Kramer on a cross-field throw on the left side for the score. It was 35-6.

Indiana put together a 91-yard march in 15 plays. Ginter received a Tofil pass for a 16-yard touchdown. The two-point play failed.

Minnesota countered with some razzle-dazzle and from its 20, worked its way down to the Hoosier 29. Hankinson hit Kramer on the sidelines, who lateraled to Colburn, who went into the end zone. The conversion was good.

Ginter scored again for Indiana making the final 42-18.

"It was the best rushing we've had in a long time (292 yards) and we never had to punt. I like that," Warmath said afterward.

Hankinson, who new Hoosier coach John Pont called the best quarterback his team had faced, said his arm "felt dead." He had thrown for 156 yards and five touchdowns.

•   •   •

For three quarters the Gophers and the Hawkeyes duked it out in the rain and mud of Kinnick Stadium in Iowa City. The only scoring had been a 42-yard field goal earlier in the third quarter by Iowa's Bob Anderson. There were 39 seconds left in the quarter when Gary Snook tried to hit Karl Noonan at the Minnesota 40. But Gopher linebacker Tim Wheeler intercepted.

Minnesota made little yardage on its first two plays, so on third down, Hankinson went to the air. He found Whitlow on a crossing pattern. However, Hawkeye defensive back Tony Williams also was converging on the ball and for a moment had his hands on it. Whitlow, determined to not only prevent an interception but to make something out of the play, wrestled the ball away from Williams and spun out of his grasp. It was wide open beyond Williams and the junior flanker went the rest of the way for the score.

From that point on, Minnesota dominated. On the kickoff following Whitlow's score, Iowa's Al Randolph was hit by Bruggers and Sakal and fumbled. Brown dropped on the ball at the 30. On the next play, the Gophers sealed the outcome when Colburn scored on a tackle trap play.

Iowa couldn't do a thing after that and the frustrated Hawkeye fans started booing Snook. When the game ended, the rushing statistics told the story: Minnesota had 257 yards to just 120 yards for Iowa.

"Whitlow sure got us out of a hole," Warmath said. "It was a great play on his part."

Warmath also praised the efforts of Brown who was back in action following his broken jaw three weeks earlier.

"It felt good to be back," said Brown, who despite missing two games would be named an All-American at the end of the year.

Gale Gillingham said he felt sorry for Snook and the booing by the Iowa fans.

Iowa players afterward expressed their anger at the reaction of the Hawkeye followers.

Minnesota was 2-0 in Big Ten play. The next week they went to 3-0 in a nail biter against Michigan.

It was homecoming at Minnesota and 58,519 were in the stands as the game came down to a two-point conversion attempt.

Michigan scored first when Rich Volk intercepted a Hankinson pass at his 46 and returned it to the Gopher 35. The Wolverines reached the 14 where halfback Carl Ward tried a sweep to the left. The Minnesota defense closed off his route and he reversed himself and was all the way back to the 35. Pressured, he unloaded a throw to fullback Dave Fisher, who was all

243

alone at the 15. Fisher took the pass and ran it into the end zone for the score. Paul D'Eramo made the point after.

Ward, however, quickly went from hero to goat. Late in the quarter, in front of the Minnesota bench, he threw a vicious headblock into linebacker Jerry Newsom after a Michigan runner had been knocked out of bounds and the play blown dead. Newsom lost three teeth and Ward was ejected. Ward, irate over the ejection, threw a temper tantrum. Regardless, he was changing to street clothes within a few minutes.

In the third quarter, Minnesota tied the score by forcing a punt from deep in Michigan territory. Minnesota took over at the Wolverine 49 and scored in four plays. From the 40, Hankinson ran an option to the eight and Holmberg went into the end zone on the next play.

In the fourth quarter, Michigan returned a kick to its 38, but McKinley Boston was called for a personal foul and joined Ward in being asked to leave the field. Michigan, however, couldn't capitalize on the good field position, getting to the 20 before being stopped. Minnesota also was stymied and was forced to punt. But the Gophers got a big break.

Van De Walker's punt bounced off the leg of Michigan's Ernie Sharpe and Colburn recovered the ball at the Minnesota 46. The Gophers scored quickly as Hankinson made good on a pass to Last at the 16. A few running plays got the ball to the one and Hankinson went in behind the block of guard and captain Paul Faust to score. Ramey made it 14-7 and there was 7:12 left in the game.

Michigan took the ensuing kickoff and put together a drive that got to the Gopher four. From there, quarterback Wally Gabler ran for the touchdown. The two-point play was the obvious call with only 1:12 left in the game.

Gabler sprinted to his left on a run-pass option play, but Bruggers closed off the lane and forced him to retreat. There were two Michigan would-be receivers in the end zone, but as

Gabler started to throw, linebacker Gary Reierson streaking in on a blitz from the other side hit the Michigan quarterback. The throw sailed out of the back of the end zone and the Little Brown Jug was back in Minnesota hands for the fifth time in six years.

"I thought our linebackers (Reierson, Wheeler, Newsom) played great," Warmath happily observed. "Colburn and Bruggers also had fine games."

He added that Michigan had some injured players who didn't help them, then quickly offered his opinion that the Ward-to-Fisher pass should have been illegal because he felt there were Michigan linemen downfield.

Reierson said he had a clear shot at Gabler and praised the work of Bruggers on the play.

In a quiet Michigan locker room, Pete Elliott said his team suffered when Ward was tossed out of the game. In the official's locker room next door, referee Howard Wirtz called the game as hard-hitting as he could remember.

•   •   •

For many years, Murray Warmath and Woody Hayes were close friends. Yet it wasn't until Warmath's 12th season at Minnesota that these legendary coaches got a chance to meet on the gridiron.

It was homecoming in Columbus and there were 84,359 on hand to watch a game that was as close as the Minnesota-Michigan battle. Minnesota scored first when defensive back Stew Maples intercepted Don Unverferth's pass at the Buckeyes' 17. A few plays later, Hankinson snuck in from the one and it was 7-0.

Ohio State started an 80-yard drive the last play of the quarter. Behind the running of fullback Will Sander, who ran seven straight times for 49 yards, the Buckeyes got to the Minnesota 25. From there, Unverferth hit a wide-open Nelson Adderley for the touchdown. Then Ohio State made it 8-7 when Arnold Fontes took the snap on a fake kick and went around end for the score.

Ohio State threatened again late in the quarter and drove to the Minnesota eight where tackle Jim Fulgham dropped Unverferth for a nine-yard loss.

The only scoring in the third quarter was a Ramey field goal of 32 yards that was set up on an interception by the Gophers' Gordie Condo.

The fourth quarter started with Ramey missing a 37-yard field goal attempt. Later, a Minnesota punt was downed at the Ohio State 10. The Minnesota defense couldn't keep the Buckeyes in the OSU end of the field. Unverferth hit five passes and moved Ohio State to the Minnesota eight where Bob Fuelk kicked 25-yard field goal for an 11-10 lead.

With 1:09 left in the game, Hankinson started a drive from his 20. He hit Last and Whitlow on passes that took the ball to the Gopher 46. After three incomplete passes, he just got a first down with a throw to Brown at the Buckeye 44. A few plays later, he hit Brown at the eight. There were no time outs left and with the clock at 17 seconds and running, Ramey attempted a 25-yard field goal. Some people thought it barely cleared inside the left upright, but the officials said no. Ohio State had won 11-10.

A dejected Warmath told the media after the game that Ohio State really won the contest in the second quarter when it manhandled Minnesota. "But I was hopeful because we were only down by a point at the half."

Hankinson said a very untimely wind shift pushed Ramey's attempt off line just enough to make the field goal no good.

"I thought we had lost the game," a grateful Hayes said. "Minnesota was as tough as we figured it would be and that Brown is one hell of a ballplayer."

Minnesota rebounded the next week when it hosted Northwestern in front of 50,000 at Memorial Stadium. Once again, it was a game down to the wire.

Northwestern scored on the opening series by going 65 yards in just four plays. Woody Campbell's 48-yard run to the

Minnesota 12 was the big play. Two plays later, Ron Rector scored from the 10. Minnesota tied the score at 7-7 by marching 71 yards. Dick Peterson scored from the one and Ramey kicked the tying point.

Northwestern went 63 yards in 12 plays with fullback Bob McKelvey plunging for the final yard. Again, the Gophers tied it, this time on a 51-yard scoring pass from Hankinson to Last. The drive took just six plays.

In the second quarter, Hankinson scored from the three for the third Gopher touchdown after a drive of 52 yards. At halftime, it was Minnesota 21, Northwestern 14.

On the last play of the third quarter, Wildcat Bob Hampton blocked a Van De Walker punt at the Gopher 15 and Holmberg fell on the bouncing ball in the end zone for a safety. The fourth quarter started with Minnesota free-kicking and Northwestern returning to the Gopher 43. It took eight plays to get to the Minnesota 17 where McKelvey broke through the middle for the touchdown. A two-point pass was no good and the Wildcats led 22-21 with 9:38 left.

It looked as if Northwestern might win when Mike Buckner intercepted a Hankinson pass at Minnesota's 34. But a couple of plays later, Larry Gates fumbled and Wheeler recovered at the 20. It took 17 plays for the Gophers to regain the lead.

Hankinson connected on seven passes. One completion to Last was for a touchdown, but was called back for a procedure penalty. From the 38, Hankinson again went to Last and found him at the 16. He then connected with Brown at the five and Peterson moved the ball to the one with less than 1:30 left.

Hankinson took the snap and started behind Paul Faust, but lost the ball. It fell underneath Faust who alertly recovered for the touchdown. The two-point attempt was not good, but a six-point lead was and the game ended with a 27-21 Minnesota victory.

"Northwestern has the best backs in the conference in my opinion," Warmath commented. "Yet, I don't think there is an end anywhere better than Brownie (Aaron Brown) and Hankinson is the best all-around quarterback in the Big Ten."

Hankinson passed for 255 yards on 14 completions.

Warmath argued that the safety on the blocked punt shouldn't have been allowed because the Northwestern player (Hampton) inadvertently kicked the ball into the end zone.

Wildcats coach Alex Agase called the fourth quarter fumble by Gates the turning point.

"Hankinson and Brown killed us," he added.

Jeff Brooke, the Wildcat captain and an Albert Lea, Minn. native, said the Gophers were the hardest hitting team he and his teammates had faced all year.

Minnesota was 4-1 in conference play and had a shot at the championship. The next week's game at Purdue would be critical.

•    •    •

It wasn't even close. Purdue outplayed Minnesota in every category and won 35-0 in front of 45,600 at Ross-Ade Stadium.

Minnesota was so dominated defensively that it finished with minus 17 yards rushing. Hankinson was forced to take to the air and completed 17 passes for 191 yards, but the Gophers never threatened to score.

Purdue scored twice in the second quarter, first on a short run of three yards by fullback John Kuzniewski and then a five-yard pass from Bob Griese to Jim Beirne.

Despite the score and no offense to that point, Minnesota wasn't out of the game through the third quarter. The Boilermakers, however, put things away with three fourth-quarter scores. Two drives culminated in short TD plunges by Kuzniewski and then Bob Cory stepped in front of a down-and-out sideline pass by Hankinson at the Minnesota 17 and returned the ball untouched for the score.

"We couldn't do a thing right," Warmath snapped. "I was concerned about not having Dave Colburn, who didn't suit up because he was hurt. We set up four of their touchdowns with mistakes that gave them the ball."

"We knew they'd throw a lot because Colburn was out, so we created a defense to stop the pass," Jack Mollenkopf said. "We focused on containing Brown on pass coverage and it worked."

Now 4-2 in Big Ten play and eliminated from any chance to catch undefeated Michigan State, Minnesota went home for the finale against Wisconsin.

The Gophers rebounded in 32-degree weather before nearly 51,000 and handled the Badgers 42-7. It was Minnesota's turn to shine defensively. The Gophers held the Badgers to just 32 yards rushing and 186 passing.

Hankinson, closing out his excellent career, scored on a four-yard run in the first quarter, capping a 55-yard drive. Later in the quarter, he connected with Brown for a 37-yard TD.

Wisconsin got its only score in the second quarter when Chuck Burt threw to Bill Fritz to tie the score at 7-7. Minnesota took a halftime lead of 14-7 when Wisconsin's Tom Jankowski fumbled at his eight and Brian Callahan recovered. Peterson scored on the next play and Ramey kicked the conversion.

There was no scoring in the third quarter, but there was an important defensive effort when Minnesota stopped Wisconsin on the one yard line. The floodgates opened in the fourth quarter when Peterson, reserve fullback John Williams and Ray Whitlow scored touchdowns, Whitlow's coming on a pass from backup quarterback Glen Wirtanen,

Minnesota finished 5-2 in the Big Ten and 5-4-1 overall.

Warmath called the season "creditable given the number of injuries we had. Today was our best game of the season."

Hankinson broke Paul Giel's single-season total yardage record with 1,583 yards and set 10 offensive records in the two seasons he played.

# Thirty-One

As the Gophers went into the 1966 season, they again faced the problem of replacing a seasoned quarterback. In addition, they turned to several sophomores from 1965 to step in to fill starting or key reserve positions. The season turned out to be slightly better than expected but, the real benefit was the experience gained by the players who would comprise the '67 team.

The 1966 season began as the Gophers traveled to Missouri and were soundly trounced by the Tigers 24-0, a game marked by Minnesota errors.

The first half was scoreless until just over a minute remained. Missouri worked the ball to the Gopher 25 and with 1:14 left, Bill Bates connected on a 42-yard field goal attempt.

Previously, Minnesota quarterback Curtis Wilson had been running the ball a great deal. He had gained 70 yards in 14 carries and in one instance, connected on a 65-yard pass to Ken Last for a touchdown, but an offside penalty brought the play back. Earlier, the opening drive of the game saw Minnesota advance as far as the Missouri 25, but a series of penalties killed that effort.

Missouri took command at the start of the second half. The Tigers went 71 yards with Charlie Brown scoring on a nine-yard run. Bates made the conversion for a 10-0 lead. Late in the quarter, Missouri went 62 yards for a touchdown and a 17-0 lead when Bates connected with Chuck Weber from eight yards out.

Missouri got its final touchdown with 41 seconds left when John Douglas intercepted a pass by sophomore substitute quarterback Ray Stephens at the Gopher 23 and returned it for the touchdown. The extra point was good.

"The play to Last which got called back really hurt us," Warmath said. "I thought we were dominating them for most of the first half, but in the end Missouri simply played better football."

Captain Chuck Killian said the Tigers had Minnesota backed up most of the day and "we couldn't get going."

Tiger coach Dan Devine said Missouri adjusted at halftime to the Gopher defense and in the second half "just played better football."

The following Saturday Minnesota returned home to beat Stanford 35-21. There were only 43,500 on hand as the Gophers dominated nearly every aspect of the game. In the first quarter, Minnesota linebacker Gene Hatfield intercepted a throw by the Indians' Gene Washington at the Gopher 48 and returned it to the Stanford 44. Several plays later, Wilson fumbled at the goal line, but end Chet Anderson fell on the ball for the touchdown. Bob Stein kicked the extra point.

In the next quarter, the Gophers got the ball at their 35 and scored in 11 plays, Dick Peterson going the final 16 yards on a pitchout. Peterson had 42 yards in the march.

Minnesota got another score late in the half as John Williams, now a defensive end, forced a Gene Washington fumble which tackle Jerry Hermann recovered at the 14. A few plays later, Wilson scored from the two and it was 21-0.

In the third period, the Indians finally got something going when Mark Marquess grabbed a Minnesota pitchout at the Gopher 47 and took it to the 36. From the 15, Dave Lewis gathered in a Washington pass for the touchdown. The kick was good to cut the Gopher lead to 21-7.

Whitlow got Minnesota back in position for another score by taking the Stanford kickoff at his three and returning it 81 yards to the Indians' 16. The Gophers worked the ball to the five where Wilson scored on a keeper play. The Stein kick made it 28-7.

Late in the quarter, Standord's Jon Huss fumbled at his 39 where Hermann again recovered. At the 10, Wilson hit wide receiver Chip Litten between two defenders for the fifth TD. Stein converted. Stanford scored two meaningless touchdowns late in the game and Minnesota had its first victory 35-21.

Warmath called the first half breaks the key to the victory and said the Gophers seemed in better condition than they had the week before.

John Ralston, the Stanford coach, called Minnesota a "solid, well-coached team which took advantage of the breaks we gave them."

Another Big Eight team was on the schedule when Kansas came to town.

Wilson was hurt early and was replaced by junior Larry Carlson, who had a good day passing, but it wasn't enough as the Jayhawks won 16-14. The problem primarily was the Gophers' rushing game. Don Shanklin scored for Kansas, going seven yards to cap an 84-yard drive in the first quarter. Wilson was hurt in the next series (a knee) and didn't return.

Kansas took over at its 43 and went to the Minnesota nine where it settled for a 26-yard field goal by quarterback Dave Bouda.

Late in the half, Carlson engineered a scoring drive. After two running losses put Minnesota at the Jayhawks' 41, Carlson hit a fourth down pass to Last for 15 yards. Whitlow followed with a leaping catch at the 13 and then went to the nine on a flare pass. Carlson hit Last for the touchdown. Jerry Bevan made the extra point and it was 10-7 at the half.

Minnesota got as deep as the Kansas seven in the third quarter, but two sacks of Carlson by George Harvey put the Gophers back at the 22. Bevan's field goal attempt was no good.

Kansas came back and went 80 yards in 22 plays. It got to the one. Minnesota stopped them three times before halfback Thermus Butler went in on the second play of the fourth quarter. The conversion attempt failed.

Minnesota started the next series its 36 and behind Carlson's arm (he would complete 11 straight passes in the half), went to the Jayhawks' two. On fourth down Carlson threw to Hubie Bryant. The ball bounced out of his hands and into the hands of Chet Anderson for the touchdown. There was 10:44 left to play, but neither team could score again.

"Carlson was a gutty player, but he wasn't getting much protection," Warmath said quietly in the Gopher locker room after the 16-14 loss. "Kansas blitzed a lot, but that wasn't surprising to us."

Jack Mitchell, the Kansas coach, said his team played near-perfect football. "We gave up the short passes. Last week when we lost to Texas Tech, we got caught on three long passes. Our secondary is young and they were a bit scared. Today, however, our rush put the pressure on Minnesota."

The Big Ten season opened the following week and it was "kiss-your-sister" time as the game ended in a 7-7 tie with Indiana in Bloomington.

Minnesota scored in the first quarter on a 32-yard pass from Carlson to Bryant. Stein made the extra point.

In the fourth quarter, Indiana's Mike Krivoshia scored from the one and the kick tied the game. Both teams had chances to win in the final minutes. With 2:58 to go, the Hoosier's Dave Karnowa missed a 36-yard field goal attempt. Minnesota drove from its 20 to the Indiana 14 and on the final play of the game, Stein's first collegiate field goal attempt was wide.

Afterward, Warmath blamed penalties, failure to generate any kind of offense and Stein's recent bout with mononucleosis as the reasons for the team doing no better than a tie. Now he had get his team to look ahead to the annual battle with Iowa.

The homecoming victory the following weekend over the Hawkeyes was satisfying for 62,600 fans, most who were from Minnesota.

It was chilly and windy as Minnesota got on the scoreboard late in the first half when it went 42 yards in nine plays. The big play was a reverse by Bryant for a gain of 11. Carlson hit Last from the 10 for the touchdown. Stein made the kick.

Minnesota's defense continued to dominate and field position played a role in the second half. Whitlow took a Chuck Rollins punt at his 43 and returned it to the Iowa 14. The Gophers settled for Stein's 24-yard field goal.

Leading 10-0, Minnesota took advantage of an Iowa mistake in the fourth quarter. Inside the five and threatening, Iowa's Ed Podolak rolled out to his right to pass, but before he could get the throw off, was hit by Gopher defensive lineman Ezell Jones. The ball popped into the air and Ed Duren, one of the Gopher lineman, grabbed the ball at the five. He headed for the far end zone.

"I thought we were going to have to time him with a calendar," Warmath remarked with a chuckle.

The big North Carolina native lumbered all the way and made it in for the touchdown. Stein made the kick and the final score was 17-0.

The Gophers had kept Iowa in poor field position most of the game. Except for the penetration to the five on the Duren play, the Hawkeyes only got as far as the Minnesota 46.

Warmath cited defensive end Stein's 14 tackles and linebacker Gary Reierson's 17 tackles, as spearheads in the tough defense. Iowa lost its 15th consecutive Big Ten game and had not scored in 15 quarters.

Duren said his 95-yard jaunt was his "onlyest" touchdown in his high school or college career. Ironically, he had missed two earlier games because of painful corns on his feet.

Warmath and his team enjoyed the shutout win. They needed to for the next week they lost in a big way.

•   •   •

In Ann Arbor the next week, a veteran Michigan team annihilated the Gophers. The Wolverines, picked as a preseason darkhorse in the Big Ten, had lost three straight and they took out their frustration on Minnesota.

In the first quarter, Michigan's Jim Detwiler scored on a one-yard plunge to finish a 67-yard drive. A couple of series later, Rich Sygar took a punt back for 68 yards and a score.

In the second quarter, Dave Baldridge got off a punt for an amazing 72 yards to the Michigan 20. It made little difference, however, as the Wolverines came back to score as quarterback Rich Vidner hit end Jack Clancy on a 21-yard touchdown pass.

Things got worse for the Gophers. With 9:22 left in the half, Michigan scored again on a five-yard pass from Vidner to Carl Ward. Vidner later threw a 57-yard bomb to Clancy and the extra point put Michigan ahead 35-0.

Michigan added two second half touchdowns. The first was when Detwiler dove into the end zone from the one to finish a 45-yard drive, and the second on an Ernie Sharpe run of four yards after a 68-yard drive.

Michigan had 456 yards and let Minnesota cross midfield only twice. The Gophers got just 34 yards on the ground and 72 in the air.

"We have no excuses," Warmath said after the game in a deadly silent Minnesota locker room. It equaled the worst defeat in Gopher history ( Indiana in 1945).

"I haven't seen a team play better than they did," he added. "We certainly contributed to their win."

Gopher assistant Butch Nash felt the frustration of Michigan was a big factor. "They gained 400 yards last week against Purdue and lost."

Pete Elliott said he wanted to control every facet of the game from the beginning. "We're a good team," he understated.

Warmath needed to see what his team was made of after such a shellacking. His test was a tough one. Ohio State was coming to town the next Saturday.

Warmath decided to try something radical. He went to the new, still untested, I formation that soon would be in vogue in football. It worked. Behind strong line play and the running of Wilson at quarterback and sophomore halfback John Wintermute, the Gophers pulled off a surprise 17-7 victory before 49,500 and a regional television audience.

Minnesota got its first score, thanks to a key defensive play. Ohio State had moved to the Minnesota 11, but Gordie Condo intercepted a Bill Long pass at the three and took it back to the Buckeye 39. Minnesota drove, but halfback Dennis Cornell fumbled at the one and Ohio State recovered. The Buckeyes couldn't move and punted to the Gopher 37.

A Minnesota drive was aided by a defensive holding call. From the five, Wilson went around end, extended his arm as he was hit inside the one, but fumbled. Wintermute alertly picked up the bouncing ball in the end zone for the touchdown. For the second time (the other time being in the Kansas game), Wilson lucked out when one of his fumbles resulted in a Gopher touchdown. Bevan kicked the extra point.

Ohio State drove again in the second quarter, but was stopped by a Tom Sakal interception at the Gopher 34. Bevan missed two field goal attempts in the quarter and Minnesota took a 7-0 lead into the locker room.

In the third quarter, Ohio State fumbled deep in its territory and Wilson turned the miscue into a touchdown by scoring from the three. Bevan made the point after for a 14-0 lead.

In the fourth quarter, Ohio State drove to the Gopher 10 where Long hit Bo Rein for a touchdown. The Buckeyes then tried an unsuccessful onside kick. Minnesota capitalized and Bevan made a 21-yard field goal a few plays later.

"We worked on the I formation last spring," Warmath said following the triumph. "We practiced it again somewhat in the fall. This seemed the time to use it and it helped that Cornell blocked so well for Wilson and Wintermute so they could get some good runs."

End Chet Anderson and tackle Ron Klick were singled out for their double-team blocking which aided the Cornell and Wintermute dives off tackle and at the same time, gave Wilson a chance to run the option.

"I felt good for the first time since the Stanford game," Wilson said. "My knee finally was sound today."

Sakal said the Gophers knew the Ohio State pass routes "by heart" and praised the coaching staff for an excellent scouting report and game plan.

Meanwhile, Woody Hayes kept the media waiting for nearly 45 minutes, then abruptly came out of the visitors' locker room and snapped, "we were beat by a better team and never got off to a good start. That's all boys." He turned and went back to his team, the door slamming loudly behind him.

With a 2-1-1 record in the conference, Minnesota was third behind Michigan State and Purdue. They faced Northwestern next.

At Evanston, they played a good game and beat the Wildcats 28-13. Again, it was Wilson's and Wintermute's running which led the way.

In the opening quarter, Minnesota moved the ball but Cornell was stopped short of a first down attempt at the 16. Tim Wheeler, however, picked off a Bill Melzer pass at the 30 and in 10 plays Cornell scored from the one with Jim Barle kicking the extra point.

In the second quarter, Sakal intercepted another Melzer pass at the Minnesota 10 and went to the 16. The Gophers moved the ball and faced a third-and-six at their 42. Hubie Bryant took the ball on a reverse and went to the Northwestern 24. Five plays later from the eight, Wilson hit Last in the end zone. The conversion was good and Minnesota was on top 14-0.

Late in the half, Whitlow fumbled a punt at his 28 and the Wildcats recovered. On fourth-and-goal from the five, Melzer passed to Larry Gates for the touchdown and with 1:57 left, it was 14-7.

On the second half kickoff, Northwestern's Chico Kurzawski was hit by Barle, fumbled and Jerry Hermann recovered at the 28. From the 20, Wilson and Last hooked up again for a TD and the kick made it 21-7.

Northwestern scored on a one-yard plunge by Woody Campbell, but the extra point try by Dick Emmerich was not good leaving the score at 21-13.

In the fourth quarter, Minnesota consumed a lot of time with an 80-yard drive. It almost was for naught when Wintermute fumbled at the Wildcats' 47, but Wilson picked up the ball and went 20 more yards. A couple of plays later from the 17, Wilson swept right end on an option and scooted into the end zone. Barle made the conversion.

Northwestern got another drive going and was deep in Minnesota territory, where on a fourth down pass play from the Minnesota six, Charlie Sanders broke through and sacked Melzer.

"The blocking was so good today that practically everything worked," Wilson said after the game.

Wheeler praised the defensive ends who "contained the Northwestern receivers."

"We need to win our last two for a chance to go to the Rose Bowl," Warmath said looking ahead. Michigan State, undefeated and ranked No. 2 behind Notre Dame, was not eligible to return to Pasadena. Purdue had lost only to the Spartans and was a game ahead of the Gophers. Minnesota and the Boilermakers met the next week in Minneapolis.

• • •

More than 49,000 were in attendance for the game in Memorial Stadium and what they saw was Bob Griese Day. The outstanding Purdue senior quarterback scored 10 of Purdue's 16 points.

The only scoring in the first half was a 30-yard Griese field goal. The Gophers couldn't get their offense going. Only their defense kept them in the game.

In the third quarter, Purdue drove 69 yards in 12 plays with Griese running for the score. A few plays earlier, it looked as if the Gophers had halted the drive. Wheeler appeared to have intercepted a Griese pass at the four. However, offsetting penalties (Wheeler for interference and a roughing call on Purdue) kept the ball in the Boilermakers' possession. The extra point kick was no good.

Late in the quarter, Minnesota got to the Purdue 13 but penalties pushed the Gophers back and Bevan missed a 42-yard field goal attempt.

In the fourth, Purdue used a 10-man rush to block a punt attempt by Dave Baldridge at the 30. Purdue drove from the 31 with Bob Baltzell scoring from the two. Griese kicked the extra point. Minnesota mounted one last effort, but again couldn't score. Purdue won 16-0.

"We lost to a better team," Warmath said. "Their only losses have been to the No. 1 and No. 2 teams in the country and Griese is simply a great player who came through with the big play when needed.

"Our defense played well, but we couldn't get Wilson untracked either running or passing."

Wheeler said the interference call on him was a correct call and added that "Griese is everything they say he is. He can run and throw and he sure keeps his cool."

In a happy Purdue locker room, Jack Mollenkopf said "this win feels wonderful. There is no better player in the country than Griese. He does it all and he is very bright."

Purdue went to the 1967 Rose Bowl and beat USC.

At Madison for the season finale, the Gophers, down after the loss to Purdue and with no hope of a Rose Bowl trip, went against a Wisconsin team inspired to win for Milt Bruhn who was stepping down after 11 seasons as the Badger head coach. He had compiled a record of 52-45-6 and won two conference championships (1959 and 1962).

During the game, Minnesota lost Wilson, Noel Jenke, Peterson and Bryant to injuries. Larry Carlson replaced Wilson. In the second quarter, Condo intercepted a Badger pass. The Gophers got to the six where they scored on a pass from Carlson to Last in the closing seconds of the half. But Carlson muffed the snap on the extra point and the score stayed 6-0.

In the third quarter, Wintermute fumbled at the Gopher 31 and Tom Domres recovered for the Badgers. Wisconsin got to the three and on fourth down, quarterback Jon Ryan hit Tim McCauley for the touchdown. Tom Schinke made the extra point that decided the game.

In the fourth quarter, Minnesota stopped the Badgers at the Gopher 20 then drove to the Wisconsin 31. The Wisconsin defense forced two incomplete passes and sacked Carlson for a loss of eight on a fourth-down play. Bruhn was carried off the field following the 7-6 victory.

"In many ways, this was our poorest performance of the year," Warmath lamented. "Even worse than Michigan. We didn't hit a lick in the second half."

Wheeler called it the biggest disappointment in his life.

"There needs to be more pride by the players," he muttered. "They've got some talent coming back, but they'll need a change in attitude by next fall."

It happened.

# Thirty-Two

As the 1967 season approached, the coaching staff made some changes before the first game, changes that paid off as the season progressed. At the same time, it took them about five games to get consistent play at a couple of positions. When that finally happened, it made all the difference in the world.

"In looking back to that year, I would say the biggest change was the decision to convert John Williams into a tackle and Charlie Sanders into a tight end," recalled Gopher athletic director McKinley Boston. "It really was a large part of the reason our offense was so successful."

Butch Nash concurred. "I didn't think we would be as good as we were. Moving Sanders and Williams was a big reason for the offensive success because they both became such excellent blockers and Charlie, of course, was a fine receiver."

Sanders became a perennial star for the Detroit Lions and Williams was the first round draft pick of the Baltimore Colts and enjoyed a long career with them and the Los Angeles Rams.

"Sanders got bigger after he got to Minnesota from high school," Warmath remembered. "We had recruited him as a halfback. By the time he graduated, he was one of the best players we ever had and as fine a person as you will ever know."

When the season opened, Larry Carlson and sophomore Phil Hagen split the quarterbacking duties. Wilson was plagued by injuries and his playing time was primarily as a halfback. When the Gophers hosted Utah to commence the 1967 season, it was Hagen at quarterback.

The game with Utah was filled with the usual first game jitters and a lack of crisp execution. There was no scoring in the first half. Minnesota had nine different possessions where it never ran more than six plays in any of the series. The Gophers got only as far at the Utah 48. Utah went to the Gopher 13, but Dennis Hale picked off a Jack Gehrke throw to stop that threat.

Two big defensive series in the third quarter helped the Gophers get on the scoreboard. First, Utah went to the Minnesota 37, but Bob Stein stopped a fourth-and-one run attempt. Next, Utah fumbled at its 22 where Wayne King recovered for the Gophers. Four plays later from the 11, Carlson hit Hubie Bryant in the corner of the end zone and Stein kicked the extra point.

Late in the period, Carlson fumbled at his 23 and Utah recovered. The visitors drove with Tim Collins scoring from the three. The snap on the extra point attempt was bad and the kick attempt was smothered.

The first play after the kickoff, Gopher back Mo Forte lost the ball and Utah recovered at the 32. It took the visitors seven plays to score with fullback Steve Molnar getting the final yard. The two-point attempt was no good and Utah led 12-7.

Late in the fourth quarter the Gophers started what became the game's winning drive. It came after the Gophers fended off another threat which ended when Utah fumbled at the Gopher six and Stein recovered at the 12.

The first two plays got two yards, then Hagen hit Curtis Wilson for seven. It was fourth-and-one and Minnesota had to go for it at the 21. Hagen kept for four. A Utah offside took the ball to the 30 and Litten caught a short pass of five for the first down. Two incomplete throws followed, then Hagen hit Sanders down the right side for 29 yards to the Utah 36. Bryant gathered in a seven yard pass and Hagen ran for five and the first down at the 24.

Two plays lost five yards and it was third-and-15 from the 29. There was 1:25 left in the game when Hagen dropped back and threw to Litten just inside the end zone. Litten fought Utah defensive back Jim Street for the ball and Minnesota had the touchdown. Stein missed the conversion and the Gophers clung to a 13-12 lead.

It wasn't over as Utah took the kickoff at its 33 and with a little over a minute left, moved to the Minnesota 35. On fourth down, Stein sacked Collins.

"We always practice a two-minute offense and on days like this, it pays off," Warmath said. "But I wasn't pleased with our play, especially the fumbling."

"I was worried the official might have thought I interfered with Street on the pass for the touchdown because we bumped each other," Litten said. "He hesitated, then signaled it was good."

Mike Giddings, the Utah coach, said his team lost to a disciplined and well-coached Gopher squad.

Offensive ineptness was the hallmark the following week as the Gophers went to Lincoln and lost 7-0 to Nebraska.

Junior Ray Stephens started at quarterback and ran the team for three quarters, but he was replaced by Hagen when the Gophers weren't moving.

The game's only score came in the third quarter. Minnesota had moved to the Cornhuskers' 40, then was forced to punt. Baldridge put one down at the Nebraska six. On third-and-four from the 12, Nebraska showed a punt formation, but quarterback Frank Patrick shovel-passed the ball to halfback Ben Gregory who went to the 19 for the first down. A couple of plays later, it looked like good fortune had smiled on Minnesota when Ed Duren fell on a fumble at the 37, but the Gophers were offside.

Nebraska moved to the Minnesota 25. On the next play Joe Orduna went off left tackle, cut to the outside and went into the end zone. Bill Bomberger made the PAT.

Clearly, Warmath was concerned about his offense, but felt the Gophers had played better in the loss than they had in the win a week earlier over Utah.

The following Saturday, things came together. Southern Methodist came to Minneapolis and the Gophers outmanned the smaller Mustangs coached by present Iowa coach Hayden Fry.

It was cold, windy and a steady rain fell most of the afternoon. Fumbles killed two Minnesota threats in the first half. But SMU wasn't doing any better as ends Stein and Del Jessen and Dave Nixon and Wayne King at linebacker, shut down the Mustangs and their fine back Jerry Levias.

The only scoring of the first half came with eight minutes left when Stein tackled SMU quarterback Eddie Valdez on a rollout in the Mustang end zone for a safety to give the Gophers two points.

In the third quarter, SMU fumbled at the 36 and Jessen fell on the ball. Hagen's short pass to Sanders and a run by sophomore fullback Jim Carter got to the 25. From there, Hagen connected with Sanders to the four. Two runs by Carter got the touchdown. The extra point by Stein was good and it was 9-0.

SMU moved the ball for the only time in the game and settled for a 28-yard field goal by Dennis Partee. The Mustangs then tried an onside kick, but John Williams scooped up the ball at the Gopher 48 and went to the SMU 44. Minnesota couldn't move and punted, but the kick was fumbled and bounced out to the 28 where Gopher guard Dick Enderle fell on it. Hagen took it to the four on a keeper and then sent Carter into the line twice for the touchdown. Stein had been shaken up earlier, so sophomore Jeff Nygren kicked the extra point.

The Gopher defense held again in the fourth quarter. Southern Methodist had to punt and it was Minnesota's ball at its 37. Hagen got the offense to the SMU 38 where it stalled and faced third-and-14. He called a pass play to Litten and found the junior receiver for the touchdown. Stein returned and made the extra point.

Warmath attributed the 23-3 victory to controlling the SMU running game. Jessen said the effort was made easier because Southern Methodist was a small team.

Hagen, who threw only four passes and completed three, one for the touchdown to Litten, said the rain dictated a running game.

Fry said, "Big Ten teams are too much for a school like ours. Minnesota was on the schedule before I came here."

•     •     •

The Big Ten season opened the following weekend in Champaign and the Gopher victory resulted from a field goal by Jeff Nygren with less than five minutes to play.

The game was marked by turnovers (four by Illinois, three by the Gophers) and tough defensive play by both teams.

There also was more quarterback shuffling by Minnesota. Hagen started, was replaced by Carlson, then Stephens. No one could move the team. Minnesota got just 52 yards in the first half. But the defense was strong once again and held the Illini to 88 total yards.

In the second half, Hagen was back calling signals and took the Gophers in for their only touchdown. Carter and halfback George Kemp got most of the 74 yards in the drive. Carter scored from the one and Nygren kicked the extra point.

Illinois came right back and went 75 yards in just seven plays. Quarterback Dean Volkman utilized split end John Wright, although a pass to Bill Huston for 29 yards was a key play. From the nine on third-and-goal, Volkman found Wright at the goal line and the Illini receiver slipped over. Dan McKissick kicked the extra point to tie the game.

The teams traded turnovers after that. Minnesota lost a fumble at midfield but got the ball back two plays later when King intercepted Volkman. Hagen was then intercepted at the Illinois 43. Illinois started a drive, but lost a fumble at the Gopher 33. Hagen took the Gophers to the Illini 19 where Terry Miller intercepted a fourth-down pass. At its 48, Illinois gave the ball back when Condo intercepted a Volkman pass and returned it to the Illini 44.

Time was running out. On a third-and-seven, Hagen hit Kemp at the 31, then sophomore Mike Curtis at the 19. Two plays got one yard and on third down, Hagen connected with Curtis at the 15, but he fumbled. The ball bounded toward the goal line and Gopher guard Andy Brown fell on it at the six. Minnesota couldn't move and with 4:59 left, Nygren kicked the winning field goal.

The ensuing kickoff was short and was bouncing around long enough for Jessen to fall on it at the 25. Minnesota drove to the six, but was stopped. There were less than two minutes left. Illinois didn't use the clock wisely, getting just to midfield when the game ended with Minnesota a 10-7 victor.

Carter gained 188 yards in 29 carries and the fullback added two receptions for 25 yards. Kemp also had played well and caught four passes for 50 yards.

The quarterback situation still was unsettled and during the following week, Warmath decided to rectify it. He did it with a bang against the reigning Big Ten champions.

•　　•　　•

"Minnesota, impeccably prepared and flawless in its execution, unarmed Michigan State 21-0 Saturday at Memorial Stadium," wrote the Sunday Tribune's John Wiebusch.

"It was quarterback Curt Wilson who threw three touchdown passes and it was a defense of strength and savvy that checked the Spartans.

"But standing tallest was a man named Murray Warmath. His game plan caught Michigan State flat-footed and exploited virtually every weakness the Spartans have."

During the week leading up to the game, Warmath and his staff moved Wilson to quarterback and put together an offensive scheme that they were confident could get the job done. Defensively, they believed they could whip the Spartans.

"Wilson always was in our plans, it was just that he was banged up in the early part of the season," Warmath said looking back on the change.

Wilson tore the Spartan defense to shreds.

In the first quarter, Minnesota showed it could move the ball, but Carter fumbled at the MSU one. However, the visitors couldn't get out from the shadow of their goalpost and punted. From the State 45, Wilson took Minnesota to their first score. His nine-yard sneak and a nine-yard pass to Litten got the ball to the 19. There he dropped straight back and rifled a pass to Litten near the goal line. The Gopher receiver grabbed the throw and broke through a State defender's grasp for the touchdown. Stein made the extra point.

It wasn't until late in the second quarter that Minnesota struck again. A Gopher punt bounced off Spartan Sterling Armstrong and Bryant recovered at the Gopher 45.

There were 41 seconds to go in the half. Wilson hit three straight passes—the first was to Curtis for 18, then to Bryant for 11 and the third was to Litten as he stepped into the end zone.

Stein kicked the extra point with three seconds left.

Early in the third quarter, runs by Carter and Kemp, plus a 15-yard personal foul on the Spartans, got the ball to the State 33. From there, Wilson dropped back and fired a perfect throw to Bryant, who was running a post pattern. The senior wide receiver dove through the air and gathered in the ball over his left shoulder and tumbled into the end zone. Stein kicked the 21st point.

When the gun sounded, Wilson had connected on 14 of 25 passes for an amazing 262 yards, breaking Hankinson's single-game yardage record by seven. The Gophers piled up 450 yards in total offense and stopped the Spartans' Big Ten winning streak at 16.

A crowd of 56,554 watched the players carry Warmath off the field in what was one of his most convincing and satisfying victories.

"Wilson was nothing short of sensational," a happy Gopher coach said. "He's a talented kid and had a fine reputation as a high school quarterback."

Bryant called the triumph the "sweetest victory of my life. This game is the key to our having a fine season."

As for Wilson, he praised his receivers and singled out John Williams for both his pass protection and run blocking.

Over in a quiet Spartan locker room, Duffy Daugherty, always gracious in victory or defeat, said "Minnesota beat us in every way. They are very big and strong. It didn't help that we lost three starters to injuries in the first half, including our quarterback Jim Raye."

The Spartan coach said the turning point was the punt which bounced off Armstrong late in the second quarter that led to the second Minnesota touchdown.

Warmath's team had given up just 29 points in five games. The following week, the Michigan Wolverines would come to town and test that statistic.

The Wolverines forced the Gophers to play come-from-behind football and then took the game down to the closing seconds before Minnesota could take back the Little Brown Jug.

Minnesota got off to a bad start, however, as it let Michigan take a quick 15-0 lead.

On the game's second series, Michigan quarterback Dennis Brown took his team from its 21 to its 41 in four plays. He then pitched out to halfback Ron Johnson, who went around right end, cut to the sideline and zipped 59 yards for the TD. The extra point kick was no good.

Minnesota got the ball and Wilson tried to hit Bryant, but Brian Healy of Michigan intercepted at the Gopher 36 and went to the five. Johnson slammed into the middle three times and scored on the last carry. The two-point play was no good, but it was already 12-0.

In the second quarter, George Hoey, an excellent return man, fielded Baldridge's punt at his 27 and behind good blocking went to the Gopher 20. The Minnesota defense held at the four and Michigan's Mike Hankwitz put three points on the board with a 21-yard field goal.

There were five minutes left to play in the second quarter and the Gophers had yet to make a first down when Kemp finally gained 11 yards. Three plays later, Wilson was grabbed by the face mask and the ball was advanced to the Wolverine 31. Wilson found Wintermute open for a 17-yard pass to the 14.

On third-and-one, Wilson went around right end and scored. The two-point pass attempt failed.

Minnesota threatened in the third quarter, but couldn't capitalize. Late in the quarter and early in the fourth, Carter carried three times from his 37 for gains of 12, 6 and 6 yards. Wilson dropped back and saw Curtis breaking into the end zone and hit him for the TD. Stein kicked the extra point and the Gophers trailed by two with 14:20 left.

Michigan got the kickoff, couldn't move and punted. Minnesota drove as deep at the 31, but a field goal attempt by Nygren was short. Michigan again failed to advance and punted to Sakal at the Gopher 49.

Wilson found Litten up the middle for 22 yards. Then on a fourth-and-one with the ball at the 13, Wilson followed an excellent block by Sanders on the left side and scored. With Stein's kick, the Gophers had scored 20 straight points to take the lead 20-15.

Michigan came right back and took the ball to the Minnesota 21, but three passes failed to connect. Minnesota got possession, but couldn't get a first down. There was one minute left when Baldridge hit a beautiful punt from his 20 that went 54 yards to Hoey who took it at his 26. He started up the middle and got some fine blocks and went along the right sideline in front of the Michigan bench. He had only Baldridge to beat, but the Gopher punter from Minneapolis West cut off his angle and knocked him out of bounds at the Minnesota 26.

Two pass attempts lost five yards thanks to a tough Gopher rush and the game ended.

"We took Michigan too lightly and I'm mad about that," said captain Tom Sakal.

Wilson said the block by Sanders that sprung him for the third Gopher touchdown was critical.

In the meantime, Pete Elliott called Minnesota a big, strong team, but he couldn't help muttering that his squad should have won.

At Iowa the next week, the Gophers went back to their old ways—just enough offense to win and plenty of defense to hold the opposition scoreless.

The 10-0 victory over the Hawkeyes in Iowa City came even though the Gophers self-destructed with three lost fumbles. In addition, the Gophers had several key players injured including Carter, Condo, Sakal, Sanders, Boston, Litten, Jessen and Wilson. Carter, Condo and Jessen were the most serious and played little, if at all. Carter was replaced by Mo Forte, who had a great game (149 yards in 27 carries), even though he lost two of the three fumbles.

Iowa also gave up the ball. On the third play of the game the Hawkeyes turned it over on a fumble, but Stein's 41-yard field goal attempt a few plays later was no good.

Iowa fumbled again and Boston recovered at the Hawkeyes' 43. Wilson then connected with Sanders for 14, was incomplete on his next pass and then gave to Kemp twice for nine yards. On fourth and one, Wilson got the first down at the 17. He then passed to Sanders at the three, who stepped into the end zone. Stein hit the PAT and it was 7-0 with 7:37 left in the quarter.

Minnesota again drove deep, but a Forte fumble at the one gave the ball back to the Hawkeyes.

In the second quarter, Iowa got to the Gopher 39, but Bob Anderson missed the field goal try. Another Minnesota threat was killed by an end zone interception. Later, Forte had a 44-yard run to the 23, but then Kemp fumbled.

In the third quarter, Hagen replaced Wilson and connected with Sanders on a 28-yard pass to the Iowa 25. Forte got to the 10 and Stein made a 27-yard field goal.

Wayne King made two big defensive plays when he stopped a fourth-down run at the Gopher 33 and then recovered a fumble at the 14 by Hawkeye quarterback Mike Cilek.

Sakal intercepted an Iowa pass in the fourth quarter at the Minnesota 22 and took it to the 44. The Gophers then ate up five minutes and appeared to be on the way for another score when Forte once again fumbled, this time at the Iowa seven with 40 seconds left. The turnover was irrelevant and the Gophers beat the Hawkeyes for the sixth time in seven games.

"Our defense played well but there is simply no excuse for our fumbling," said a rather unhappy Warmath. "Our fans here were unhappy and I never thought I'd see the day when they would boo us for beating Iowa, but given the way we played...."

The Purdue game was next and along with Indiana, the two teams were undefeated in conference play. Minnesota headed for West Lafayette against what Warmath called the best talent in the Big Ten.

Minnesota came into the game as the best defensive team in the conference. They had given up the fewest points, fewest first downs, fewest rushing yards, fewest total yards and had the most interceptions. All this made little difference.

Purdue had 475 yards in total offense. Mike Phipps, the sophomore heir to Bob Griese, passed for 235 yards and one touchdown. The great LeRoy Keyes, perhaps the most versatile back in the country that year, scored three times, rushed for 96 yards and caught six passes for 65 yards. Fullback Perry Williams ran for 90 yards in 22 carries.

The final score was Purdue 42, Minnesota 12.

Things started well for the Gophers when Ron Kamzelski recovered a Phipps fumble in the first quarter at the Purdue 17. Stein got the game's first points by making a 31-yard field goal.

Purdue came back and sustained a 59-yard drive with Keyes scoring from the two. The extra point kick was good. The Boilermakers got close again, but fumbled at the six and it went through the end zone for a touchback.

A series later, from their 39, the Gophers scored again as Bryant went 59 yards on a Statue of Liberty play around right end. Stein made it 10-7 with his extra point.

In the second quarter, Purdue scored twice. First, Kemp fumbled at the Minnesota 44 and several plays later Keyes took a pitchout from Phipps and scored the touchdown. Minnesota got to the Purdue 27, but couldn't score. Then with 58 seconds left, came a heartbreaker for the Gophers. From his six, Phipps first hit tight end Marion Griffin for 37 yards, then threw a 57-yard bomb to Jim Beirne for a score. It was 21-10 at halftime.

Purdue continued the assault in the second half. Williams and Keyes were the main contributors on an early fourth-quarter touchdown, a one-yard plunge by Keyes. Minnesota added two points on a safety when Wintermute's option pass was intercepted by Bob Corby. Corby went from the end zone out to the two, then went back into the end zone evading a tackler where he was pulled down for the safety.

The safety made no difference because in the final quarter, Purdue marched 77 yards in 11 plays and Keyes scored his third touchdown on an eight-yard run. With 24 seconds left, substitute Boilermaker quarterback Don Kiepert threw a four-yard pass to Bill Liber for the game's final score.

Warmath said that Purdue was the best team Minnesota faced all year and that his squad was "totally dominated. Phipps is further along as a sophomore than Griese was."

Jessen believed Keyes was everything they said he would was.

Minnesota had to look ahead to the arrival of undefeated Indiana.

•　　•　　•

One of Warmath's great attributes as a coach was his ability to rally his team after a big loss and get a victory the next week. He did it in 1954 after the 34-0 defeat at Michigan by coming back against defending conference champion Michigan State. In 1956, he beat Michigan State a week after losing the big game to Iowa. In 1960, he clinched a title share and a trip to the Rose Bowl with a victory at Wisconsin after Purdue had beaten the Gophers the week before. In 1966, he upset Ohio State seven days after being routed by Michigan.

The challenge in 1967 was to beat Indiana after the devastating loss at Purdue. Again, he met the challenge.

The Gophers were in second place with Purdue and Indiana on top of the conference at 5-0. Indiana was the darling of not just the Big Ten, but the nation. Led by sophomore sensations Harry Gonso and John Isenbarger, they had pulled several games out of the fire and were legitimate contenders for the conference championship and the right to be the Rose Bowl representative.

The game started with Indiana driving early but being stopped at the Minnesota 35. They punted, pinning the Gophers back on their five. Minnesota moved the ball out to the 37 where Kevin Duffy picked off a Curt Wilson pass. A few plays later, however, Jessen forced Gonso to fumble and the Gophers recovered at the Hoosiers' 40.

Wilson connected with Sanders for nine yards. Wintermute went to the 22 on two carries. A couple of plays later, Wintermute broke a tackle and went to the six. On the next play, Wilson faked the dive to Carter, kept the ball and went around right end for the touchdown. Stein kicked the point after touchdown.

Indiana appeared on its way to tying the score when Gonso hit wide receiver Jade Butcher for 26 and 21 yard gains to the

Minnesota five. After Jessen dropped Gonso for no gain, an apparent touchdown pass was called back for an ineligible receiver downfield. Another penalty put Indiana back upfield where a 57-yard field goal try was way off the mark.

In the third quarter, Indiana evened things when key passes to Al Gage and Butcher put the Hoosiers at the Minnesota one. Gonso took it in on an option and Dave Kornowa made the PAT to tie the score.

Minnesota put together an 11-play drive of 68 yards for a score. Wintermute twice got first downs on third down plays. Wilson was successful on a pass of 19 yards to Curtis at the Indiana four. On fourth-and-goal from the one, Wilson ran the option to the right and scored. Nygren's extra point attempt was blocked by Jim Sniadecki.

In the fourth quarter, things got off to a bad start when Minnesota's Ron Kamzelski punched a Hoosier player and was ejected. Minnesota held at its 21 on a fourth-down play. Wilson came in and continued his brilliant play, taking the Gophers to another touchdown in 12 straight running plays. The big gainer was his 24-yard keeper. From the three, Wilson scored his third touchdown and Nygren again had his kick blocked by Sniadecki. It was 19-7 with 7:24 left.

Indiana went brain dead on the ensuing kickoff. It watched the Gopher kick bounce around and allowed Dennis Hale to grab the ball at the 23. Minnesota took advantage of the mistake when Wilson on fourth-and-four from the 17, threw one of his few passes of the day. The ball bounced out of Bryant's hands to Sanders in the end zone. Nygren made the point after to essentially put the game away at 26-7.

Minnesota scored again when Bill Laakso, substituting at tackle for the departed Kamzelski, recovered a bad pitchout by Gonso at Indiana's 23. Runs by Carter and Wintermute took the ball to the one and Wilson scored his fourth touchdown with 69 seconds left. Nygren split the uprights to make the final 33-7.

"We had a great week of practice and the kids wanted this badly," Warmath said. "We were stronger than Indiana and forced Gonso to pitch the ball rather than keep it and run. When we stopped them at the 21 at the start of the fourth quarter with the score tied, it seemed to really pick us up."

Sakal felt a Minnesota team had never played better against such quality opposition in his three years at the school. Wilson ran to the outside because it was apparent the Indiana defense was stacking the middle to stop Carter and Wintermute. Still, Carter rushed for 94 yards and Wintermute for 135. The defense, meanwhile, had limited Gonso to 61 yards rushing and just 66 via the pass.

"I could write the 'Don'ts of College Football' based on our play today," said Hoosier coach John Pont. "Minnesota was strong and tough and we made too many critical mistakes. I've never seen anybody run as hard as Carter did today."

The season's final week was filled with high drama. Indiana, with one loss, would meet undefeated Purdue and Minnesota would host winless Wisconsin.

The Gophers tried to concentrate on the Badgers while listening for an announcement from Julie Perlt over the Memorial Stadium public address system for the result of the Hoosier-Boilermaker clash. A victory by Purdue would give the Boilermakers the title outright. If Minnesota beat Wisconsin as expected, the Gophers would go to the Rose Bowl since Purdue couldn't repeat and Indiana would have two losses.

Minnesota scored first with less than five minutes gone in the game. Ed Duren recovered a Dick Schumitsch fumble at the Wisconsin 29. Dick Peterson, playing his first game of the season after being hurt, got two big first downs and then scored from the two. Stein made the conversion.

Minnesota drives to the Badger 35 and 28 resulted in no scores. Wisconsin went to Minnesota's 30, but Noel Jenke intercepted a John Boyajian pass at the 12.

In the second quarter, Wisconsin settled for a 28-yard field goal by Tom Schinke after the Gopher defense stopped a drive at the 10. Schinke made another field goal, this time of 30 yards, with 1:15 left to make the score 7-6 for Minnesota.

The Gophers took the second half's opening kickoff and went 77 yards in 20 plays. Wintermute carried for 37 yards and Carter 21. Bryant caught a Wilson pass for 16 yards to the Badger four. Wilson scored two plays later and Stein made the conversion.

Right after that came word that Indiana had upset Purdue. It would be the Hoosiers in Pasadena on New Year's Day, not the Gophers. A massive groan went through the crowd of 47,000.

"After the announcement, we seemed to get fired up," Sakal said following the game. "We certainly wanted a share of the title."

Wisconsin ran two plays after taking the kickoff before Jenke picked off a pass at the Gopher 42 and ran it back to Wisconsin's 33. With 26 seconds left in the third quarter, Wilson scored from the one and Stein converted.

In the fourth quarter, Minnesota got to the Wisconsin four but was turned back. Seven plays later, Boyajian hit Stu Voigt on a 51-yard throw and suddenly, with the successful two-point conversion, it was 21-14 with 5:09 left.

Minnesota couldn't move and a Baldridge punt went to the Wisconsin 17. A pass to Tim McCauley on the first play from scrimmage went for 39 yards to the Gopher 44. But Hale intercepted a pass two plays later and ran it 25 yards to the Badger 40.

Wilson was hit late on a pass play and Gopher tackle Ezell Jones got into a fight with two Wisconsin players. Both benches cleared and several hundred fans thought it would be a good idea to join in. It took several minutes for order to be restored. Voigt, meanwhile, was ejected.

Wisconsin got the ball back and was driving when the game ended. Just to keep things interesting, another fight broke out.

Finally, both teams left the field, although Wisconsin was held back until Minnesota was some distance away in order to prevent any more fights.

Minnesota may have won a share of the Big Ten title with Purdue and Indiana, but it was a very quiet locker room after the victory over Wisconsin. Every player said they would have settled for second place and a Rose Bowl trip as opposed to a title share.

Few players felt like conversing with the media and Warmath said Indiana would certainly go to Pasadena. He called the two brawls "red-blooded American boys just having a fight."

The team picked up and the student and equipment managers packed up to say good bye to what certainly had been a very good season. Stein was named All-American and Wilson was third in conference scoring. Several other players won post-season conference recognition and/or went on to play in post-season all-star games and advanced to professional football careers.

Shortly after the season ended, Warmath was elected president of the American Football Coaches Association for 1968. It was a reflection of the high esteem in which he was held by his fellow collegiate coaches.

As 1967 ended, perhaps the most alarming fact was that this fine team got just above average support from the sports fans of Minnesota. The media noted that the Gophers averaged just 48,000 fans for six home games, the worst average in the history of six-game home stands. It was the harbinger of things to come.

# Thirty-Three

While Wilson, Sanders, Williams, Condo, Sakal, Bryant, Baldridge, King, Peterson, Duren and Boston had all moved on following the 1967 season, Warmath still had a nucleus of fine players returning in 1968.

Carter, Wintermute, Kemp and Forte were four solid runners, Hagen and Stephens were experienced quarterbacks, Steve Lundeen was the returning center and Dick Enderle and Tom Fink the returning starting offensive guards. Litten was back at wide receiver. Defensively, Stein and Jessen came back to their defensive end spots. Kamzelski returned to defensive tackle, Jenke (that year's captain) and Dave Nixon were veteran linebackers and Hale and Nygren were experienced secondary men. The opening weeks of the season had a lineup of formidable opponents—beginning with the 1967 national champions.

"He came. He saw. He conquered."

This was the opening of the report by the Tribune's Jon Roe on the game between Minnesota and Southern Cal. The "he" was the legendary O.J. Simpson. In the first game of 1968 for both Minnesota and USC, the Trojan great had 375 all-purpose yards in leading USC to a comeback victory over the Gophers, 29-20.

Simpson was a consensus All-American the previous year and in 1968 would win the Heisman Trophy. He had a brilliant opening game at Memorial Stadium before nearly 61,000 fans, but not without a tough fight from Warmath's team.

Minnesota took a 10-0 lead in the first quarter. Simpson fumbled early at the USC 15 and Walt Prybl, a defensive back, recovered. Four plays later, Hagen hit tight end Ray Parson, a junior from Uniontown, Pa., and Stein made the extra point.

Stein set a school record late in the quarter when he made a 40-yard field goal.

In the second quarter, USC's Mike Battle intercepted a pass from Hagen and went from his 46 to the Gopher 46. On second and 12, Simpson took a handoff, hit off left tackle, burst to the outside and streaked into the end zone. Quarterback Steve Sogge's two-point pass attempt to Ron Ayala was no good.

Simpson fumbled again, this time deep in Gopher territory, but Minnesota couldn't move and punted to its 37. Bob Chandler and Simpson caught 10-yard passes. There was a gain of three and then Simpson ran for two seven-yard gains, the second one for the touchdown. The extra point kick by Ayala was good and the Trojans led 13-10.

Late in the half, the Gophers went 74 yards and with one second left, Stein made a 27-yard field goal to tie the game.

There was no scoring in the third quarter. In the fourth quarter there was both tough defensive play by both teams as well as a barrage of offensive fireworks.

Minnesota was held to just one first down in the third quarter. Noel Jenke led a Gopher defensive unit which stopped Southern Cal at the Minnesota 19. Jenke knocked down two passes in the Trojans' futile drive.

There were less than eight minutes to play when Ray Stephens fumbled at the Minnesota 22. Ayala kicked a 29-yard field goal and USC led by three. Then came one of the most electrifying plays in years at Memorial Stadium.

Kemp took the Trojan kickoff and headed up the middle. Suddenly, at the 20, he turned and threw an overhand lateral to Wintermute, standing at the 17 along the right side of the field. The vast majority of the USC players had converged toward Kemp and were caught flat-footed.

Wintermute went up the sideline. At the Trojan 30, Walt Bowser blocked the one lone Southern Cal defender who had a shot at Wintermute. Wintermute waltzed in for the touchdown.

Gopher fans went berserk as Minnesota went ahead 20-16 with 7:34 left.

But USC—and Simpson—weren't through.

Minnesota got the ball back after stopping the Trojans once, but was forced to punt. Battle took the kick and went to the Minnesota 45. Simpson gained 20 yards. From the seven, he swept right end and scored. The point after attempt was blocked.

Down by two and with time slipping away, Minnesota was forced to go for a first down on fourth-and-one at its 37. The Trojan defense stopped Carter short. Starting at the Minnesota 37, USC quickly scored with Simpson tallying his fourth TD, again on a seven-yard run. The final was 29-20.

"Simpson has been misrepresented," Warmath told the media after the game. "He's better than they said he was."

The Gopher coach said the USC star seemed to get stronger as the game progressed. He cited the old axiom of Bob Neyland: position and possession win football games.

"We lost to the best team in the country, but we gave them one hell of a fight," Jenke said.

Simpson praised the Gophers, saying he had never been hit harder than he was that day. Quarterback Sogge said the Trojans stopped themselves several times but always felt that with Simpson they could move the ball.

John McKay, the Trojan coach, praised both teams and said it was the tough, close game he expected.

Things didn't get any easier the following week when Nebraska came to town. Once again, it was late in the game before the outcome was determined.

In the first quarter, Jenke picked off an Ernie Sigler pass at the Minnesota 48 and took it back to the Cornhusker 38. A facemask call took the ball to the 23. Six plays later, Mo Forte scored from the two and Stein made the extra point.

In the second quarter, Cornhusker Tom Heller fumbled a Bowser punt at the Nebraska 17 where Andy Brown recovered for the Gophers. It was another Forte plunge of two yards and a Stein conversion that gave the Gophers a 14-0 lead. Late in the half, Nebraska got on the scoreboard. They went 61 yards in five plays, the big gain a Sigler-to-Jim McFarland pass for 43 yards. Joe Orduna scored the TD from the two and Paul Rogers made the PAT.

The third quarter was marked by threats, but no scoring. Minnesota had a pass intercepted and Nebraska lost a fumble.

In the final quarter, Dana Stephenson intercepted Stephens at the Gopher 45 and ran it to the 17. Two plays later Sigler hit McFarland for the touchdown and the extra point tied the game.

Minnesota stopped Nebraska's Dick Davis on a fourth and one at the Gopher 40. Then Sherwin Jarman intercepted Stephens and Nebraska had the ball at its 47 with 5:33 left.

A pass to McFarland and a run by Orduna got the ball to the Minnesota two where the Gophers stiffened. On fourth down, Rogers kicked a field goal and Nebraska was ahead by three. Minnesota drove late and got to the Cornhusker 39 when referee Howard Wirtz let the clock run out after a Gopher first down. The final was 17-14.

"The officials blew that call," Warmath snapped.

Wirtz had a rather strange excuse when he said the clock was "only stopped to move the chains, not conserve time." The rules, however, call for the clock to be stopped after a first down and then restarted once the chains have been set in place for the next series.

"We played well, but their defense was better than our offense," Warmath added.

Bob Devaney said the late second quarter TD by his team was the key.

Wake Forest came to town the following Saturday and once again it was a nail-biter. However, this time things worked out for Minnesota. There were only 39,000 in attendance due to a steady downpour. These who were on hand saw a fine Gopher comeback.

Things started on an up note when Minnesota's Doug Roalstad intercepted a Freddie Summers pass at the Gopher 42 and ran it back to the Wake Forest 30. However, a clip on the play brought the ball back to midfield. From there, Forte and Kemp spearheaded a drive that went to the one where Forte scored the touchdown and Stein kicked the point after.

In the second quarter, Hagen fumbled at the Wake Forest 41 and it took the visitors six plays to go 59 yards for the TD on a Fred Augerman-reception of a 19-yard pass from Summers. The kick was wide.

The second half started with Wayne King intercepting a Summers pass at the 36 and running to the Wake Forest 15. The Gophers settled for a 25-yard Nygren field goal.

Wake Forest came back and went 72 yards in 12 plays. The big play was a 25-yard pass to Ron Jurewicz. On fourth-and-goal from the two, Jurewicz took the ball in for the score. Jeff Wright broke up Summers' pass for two points and Wake Forest led 12-10.

In the fourth quarter with less than 12 minutes to go, Wintermute fumbled at the Gopher 21. Dan White recovered for the Demon Deacons at the 24. Jack Doblin made an eight-yard gain after the Gophers forced a fourth-and-one at the 15. A few plays later, Summers snuck in from the one. Tom Deacon's kick put Wake Forest in front 19-10.

Minnesota came right back to narrow the lead. An 80-yard, 12-play drive was aided by a 42-yard pass interference call against Dick Bozoian on Bowser. That put the ball at the 13. Carter hit the middle three times before scoring. Nygren made the point after and there was 7:33 left with Minnesota down 19-17.

The Gopher defense stopped Wake Forest and got the ball back on a punt at its 25. Eleven plays later, Minnesota took the lead. There were two big passes from Hagen to Litten in the drive. The first came on a third and five at the Deacons' 48. Litten caught that pass for 16 yards. Then with fourth-and-six at the 28, Hagen hit Litten again, this time for the touchdown. The point after made it 24-19.

But Wake Forest wasn't finished and had two drives in 90 seconds. The first came after the kickoff when they drove into Gopher territory, but linebacker John Darkenwald batted down two passes.

Hagen, however, fumbled and the visitors had it at the Gopher 30 with seconds left. Three passes were incomplete and on fourth down Jenke blitzed and sacked Summers. The game was over and Minnesota had its first victory of the season.

"We had our troubles, but showed a lot of courage in coming back," Warmath commented. "The five interceptions helped, but that Summers (49 pass attempts) can make any team go."

He added that his team was banged up, the worst injuries being to Stein and offensive tackles Jim Wrobel and Alvin Hawes.

Bill Tate, the Wake Forest coach, said the interference call on the pass attempt to Bowser hurt his team and was the turning point.

"Blacken the Illini-I" was the homecoming slogan the next week for the fourth consecutive home game.

Minnesota won the battle of two tough defenses.

In the first quarter, Carter took a two-yard TD pass from Hagen to cap a 55-yard drive which took nine plays. A 23-yard toss to Litten was the drive's big play. Stein made the extra point kick.

The next score came in the second quarter when Illinois punted from deep in its territory. Roalstad took the ball at his 39, faked a reverse to Dennis Hale, got a couple of nice blocks and went 61 yards for the touchdown. Nygren made the kick and it was 14-0.

Illinois got on the scoreboard later in the quarter when Don McKissick made a 40-yard field goal.

In the third quarter Illinois fullback Rich Johnson swept right end for five and a touchdown to finish off a 59-yard drive which took 11 plays. McKissick made the point after.

Late in the fourth quarter, Minnesota took the ball from its 23 to the Illini 15 where Stein made a 32-yard field goal and the score went to 17-10. Hagen completed seven consecutive passes and had a total of 11 in a row when combined with the drive before.

After the game, Warmath cited his defensive unit for their solid play.

The Gophers finally left town and went to East Lansing. Minnesota lost the statistical battle, but got another big punt return from Roalstad and made a couple of tough defensive stands with its backs to the wall to earn a 14-13 victory over Michigan State. It was Michigan State's homecoming and 74,321 were on hand.

On the first series, State went from its 29 to the Gopher six. Steve Thompson, the sophomore defensive tackle, broke through and blasted Spartan quarterback Bill Triplett, knocking the ball loose and King recovered. Later, State drove to the Gopher one but halfback Tommy Love fumbled.

In the second quarter the Gophers were backed up on their 15 and a Bowser punt went only 17 yards. The ball bounced off State's Wilt Martin and Wrobel recovered. Passes to Litten and tight end Leon Trawick were part of the drive that reached the Spartan 10. But on third down, Al Brennan intercepted Hagen and went to the Minnesota 25. As he was hit, he lateraled to Bill Dawson who went to the 15.

From the 13, Triplett hit Frank Foreman for the touchdown. The PAT was good and the clock showed just 32 seconds left in the half and the Spartans ahead 7-0.

Roalstad put Minnesota on the scoreboard in the third-quarter when, for the second week in a row, he returned a punt for a touchdown. He took the Spartan kick at his 42 and made what Warmath later called one of the nicest returns he had ever seen as he kept his balance all the way along the sideline. Stein tied the game with his conversion kick.

Minnesota got another score in the quarter when from the 50, they moved the ball in six plays to the State three. The drive featured passes of 15 yards to Litten and 18 to Kemp. From the three, Hagen threw to a diving Carter in the end zone and the PAT gave Minnesota the lead at 14-7.

Michigan State made two fourth-quarter drives. One got them back into the game, the other lost it for them.

The first started at their 12 and it took just seven plays to score. From their 32, Love gained 49 yards to the Gopher 19. Two plays later from the 17, Triplett connected with Foreman for the second time and a second touchdown. Duffy Daughtery went for the lead and called a two-point pass play. But defensive tackles Thompson and Jim Pahula crashed through and sacked Triplett. There was 2:34 left and Minnesota held a fragile one-point lead.

Minnesota couldn't move after receiving the kickoff and Bowser had to punt. State worked its way to the Gopher 24. But, Stein and Jessen sacked Triplett at the 36. Out of field goal range, State had to try a pass. Wright knocked it down and the Gophers ran out the clock.

Jessen said after the game that the sack by him and Stein was the only blitz they ran all day. Both Pahula and Thompson said missed blocks by State offensive linemen allowed them to get to Triplett on the critical two-point play.

Daughtery said the call was the right one. "You always play for the win in a situation like that."

"I think Roalstad's run was the key to our win because it got us back in the game right away," Warmath said. "I'm proud of the kids for the way they played and grateful for the win."

The next week, there was little to be proud of or grateful for. Warmath must have felt as if the 1966 game at Ann Arbor was still being played two years later.

At Michigan, Minnesota suffered the through one of the worst first halves in Warmath's 14-plus seasons. Michigan ran off 54 plays to Minnesota's 24 and in the process scored 30 points.

The final was 33-20.

The Wolverines scored twice in the opening quarter. First, Roalstad fumbled a punt at the Gopher 10 and two plays later quarterback Dennis Brown hit end Paul Satroba for an eight-yard scoring pass. The point after was no good.

George Hoey, whose punt returns in the 1967 Minnesota triumph had terrorized the Gophers, took a punt from his 15 to the Minnesota 46. On fourth-and-nine at the 33, Brown passed to end Jim Mandrich for the first down and then halfback Ron Johnson went in from the one. Jenke knocked down the pass attempt for two points.

In the second quarter, Tom Curtis intercepted Hagen and from the Gopher 45, Michigan scored in nine plays. Again, it was Johnson scoring from one yard out. A run for two points was stopped.

Next it was Brian Healy who picked off Hagen's pass. From the 48 of Minnesota, the Wolverines scored quickly, the touchdown coming on a 23-yard pass from Brown to end Bill Harris. The only problem Michigan had all day was making points after touchdowns. The fourth attempt (a two-pointer) again was no good.

Tom Killian added six points on 24 and 32-yard field goals. The last one came on the final play of the half and put the Wolverines ahead 30-0.

Michigan opened with another field goal in the third quarter as Killian made a 31-yard attempt which was set up after Hagen had fumbled at the Wolverine 47.

In the fourth quarter "it was all Minnesota." It looked as if Michigan would score again, but it was stopped at the two. From the 12, Stephens unloaded a long throw to Litten along the sideline and he went all the way for the touchdown. The two

286

point play was no good. The Gophers got the ball back at their 27 and went the 73 yards in just seven plays as halfback Barry Mayer scored from the five. Another two-point attempt failed.

Late in the game, Minnesota linebacker Rich Crawford intercepted a Michigan pass at the Wolverines' 35. Stephens found Leon Trawick in the end zone for a 12-yard touchdown. For the first time in nine attempts all day, a conversion attempt was successful as Stephens passed to Carter for the two points.

"We played terrible football," a dejected Warmath said after the game. "I've never seen a quarterback throw any better than Brown did today. Turnovers, especially the five interceptions, killed us."

Guard Dick Enderle said the Michigan defensive line "was very, very quick."

Iowa had beaten Minnesota just once in eight previous meetings, so when the Hawkeyes arrived in Minneapolis the following week with a 15-game losing streak, it appeared Minnesota would get back in the win column. The fact that Stein, Thompson and John Darkenwald were not dressed for the game due to injuries didn't help, but an early 20-7 lead did.

Iowa opened the game by taking the kickoff to its 40 and scored in 13 plays. Larry Lawrence, the Iowa quarterback, took it in from the three and Marcos Melendez kicked the extra point.

Minnesota came back on the third play from scrimmage as Barry Mayer bolted 60 yards for the touchdown. Nygren tied the game with his conversion kick.

On the fourth play of the second quarter, Stephens hit Ray Parson for an 11-yard touchdown culminating a 55-yard march. The possession came after Jenke picked off a Lawrence throw at his 25 and took it back 20 yards. Nygren's extra point attempt was no good.

Minnesota stopped Iowa at the Gopher 20 and drove the 80 yards for the touchdown. Mayer carried for 32 yards during the march that ended when Carter went in from the one and Nygren made the PAT. Iowa got on the scoreboard one more time before the half, going 51 yards in nine plays. Ed Podolak scored on a three-yard sweep of right end and Melendez made the PAT and the Gophers led 20-14.

The second half came down to the sudden emergence of the Iowa defense. The Gophers started poorly, getting bogged down in their end of the field, then punting to only the Hawkeye 46. Fullback Tim Sullivan made big runs of 11 and 20 yards and on the eighth play of the drive, Lawrence went off tackle for four yards and the score. Melendez made the conversion and it was the Hawkeyes by one point.

Minnesota again was deep in its end of the field and a delay of game penalty pushed them back to the one where they had to punt. Bowser got off a good punt which put Iowa back to its 49. From there, Lawrence executed another drive that included a 16-yard pass to end Ray Manning at the 29. Sullivan put together two runs of nine and 11 yards. On the third play of the fourth quarter, Lawrence ran in from the nine on a keeper for the touchdown. The extra point was good.

Iowa added to the lead a couple of series later when Mike Phillips intercepted a Hagen pass at the Gopher 34 and took it back eight yards. Bill Powell's run of 14 was the big play that set up Lawrence on another keeper, this one from the eight for the touchdown. The kick was good and Iowa led 35-20 with 6:18 left.

Minnesota rallied on three plays—a 53-yard pass from Stephens to Litten, a 14-yard throw to Terry Addison and a run of three yards by Stephens for the touchdown. Carter ran for two points to make it 35-28 for Iowa. It was too late, however, as with only 1:56 left, Charles Bolden intercepted a Stephens pass to secure the Hawkeye victory.

"We utilized flat passes to our backs and ran some old double-wing blocking formations with two backs flanked out and it seemed to work for us," said Iowa coach Ray Nagel. "The delay of game call in the third quarter that put Minnesota back on their one and forced them to punt really helped us."

"Iowa had better overall speed than we did," Warmath summarized. "Again, we made too many mistakes at the worst possible times."

Warmath knew a victory the next week was critical or the 1968 season could disintegrate fast.

•   •   •

The Monday before the game against Purdue, the Gopher coaching staff put a picture of a specific Purdue player on the locker of every starting Gopher player. Below each picture was the following caption: "this is the man you have to stop Saturday for us to win. You have to dominate him from the beginning and punish him for 60 minutes. You have the ability and you must get the desire to do it. Get ready mentally and we will win."

The Gophers were ready.

On the first Minnesota possession and with ball at the Purdue 49 on third-and-one, Carter took a handoff up the middle. Between the line of scrimmage and the goal line, he knocked over three Boilermaker would-be tacklers. He didn't side-step them or break a tackle. He literally ran over them.

When he got into the end zone at the open end of Memorial Stadium, he made a celebration toss of the ball into the packed bleachers. Nygren made the kick and was it was quickly 7-0.

The pace continued. On the next series, Jenke intercepted a Mike Phipps pass intended for LeRoy Keyes at the Purdue 47 and took it to the 37. A Stephens run of 11 was the key play and from the one Carter plunged into the end zone. Nygren made the conversion.

On the first play after the kickoff, reserve quarterback Don Kiepert fumbled and Steve Thompson recovered at the Purdue 33. It took six plays to get to the two, the big gainer being a 14-yard throw from Stephens to Parson. On fourth-and-goal,

Carter crashed into the end zone for his third TD and Nygren's extra point kick made it 21-0.

The onslaught slackened somewhat in the second quarter as the Gophers scored only once. Purdue had a fourth-and-two at the Gopher 48, but Jeff Wright came up and stopped Keyes for a one-yard loss. Mayer made a run of 11 and Carter rambled for 14. From the three, Stephens went into the end zone following a fine block by Litten. Nygren made the conversion, it was 28-0 and a national television audience had to be in awe of the Gopher juggernaut.

Purdue scored the only touchdowns of the second half. Perry Williams went in for the first TD in the third quarter after a Jim Kirkpatrick punt return gave the Boilermakers good field position at the Minnesota 39. The extra point kick was good. Then early in the fourth quarter, Purdue went 81 yards in 15 plays (aided by a roughing the kicker call on Minnesota that kept the ball in Purdue's possession). Tight end Marion Griffin caught a Phipps pass of nine yards for the score.

After that, the Gophers kept the pressure on, forced Purdue into poor field position, and were driving for another score when the game ended with Minnesota a 28-14 victor.

In a happy locker room, several of the Gophers alluded to a meeting they had without the coaches earlier in the week when they talked through some problems and dedicated themselves to a victory.

"One thing we didn't do was play give-away football today," Stein explained.

Alvin Hawes, the offensive tackle, said a major factor was running at the big, but slow, Purdue tackles. Along with Ezell Jones at the other tackle spot, guards Enderle and Fink and center Lundeen, Minnesota had blown the Purdue defensive line off the line of scrimmage.

"We had no offensive breakdowns, " Fink added.

Carter called the line play great and singled out Stephens for his excellent play calling and good ball handling.

"We had a good game plan, but those work only if they are executed and the kids played very well today," Warmath said. "It was our most consistent play all year."

He praised the defense which limited Keyes to only 48 yards in 15 carries.

The Purdue victory seemed to be the catalyst the team needed to finish the rest of the season undefeated.

Minnesota traveled to Indiana the next week and won 20-6 in a unique moment in Hoosier sports history. It was the first time it had ever rained during a game at the eight-year-old stadium.

Carter and Mayer led the way for the Gophers combining for 250 yards in 56 carries and scoring three touchdowns in seven and a half minutes in the third quarter.

The defense sparkled as Thompson had 16 solo tackles, Crawford 15 and King 12. Stein and Jessen prevented Harry Gonso from running the option to the outside.

The only first-half scoring came midway in the opening quarter when Gonso on fourth-and-one from the Minnesota 44, hit tight end Al Gage at the 20 and he went for the touchdown. Jenke blocked the extra point try.

In the third quarter, Minnesota got the ball at the Indiana 49 and scored in five plays. From the 37, Mayer got 28 yards on a sweep to the nine and Carter bolted up the middle on the next play for the touchdown. Nygren missed the kick.

Minnesota held Indiana and forced a punt. The Gophers started at their 33. Mayer had runs of 12 and nine yards and Hagen hit Parson on a 14-yard pass which eventually put the ball at the five. From there, Carter went in for the score. It was 13-6 following Nygren's PAT.

The Gophers quickly scored again. Rick Thompson lost a fumble at the 19 on the Hoosiers' first play from scrimmage. Four plays later, Carter scored from the three and Nygren made the extra point.

There were two big events in the fourth quarter. The first was a drive by Indiana that got to the Gopher six. But Gonso was rushed hard by Jenke and lost the ball at the 19. In the last minute of the game, a fight broke out between the teams which lasted nearly seven minutes.

In the locker room following the 20-6 victory, Warmath praised the defense for its adjustments at half. He cited the tough play against the pass. Gonso only completed five of 22. "We played very well offensively in the third quarter and took advantage of breaks."

Enderle added that the team changed to longer cleats at halftime which gave them better footing in the second half on the wet, muddy field.

"I think the line play was as good as last week," said Carter.

Assistant coach Mike McGee praised Parson, saying he was the best blocking tight end in the country.

The Gophers went to Madison to face winless Wisconsin hoping to get their sixth victory of the year. They did, but it wasn't easy.

Minnesota got off to a roaring start, scoring on the second play of the game when Hale stepped in front of a John Ryan pass at the Badger 41 and dashed along the left sideline into the end zone. Nygren made the extra point after just 48 seconds.

Minnesota returned the favor a short time later when Roalstad fumbled a punt at the Gopher 25. Wisconsin scored when Stu Voigt on a fourth-and-one, got into the end zone on an end-around play. The point after try was no good.

The Badgers scored before the quarter ended when they went 63 yards in eight plays. From the 21, fullback John Smith got 20 yards on a draw play and Ryan snuck in from the one. Again, the extra point attempt was no good.

In the second quarter, Minnesota marched 80 yards in 13 plays. Carter made runs of 21, 19 and eight and Mayer scored on a sweep from the two. Nygren's kick was good to make it 14-12.

With nine seconds left in the half, Dan Crooks kicked a 30-yard field goal to put Wisconsin ahead 15-14.

In the third quarter, Minnesota took the opening kickoff to the 26 and scored five plays later. Pass interference committed against receiver Terry Addison of Minnesota at the Badger 13 was the big play. From the nine, Hagen took the ball on a rollout and scored. A two-point pass was not good.

Minnesota added to the lead later in the quarter when Nygren made a 20-yard field goal. The Gophers consumed a lot of time as they had gone from their eight to the Badger three before being forced to settle for the three points.

"It was not a very well-played game on our part," Warmath told the media following the 23-15 win. "Wisconsin did a nice job of preparing for us."

Carter attributed the victory to the better line play by Minnesota. Badger coach John Coatta said the Addison interference call was a turning point, but added that Minnesota's overall play was "outstanding".

The Gophers ended the year 6-4, 5-2 in Big Ten play. Stein was named second team All-American.

The season ended on a tragic note when Francis Paquette, a sophomore end from Superior, Wis., was killed very early the next morning in a car crash near Fergus Falls after the team had returned from Minneapolis. He and Chip Litten had decided to visit Litten's parents in Fargo and Paquette lost his life when Litten's car overturned. Litten was not seriously hurt.

# Thirty-Four

The 1969 season got off to a rough start. However, the team finished strong and managed to wind up in fourth place in the Big Ten.

For the second time in history, the Gophers played a night game, opening in Tempe against Frank Kush and Arizona State. It was not a pleasant evening as the Sun Devils picked apart the Gophers, particularly through the air, and walked off with a 48-26 victory. Arizona State quarterback John Spagnola passed for an incredible 339 yards, 277 in the first half alone.

Minnesota scored first. A run of 34 yards by Carter and a 21-yard Hagen-to-Parson pass moved the Gophers to the ASU five where Carter scored. Nygren kicked the extra point after only 1:10 had elapsed. But with less than 10 minutes to play in the quarter, Arizona State's Dave Buchanan returned a punt 72 yards for a touchdown. Spagnola followed with a 75-yard TD throw to Mike Brunson. Ed Gallardo made his second extra point to put the Sun Devils ahead 14-7.

Carter, Mayer and Parson led a Gopher drive which took nine plays to go 60 yards. Carter took it in from the six and Nygren's kick tied it. However, the Sun Devils scored twice more in the quarter. First, Spagnola hit Calvin Demery for a 14-yard scoring toss. State then went 72 yards in five plays with Buchanan scoring on a 10-yard run. The big play in the series was a 36-yard pass reception by Ron Corothers. The extra point kick made the score 28-14.

In the third quarter, Prentiss Williams intercepted Hagen at the Arizona State 14. A halfback pass from Buchanan to Corothers got 44 yards before Buchanan skirted right end from

294

the three for the score. In the fourth, Demery made a leaping catch of a Spagnola throw for a 28-yard touchdown reception. It climaxed an 82-yard drive of eight plays.

Minnesota got a touchdown midway through the quarter when it went 73 yards in 10 plays with Hagen passing to sophomore end Kevin Hamm for a six-yard TD. The two-point attempt failed. Arizona State scored a late touchdown and missed the conversion attempt.

"They have great overall team speed," said Warmath. "We were in it early, but they just got away from us."

Things didn't really improve the following week when Ohio University came to town. The Gophers didn't lose, but they had to settle for a tie against a team they were favored to beat. There were 737 yards in total offense, thanks in large part to the Bobcats' quarterback, Cleve Bryant, and end Todd Snyder.

Ohio scored first, going 80 yards in 11 plays with Bryant sneaking in for the score. Jim Kensinger made the extra point kick. Walt Bowser took the kickoff 69 yards to the Bobcat 17 and Mayer went off tackle from the five a few plays later for the score. Nygren made the PAT.

A personal foul on Nygren aided the Ohio cause during a 79-yard, 12-play drive. Snyder took Bryant's pass from the four for the touchdown and the conversion was good.

In the second quarter, Jeff Wright took a punt at his 38 and went to the Bobcats' 19. Six plays later, Mayer scored from the one and the extra point kick knotted it at 14-14.

Carter followed with a short plunge for another touchdown on a 57-yard march which was highlighted by two key third down catches by Addison. The kick put Minnesota in front 21-14.

Back came the Bobcats. From their 37, they went to the five, thanks to runs by Dave Leveck and catches by Snyder. Harvey Mitchell scored on a five-yard run. The conversion tied the game.

The Gophers went ahead in the third quarter when Hagen scored from the one after a drive of 59 yards that used 12 plays.

Ohio followed suit with a drive that began at its 27. Thirteen plays later on a third-and-goal from the seven, Snyder made a dandy leaping catch of Bryant's pass for the score. It was 28-28 following Kensinger's extra point kick.

The Gophers retook the lead moving from their 26 to the Ohio 15 in five plays. Big runs by Carter for 36 and Mayer for 22 sparked the drive. From the 15, Hagen connected with Parson for the touchdown and it was Minnesota on top 35-28.

The only scoring in the fourth quarter was by Ohio. The Bobcats took the ball 65 yards in 15 plays. Bryant threw a 14-yard touchdown pass to Snyder and the extra point made the final score 35-35.

Warmath called Snyder and Bryant the best passing and catching combination he had ever seen. Bryant hit 18 of 27 passes for 194 yards and three TDs. Snyder caught the three touchdown throws and had 12 catches for 122 yards. Hagen was no slouch himself as he was 15 of 25 for 152 yards.

Things didn't get any easier the next week as Nebraska came to Memorial Stadium and left with a 42-14 victory. In the process they ran for 335 yards and passed for 256. The Gophers inability to execute the basics contributed to the Cornhusker victory.

"We didn't block or tackle," Warmath stated simply following the loss.

Actually, it was a close game in the first half in front of more than 52,000.

Hagen was hurt so Walt Bowser and sophomore Craig Curry handled the quarterback duties. Minnesota scored first on a four-yard run by Carter. The Cornhuskers came right back with Jeff Kinney throwing a halfback option pass of 12 yards to Guy Ingles.

In the second quarter, Nebraska looked like it was going to go ahead when it marched to the Gopher one. Jerry Tagge, the fine Nebraska quarterback, threw a flat pass to his right, but sophomore defensive back Gary Hohman stepped in front of the throw and it was clear sailing down the left sideline for 99 yards and the touchdown. The extra point by Nygren made it 14-7.

The Cornhuskers tied the game later in the quarter on a 36-yard pass from Tagge to Larry Frost.

It was all Nebraska in the second half. Kinney scored on a one-yard plunge and Frost gathered in another throw from Tagge, this time for 43 yards to make it 28-14. In the fourth, Kinney made another two-yard touchdown run and reserve back Jim Hughes scored from the 24.

"Their offensive line just killed us," moaned Warmath following the loss.

The Big Ten season opened the following week in Bloomington, Ind.

•    •    •

Nearly 51,000 attended the conference opener for the Gophers and the Hoosiers. Minnesota won the first half. Indiana won the game.

Mayer had scored on a 46-yard run midway through the second quarter. The Gopher defense had allowed Indiana only three first downs in the half. The second half belonged to the Hoosiers and halfback John Isenbarger, who had fumbled twice in the first half.

At the start of the fourth quarter, quarterback Harry Gonso threw a 49-yard TD pass to Larry Highbaugh and Don Warner made the point after to tie the score. On the first play after the kickoff, Bowser fumbled and Indiana recovered. Two plays later, Isenbarger went for 15 yards to the Minnesota five and scored on a sweep to the right on the next play. Warner added the extra point.

Late in the fourth quarter, George Kemp gave the Hoosiers another opportunity when he fumbled at the Gopher 15. Warner made a 27-yard field goal with 39 seconds left and the final was Indiana 17, Minnesota 7.

"We had too many turnovers in our end of the field," Warmath said.

"It was a terribly rough, but clean game," Gonso commented, undoubtedly referring to the 1968 game which ended with a major brawl between the teams.

Things didn't get any easier the next week when Ohio State, the defending national champions, paid a visit to the Gophers. Pegged as perhaps one of the greatest teams ever, the Buckeyes featured a gallery of stars, many of whom had taken Ohio State to the top with a resounding victory over Southern Cal and O.J. Simpson in the 1969 Rose Bowl. When the Buckeyes came to Minneapolis, they were ranked No. 1 and stayed there until upset by Michigan in the last game of the season.

Ohio State took advantage of five fumbles and survived 400 passing yards by Hagen to win 34-7. Jim Otis, the big, strong Buckeye fullback scored twice in the first quarter on runs of eight and two yards. After the first touchdown, Stan White was wide with his extra point kick. After the second, quarterback Rex Kern hit Larry Zalina for a two-point conversion.

In the second quarter, Kern was injured and his replacement, Kevin Rusnak, filled in nicely. After Mayer fumbled at the OSU 13, Rusnak engineered an 87-yard march for the third Buckeye score. It came on a 25-yard pass to end Bruce Jankowski. White again was wide with the point after.

Down 20-0 in the third quarter, Minnesota finally got a score after Rich Crawford, the Gopher linebacker, grabbed a Rusnak fumble in midair at the Gopher 21 and took it to the Buckeyes' 28. Carter scored from the six and Nygren kicked the extra point.

Ohio State scored twice in the fourth quarter. Leo Hayden got a touchdown from the seven and Ray Gilliam scored from the one. White made both extra point kicks.

"Our quickness was the difference," Hayes said following the game. "Minnesota, however, was as tough a team as we have played."

"I thought we had an outside chance to win, but they are extremely talented," Warmath said after Ohio State had won its 18th straight game. "It was a pleasure just to play them."

Although it wasn't known at the time, the Big Ten Champions of 1969 came to Memorial Stadium the next week. It was the first season for the team coached by Glenn "Bo" Schembechler and it was it was a game of two completely different halves.

In the first quarter, Nygren made a 25-yard field goal after a Michigan punt was partially blocked. Michigan came back in the second quarter and scored as quarterback Don Moorhead connected with halfback Billy Taylor for eight yards. Frank Titus made the extra point.

The Gophers got two more field goals. The first was by sophomore Mel Anderson. It was for 43 yards and a Minnesota record. The second was a 37-yarder with one second left in the half. It was set up when, with 23 seconds left, Bowser took a punt to the Minnesota 45. Passes to Parson and Kemp got the team in position for Anderson's successful attempt.

The 9-7 halftime lead didn't standup for long. Taylor scored twice for the Wolverines. The first was on a three-yard run to cap a 75-yard, 11-play drive. The second was the ninth play of a 66-yard march with Taylor scoring from the one. Titus made both conversions.

In the fourth quarter, Barry Pierson intercepted Hagen at the Minnesota 44 and brought it back three yards. Taylor went 21 on the first carry and four plays later Moorhead scored on a short keeper. The kick was good. Hagen was intercepted again at the Gopher 44, this time by Mike Taylor. Billy Taylor made another long run to the 21 and from the 10, Lance Scheffler went around left end for the score. The kick made the final score 35-9 in favor of Michigan.

"I'm not very proud of the way we played in the second half," Warmath said quietly afterward. "Michigan stopped us cold, especially our passing game, in the second half."

Hagen called the Wolverine blitz "very tough", adding they went after him "harder than any team all year."

The Gopher staff, off to a 0-5-1 start, the worst since 1958, knew a win was needed soon.

The Iowa game, marked by the play of Carter, Bowser and Mayer, ended the string of losses. Minnesota needed their strong play because the Gophers lost five fumbles.

It was an Iowa fumble, however, at the Minnesota 16 in the opening quarter recovered by Gopher defensive back Ron Anderson, that got things started. Minnesota went 84 yards in seven plays as Hagen threw passes to Kemp for 45 yards and Parson for 26. Carter scored from the three and Nygren's conversion gave Minnesota a 7-0 lead. In the second quarter, Iowa's Tom Smith fumbled and Crawford recovered at the Hawkeye 21. An interference call put the ball on the one and Carter scored. The kick was good by Nygren.

It stayed at 14-0 until the third quarter when Minnesota drove 64 yards in nine plays. Mayer's 28-yard run and Carter's 10-yard run and 14-yard pass reception highlighted a drive that took the Gophers to the one where Carter scored.

Trailing 21-0 in the fourth, Iowa gambled on fourth and seven from their 38. Kenny Reardon tried to run for the first down, but Crawford, Anderson, Leon Trawick and Bill Light stopped him back at his 27. Mayer's pass reception got to the one where Carter blasted through the line once more. The PAT was good.

Iowa finally scored after recovering Minnesota halfback Dick Humleker's fumble at the Gopher 46. Dennis Green (the Minnesota Viking coach) scored from the five and Mike Cilek passed to Dave Krull for the two-point conversion.

The Gophers scored once more when the reserves put together a 65-yard march in 10 plays. Quarterback Craig Curry passed to fellow sophomore, fullback Ernie Cook, for the TD. Nygren's fifth conversion of the day made it 35-8.

"I guess I was kinda ornery," Warmath responded when asked about the first Carter touchdown when a field goal might have been the more logical call. Clearly, Warmath wanted to win and had no hesitation about getting as many points as possible.

Carter, the team captain, said the victory "was long overdue. I don't know why we couldn't do this well earlier in the season."

Bowser had three interceptions and it was the first time he had played defense since coming to Minnesota.

Mayer continued to show his fine running, gaining 135 yards on 32 carries.

Warmath cited the play of Ron King, the younger brother of Wayne King, and fellow sophomore Bill Light, both of whom played good games at linebacker.

The Gophers continued their improved play the next week.

This time it was a sophomore contribution that was at the heart of Minnesota's triumph over visiting Northwestern.

Cook was the fullback for most of the game after Carter was hurt. Humleker substituted for Mayer, who had been hurt that week in practice and didn't dress for the game.

It was the Wildcats who struck first. Mike Adamle capped a 78-yard drive with a three-yard TD run. He also had runs of 14 and 15 yards in the march. The PAT by Bill Planisek was good.

Minnesota came back as Hagen completed two big passes— 19 yards to Humleker and four yards to Parson for the TD to end a 68-yard drive. A poor Northwestern punt gave Minnesota the ball at the Wildcat 39. Hagen found Parson for 23 yards and then Humleker for nine and the score. Nygren made the PAT.

Gary Hohman scored his second touchdown of the year when he intercepted Maury Daigneau at the Wildcats' 38 and went all the way for the touchdown.

After the kickoff, Adamle scored again as the Wildcats went 59 yards. Adamle had runs of 15 and 18 and then scored from the five. The kick was good.

In the third quarter, Northwestern tied the game when it scored in eight plays to cap a 71-yard march. The big gainer was when Daigneau hit Adamle with a 57-yard pass to the Gopher five. On fourth-and-goal from the one, Daigneau snuck for the score and Planisek's kick tied it at 21-all.

At the start of the fourth quarter, Minnesota's Trawick recovered a fumble by Mike Hudson at the Northwestern 49. It took eight plays, Cook's TD run from the six and Nygren's extra point kick to put Minnesota ahead for good at 28-21.

After the game, Cook pointed out that his choice of schools had come down to Minnesota and Northwestern. Earlier, he had been the first black offered a football scholarship at Florida State.

"But racial tensions flared up and my parents urged me to go somewhere where things were much better for blacks. I chose Minnesota in large part because of Coach Warmath and Minnesota's fine medical school," said Cook who today is a physician practicing in Daytona Beach, Fla.

Cook had made 141 yards on 25 carries that day and Humleker added 74 in 14 rushes.

"Parson was gutsy," Warmath pointed out. "He played on a bad leg that most people couldn't walk on. I also was very pleased with our line play today."

At Michigan State the following Saturday, nothing much happened for three quarters. Neither team could capitalize on the other's turnovers. Minnesota had only 24 yards and two first downs in the first 30 minutes while Michigan State was slightly better with six first downs and 105 total yards.

State finally took advantage of a break, with just 44 seconds left in the third quarter. Bill Dawson blocked a Walt Bowser punt after Minnesota stalled at its 30. The ball bounced backward where his teammate, Rich Saul, grabbed it at the 12 and ran into the end zone. The kick was good.

A break for Minnesota at the start of the fourth quarter helped even the score. Forced to punt, the ball was fumbled by the Spartans' Jay Breslin and Steve Thompson recovered at the 26. Two passes by Hagen got the Gophers on the scoreboard. The first was to halfback John Marquesen for 10 yards and then the 16-yarder to Terry Addison for the score. Nygren tied it with his extra point kick.

The Spartans drove to the Gopher four, but had to settle for a 21-yard field goal by Gary Boyce.

A State miscue on a Gopher punt put Minnesota in front. Eric Allen was hit by Parson after fielding the ball and he fumbled at the Minnesota 46 where Bill Christison fell on it. Several plays later, Hagen found Parson at the nine. The big end broke a tackle and went into the end zone. Nygren made it 14-10.

State drove to the Minnesota four after returning the kick to its 30. With a little over three minutes left, they went for the Gopher end zone. Don Highsmith got one yard. On second down, he was stopped for no gain. On third down, Ron Slank was hit by Hohman and Trawick for a one-yard loss and the fourth down pass by Spartan quarterback Bill Triplett was intercepted by Hohman. The Gophers ran out the clock.

"We were strong when we had to be and our defense won the game," a happy Warmath said after the close win. "The goal line stand at the end was the obvious difference in the game."

Hagen was only six of 22 in the passing game, but had the two touchdown throws.

"The cold weather made it tough to throw," pointed out the senior Minnesota quarterback.

An unhappy Duffy Daughtery said his team "should never have lost this game. We gave it away."

Minnesota added to their three-game winning streak the last game of the season when they hosted Wisconsin and won 35-10 in front of less than 41,000 spectators. Mayer rushed for 216 yards in 30 carries and Cook scored three times.

In the first quarter, Hagen hit Hamm for 20 yards and a touchdown on the first possession of the game, a drive of 67 yards in just six plays. Roger Jaeger kicked a 29-yard field goal for the Badgers to make it 7-3 after Minnesota had missed a similar chance earlier from the Wisconsin 20.

In the second quarter, Cook scored from the one. Mayer had runs of seven, 10 and 12 yards and Parson made a nine-yard reception in the drive that started at the Minnesota 36. Cook scored again, this time from eight yards out following a 20-yard pass to Parson. The drive started with Minnesota taking over at the Wisconsin 28 following a terrible Badger punt from the 16. Nygren made the extra point and it was 21-3.

Wisconsin cut it to 21-10 when Alan Thompson went in from the two to finish a nine-play, 68-yard march. Stu Voigt's two pass receptions of 24 and 15 yards were the big gainers in the drive.

There was 1:23 left in the third quarter when Cook returned the Badger kickoff to the Gopher 40. Mayer made 19 yards on two runs and Craig Curry came in at quarterback and went for 12 yards on a keeper. Hagen hit Marquesen at the Badger eight and got an additional four yards when a personal foul was called on Wisconsin. Cook scored his third TD and Nygren made it 28-10 with the extra point kick.

The only other score came in the fourth quarter when Nate Butler of Wisconsin fumbled a punt at his 15 and Gopher lineman Vern Winfield recovered. Curry scored and Nygren split the uprights to make the final 35-10.

"We were a good November team," Warmath said referring to the four straight victories during the month. "Today, the late first-half touchdown really helped us."

Mayer, who had missed the Northwestern and Michigan State games, said his runs off tackle behind the weakside pulling guard were working all afternoon.

"We could run Mayer against their 5-3 defense," added Hagen who had played his last game as a Gopher.

304

# Thirty-Five

Besides Hagen, Minnesota graduated Carter, Kemp, Parson, Trawick, Nygren, Curtis, Pribyl, Pahula, Christison and Wrobel.

Minnesota opened the 1970 season in a nationally-televised game against Missouri from Columbia. The game turned out to be "The Joe Moore Show" as the speedy Missouri halfback ran for three touchdowns and 156 yards in the 34-12 win over the Gophers.

Minnesota took the early lead on a hot September Saturday. In the opening minutes, linebacker Bill Light intercepted a Missouri pass at the Tigers 12 and took it to the nine. From there, quarterback Craig Curry passed to fullback Ernie Cook in the corner of the end zone for the score. The point after attempt by Mel Anderson was blocked. Later in the period, Louis Clare, a sophomore from Mississauga, Ontatio, kicked a 32-yard field goal and the Gophers were ahead 9-0.

The score remained 9-0 until the third quarter when Bowser had his 53-yard punt returned 39 yards by Missouri's Mike Fink to the Gopher 40. Moore carried six out of the eight plays that followed and his two-yard plunge made it 9-6. The extra point kick was wide.

Clare nailed another field goal, this one from the Missouri 28, which came at the end of a drive that started at the Gopher 25. Curry had connected on passes of 29 and 18 yards along the way.

Missouri made a big play on fourth and five at the Minnesota 36. Mel Gray, the Tiger speedster (9.2 in the 100 yard dash), took a pitch out and went all the way for the score. Jack Bastable kicked the conversion to make it 13-12. In the fourth quarter, a short punt by Bowser gave Missouri possession at the Minnesota

39. It took five plays to reach the one where Moore dove for the touchdown. The kick was good and it was 20-12 for Missouri.

After another short punt by Bowser, Moore was in the end zone a few plays later. This TD came on a 13-yard run. The point after was good. Curry added to the mistakes with a fumble at his 30. A few plays later, Bill Mauer capitalized on the break when he scored from the one. The successful kick made the final 34-12.

After the game, the Minnesota players complained that the heat had gotten to them in the second half, an excuse that didn't sit well with Warmath. "We should be stronger in the second half," he stated emphatically.

Ron King said the run by Gray seemed to "take the heart out of us."

"We adjusted our defense at the halftime and that's what won it for us," said Missouri coach Dan Devine.

The next week back in Minneapolis, Memorial Stadium debuted its new artificial surface. Heralded as not only a means by which to reduce maintenance, it also was supposed to make the game faster (it did) and reduce injuries (it clearly didn't).

Regardless, the Gophers enjoyed the first time they played on it as they routed Ohio University 49-7 in front of a crowd of approximately 39,000. It was the running game that prevailed as Minnesota had the ball for 77 plays and only threw 10 passes. The Gophers got 35 first downs, a new school record. It was also the most points ever for a Warmath team.

In the first quarter, Mike White of the Gophers intercepted Steve Skiver at the Ohio 44. Ten plays later, Cook went in from the two and Clare made the conversion. Clare scored a touchdown himself on a 16-yard run later in the period to cap a 10-play drive which had begun at the Minnesota 22.

In the second quarter, Minnesota got the ball at its two after stopping the Bobcats on a fourth-down play. Ten plays later, Curry kept the ball from the 19 and went in for the touchdown.

Mayer's 39 yards in four rushes led the drive. Then with two minutes to go in the period, Minnesota went 70 yards in seven plays with Curry connecting to end Bart Buetow from eight yards out and the touchdown. Curry's run for 26 and pass to John Marquesen for 19, were keys to the march. It was 28-0 at the half.

In the third quarter, Mayer scored on a 21-yard scamper after Minnesota started at its 31. With a little less than six minutes left, Humleker scored from the six. He had an earlier run of 21 and reserve quarterback Bob Morgan had two keepers totaling 19 yards.

The final Minnesota score came in the fourth quarter following an Ohio touchdown by Bill Gary of two yards. Late in the game, Minnesota's Mike Perfetti intercepted a pass at the Bobcats' 43. From there, it took 10 plays to reach the five where Morgan scored on a fourth-down keeper.

"The turning point was the opening kickoff," said Bobcat coach Bill Hess. "We were outplayed and outcoached."

"We had the size and strength to wear them down," Warmath added.

Curry said the Gopher offense was able to move up the middle and captain Jeff Wright pointed out the team was ready to make up for the Missouri loss.

Nebraska still was on the schedule and when the Cornhuskers came to town it was more of the same as far as Minnesota was concerned.

The Cornhuskers scored on the opening drive as they moved the ball from their 23 to the Gopher four in nine plays. From there, sophomore halfback Johnny Rodgers went in for the score. The kick was good.

Minnesota got its first score two series later. After taking over at its 49, Mayer got six and then Cook ran right up the middle for 45 yards and the touchdown. Clare made the point after to tie the game. Late in the quarter, Buetow fumbled at the Gopher 34 and Nebraska recovered. From the 14, Joe Orduna hit Guy Ingles for the score on a halfback pass. The kick was good.

Early in the second quarter, Clare made a 35-yard field goal, but Nebraska came back thanks in part to a 25-yard pass to Rodgers. Tagge snuck into the end zone from the one. The final touchdown came in the fourth quarter when the Cornhuskers marched 59 yards in 16 plays and Tagge passed to Ingles from the three for the score. The kick made the final score 35-10.

"Rodgers is the best sophomore I've seen in years," Warmath observed following the game.

The fleet Nebraska back praised his line for opening "huge holes" and Tagge said even though beaten, "Minnesota hit hard."

The Big Ten season opened the following week in Minneapolis against Indiana as Minnesota posted its first shutout in 27 games thanks to six pass interceptions and two fumble recoveries.

In the first quarter, Indiana got to the Gopher 22, as far as the Hoosiers would get all day. Wright stopped the drive when he intercepted a pass. Later, Bowser put Indiana back at its 16 with a long punt. Defensive back Ron Anderson dropped Hoosier quarterback Greg Brown for a loss at the one and then tackle Steve Goldberg nailed Indiana halfback Rick Thompson in the end zone for a safety.

Following the free kick, which Bowser brought back to the Indiana 32, Minnesota scored in three plays as Mayer ran in from the 24 on a pitchout. Clare made the extra point.

In the second quarter, Curry scored from the one after leading a drive that began at the Gopher 47. He threw to wide receiver George Honza for 32 yards on a third-and-11 and then to Buetow for 10 yards to get the Gophers into scoring position. Clare's kick was good.

Minnesota's last score came in the fourth quarter when Wright picked off another throw at the Hoosiers' 34 and took it to the nine. Curry scored in two carries, Clare made the extra point and the final was 23-0.

Along with Wright, Bowser and Bill Light had two interceptions apiece.

"We forced the mistakes today," a pleased Warmath said. "We established our defense early and played very well."

Bowser said the defensive line rush was the main reason for the interceptions and Curry was pleased that the option worked well all day.

Indiana coach John Pont called his team's play "a comedy of errors."

The next week in Columbus, it was Ohio State that established itself early. The Buckeyes scored the first four times they had the ball and then sat back and finished the day with a 28-8 victory before 86,667.

"It was the best first half we have ever played at Ohio State," Woody Hayes stated later.

In the first quarter, Rex Kern scored from the seven after an 80-yard drive that used 11 plays. The second Buckeye score came after forcing Minnesota to punt and then marching from the Gophers' 41. The touchdown came on John Brockington's one-yard plunge.

Brockington came right back on the next possession and tore through the Minnesota defense for a 62-yard touchdown run.

At the start of the second quarter, Mike Sensibaugh intercepted a Curry pass at the Buckeye 12 and returned it the his 33. Kern got the fourth Ohio State score on a 10-yard run. Fred Schram made his fourth consecutive extra point kick and it was 28-0.

Minnesota played well in the second half and got the only score when it went 92 yards in 14 plays. The touchdown came on an 11-yard pass from Curry to Kevin Hamm following earlier completions to Marquesen and tight ends Doug Kingsriter and Jim Brunzell. The two-point play was good.

Warmath called Ohio State "a wonderful team that simply executes beautifully. I was proud of our kids because even though we were outmanned, we didn't quit and that showed in the second half."

309

Hayes praised Warmath and Minnesota. "They were tough and actually wore us down in the second half."

· · ·

Things didn't get any easier the next week when Minnesota traveled to Michigan.

Unlike the setback at Ohio State, the Gophers stayed close until late in the third quarter.

Billy Taylor, who had created havoc in 1969 when Michigan beat Minnesota in Minneapolis, scored first. In the opening quarter, he went in from the 17 on a run up the middle. It came on the fifth play of a 44-yard drive. Tim Killian missed the extra point try.

The Wolverines scored again on the first play of the second quarter when Fritz Seyferth went in from the three after Michigan got the ball at the Gophers' 36 following a Curry fumble. Rich Crawford batted down the two-point pass by quarterback Don Moorhead.

Doug Kingsriter came through on the ensuing drive for Minnesota. The march went 80 yards in just eight plays, thanks to his two great catches. The first was for 45 yards when he pulled the ball away from defender Tom Darden. A few plays later, Kingsriter made a fabulous one-handed touchdown catch of 16 yards. Clare made it 12-7 with his kick.

Michigan increased the lead when they went 80 yards in 10 plays. Moorhead ran for 39 on a keeper and Seyferth scored from the four. A running play for the two points was stopped short.

The Wolverines made it 25-7 in the final quarter when Darden intercepted a throw by Curry at the Gopher 37. Seven plays later, Seyferth scored for the third time on a four-yard run. Dana Coin kicked the extra point.

Seyferth scored again on a six-yard run to finish off a 65-yard drive. Minnesota scored on a 74-yard march as Curry hit four passes and then gave to Cook, who ran for the score from the four. A two-point attempt failed.

310

The last touchdown came when Michigan's Lance Scheffler scored from the two following Jim Betts' interception of Curry at the Gophers' 30. Coin's extra point kick made the final 39-13.

"Michigan's last touchdown of the half was the turning point," Warmath pointed out. "It would have been a lot better to be down by five rather than 11 at that stage of the game. We were outplayed in every department today."

Warmath said he felt Michigan was the equal of Ohio State.

Things stayed sour the next week with a 14-14 tie with Iowa. It was a cold, damp day in Minneapolis with over 51,000 in the stands as Iowa won the battle of the stats by getting 369 yards in total offense to just 190 for Minnesota. Both teams had a lot of penalties and turnovers.

Minnesota scored in the first quarter on a Curry-to-Kingsriter pass from the 10 which was set up earlier on an interception by Light. Clare made the PAT.

Not until the third quarter was there another score. The Gophers got the ball at the Iowa 40 after forcing the Hawkeyes to punt from their five. In seven plays (and with the help of two major penalties) Minnesota went ahead 14-0 following a one-yard quarterback sneak by Curry and Clare's extra point kick.

The Hawkeyes, however, came back. In the fourth quarter, fullback Tim Sullivan led a 17-play drive from the Iowa 30 in which every play was a run. He scored from the one and Marcos Melendez made the extra point. A 34-yard run by Levi Mitchell was the big play in the following drive of 56 yards. Sullivan rammed it in from the one and the kick was good to make it 14-14.

The Iowa coach, Ray Nagel, said Minnesota was outplayed and he felt his team should have won.

Warmath agreed, citing the good Hawkeye line play.

"I'm baffled," said Wright. "We appeared to have it locked up and then let it get away in the fourth quarter."

At Northwestern the next week, things didn't improve. A solid Wildcat team, behind Mike Adamle, beat Minnesota 28-14.

311

The Gophers again blew a 14-0 lead. Wright blocked a punt by Marty McCann and Mike White returned it 38 yards for a touchdown. Later, Curry capped a 72-yard march by scoring from the four. In that series, Mayer went down for the rest of the season with a dislocated shoulder.

Northwestern rallied in the second quarter when a 93-yard, 16-play drive ended on Adamle's one-yard TD plunge. Adamle scored again on a one-yard run in the third quarter after a 14-play drive of 80 yards. A Marty Daigneau-to-Barry Pearson pass of 22 yards was the key play that came on third down at the Gopher 29. Bill Planisek's kick tied the game.

In the fourth quarter, Adamle added his third and fourth TDs. The first was a one-yard run to finish a 77-yard drive and the other a five-yard run. The final was 28-14.

"Fumbles again," Warmath said in looking back on the loss. "We're also beat up pretty bad. Besides Mayer, we lost Cook and White for big chunks of the game as well."

He called Adamle one of the "great backs in the country."

Adamle felt Northwestern's overall speed was the difference and his coach, Alex Agase, said he had a good team that seemed to know how to come back when down.

If Warmath and his team needed anything now it was a "Michigan State fix". The Spartans came to town the following Saturday and Warmath had an outstanding record against Duffy Daugherty. He had beaten him in six consecutive games and eight of the 10 times they had played since 1954. He added to that dominance in 1970 with a 23-13 victory in front of nearly 43,000.

Clare got Minnesota on the scoreboard first with a 23-yard field goal to finish the opening drive. Then in the second quarter, Bowser intercepted Mike Rasmussen at the Gopher 30 and took it to the Spartans' 47. Cook went in from the one and Clare hit the PAT to make it 10-0.

In the third quarter, it was Bowser again who was the defensive hero. State was driving and at the 18, halfback Eric

Allen was hit and the ball popped up in midair. Bowser grabbed the ball at the line of scrimmage before it hit the ground and went 82 yards for the score followed by a group of whooping and cheering teammates. The kick was wide.

State came back and Allen scored from the two. The big play in the 54-yard drive was a 20-yard, third-down pass from Rasmussen to tight end Billy Joe DuPree. The point after by Borys Shlapak was good.

In the fourth quarter, Wright picked off an Allen halfback option pass in the end zone. From the 20, Minnesota drove for a touchdown in nine plays. Curry hit Kingsriter for 44 of those yards. Cook scored from the one and Clare's extra point kick made it 23-7. The Spartans scored later on a two-yard sweep by Earl Anderson. Wright knocked down the two-point pass attempt.

The Gopher team gave game balls to Mayer and Warmath with Wright calling the Gopher mentor "the best coach in the land." Warmath was moved, calling the gesture one of the most gratifying moments in his football career.

Wright called his three interceptions part of the best game he had played. Bowser pointed out that the return of the Allen fumble was his first TD as a Gopher. Cook was excited because his father had seen him play college ball for the first time.

Several of the players said they wanted the win for Warmath because there were some negative comments by the local media since the team had only won twice coming into the game.

Now the task was to sustain the momentum at Wisconsin.

For the first time in eight seasons, neither team was in the upper division of the Big Ten. Wisconsin, however, played like they should have been.

The Badgers amassed 477 total yards as quarterback Neil Graff passed for 191 yards, completing 11 of 19 passes. The Gophers struck first, however, when they recovered a fumbled punt by Wisconsin's Neovia Greyer at the 11. Cook scored the touchdown a few plays later from the one. Clare made the conversion kick. Graff tied the game, scoring on a one-yard run and the PAT was good.

A Marquesen fumble at the 25 on the first play from scrimmage of the second half, set up a Graff-to-Larry Mialik touchdown pass from the six. The conversion attempt was no good.

Graff hit Albert Hannah for a 23-yard touchdown after Curry had fumbled at the Minnesota 44. A two-point attempt failed.

Minnesota narrowed it to 19-14 at the start of the fourth quarter when Curry connected with Hamm for 42 yards and a touchdown. Minnesota had started at its 17 and Kingsriter had two 12-yard catches in the drive.

After that, it was all Wisconsin. First, Rufus Ferguson scored from the 29. Then, on a fake punt, end Terry Whitaker scored on a 27-yard pass. Minnesota moved to the Badger 34, but was stopped. Wisconsin drove, ate up time in the final drive and Lance Moon scored from the one. The final was 39-14.

"Nothing seemed to go right this year," said Wright in a quiet locker room. It was pointed out that Tim Alderson, the regular defensive cornerback for the Gophers was hurt in pre-game warmups and the only person to play his position was Mike White, himself hobbled by a bad hamstring pull. White was not at full speed and it showed when Graff connected with Hannah for 52 yards on the critical third-down play which set up Ferguson's 29-yard TD run in the early minutes of the fourth quarter. Until then, Minnesota was in the game.

The Gophers finished 3-6-1. The Wisconsin victory landed the Badgers a fifth-place finish in the Big Ten standings. Minnesota was seventh. It had been that kind of year.

# Thirty-Six

The 1971 season was to be Warmath's 18th—and last—at Minnesota. There was some speculation in the local media that he might step down once the season concluded. If that was the case, he never let on to anyone publicly. Privately it was his intent to keep on coaching in the game he loved.

Warmath went into that fall's campaign facing a new challenge: an eleven game schedule. He wasn't alone. Most of the big time schools had expanded their seasons. In a peculiar twist of scheduling, which was to last through 1976, Minnesota opened against a Big Ten team, in this case Indiana.

The game was at home and on a beautiful day, played before a sparse crowd of 28,459.

The Gophers took advantage of good field position, getting the ball four times inside the Hoosiers' 30 and turned each possession into a touchdown. In turn, they held Indiana to just 109 yards rushing. Mike Perfetti averaged 45 yards a punt with one going 65 yards.

The Hoosiers' Rich Hoffman fumbled on the second play of the game and Perfetti pounced on the ball at the 30. Curry, who would finish the season as the Big Ten's total offensive yardage leader, hit tight end Kingsriter for a 17-yard pass on the drive that culminated with Ernie Cook scoring from the one. Mel Anderson kicked the point after.

In the second quarter, another Hoosier fumble set up the next Minnesota score. Winfield jarred the ball loose from Dan Linter and Todd Randall fell on it at the Hoosier 12. An 11-yard pass to Kingsriter from Curry was good for the touchdown. Anderson converted. The Gophers created another opportunity when end

Tom Chandler blocked a punt which Scott Irwin recovered at the Indiana 17. Three plays later, Curry connected with Kevin Hamm for a 13-yard score. Anderson again was good with the extra point kick.

In the third quarter, Minnesota defensive back Alderson intercepted Greg Brown's pass at the Gopher 21 and returned it 53 yards to the Hoosier 26. Curry connected on two straight passes, the first to Hamm for 15 yards and the second to Cook for 11 yards and the touchdown. The PAT was good. Minnesota won 28-0.

Curry praised the Gopher defensive unit for getting the ball in such good field position.

Despite the victory, Warmath pointed to many mistakes and speculated that those would have to be corrected if the Gophers were to have any chance the following Saturday in Lincoln against the defending national champion Nebraska Cornhuskers.

Minnesota went to Lincoln to face what many experts now consider perhaps the greatest college team in history. The Cornhuskers would go on to win their second consecutive national championship that year. They were loaded with players such as backs Johnny Rodgers and Jeff Kinney, quarterback Jerry Tagge and linemen Rich Glover and Larry Jacobson.

A crowd of just over 68,000 was on hand. They saw Nebraska wear down Minnesota for the victory, but not without a fight.

Midway through the first quarter, Rodgers caught a 28-yard touchdown pass from Tagge to finish a drive that started at the 50. Rich Sauger made the point after. Five plays later, Minnesota fumbled at its 20 and in five plays Nebraska went ahead 14-0 following Kinney's short touchdown run and Sauger's kick.

Minnesota came back in the second quarter when it went from its 22 and scored in 14 plays. Junior halfback Jim Henry ran for the touchdown from the six. Runs of 22 yards by Curry and 21 yards by Cook sparked the drive. Anderson made the extra point.

The Gophers looked as if they were going to even things up when they put together a drive that reached the Nebraska 10. But, Curry was thrown for a three-yard loss, a pass attempt was incomplete and Anderson missed a 27-yard field goal attempt.

Taking over at their 20, the Cornhuskers scored in just seven plays. Tagge connected with Jerry List for 22 yards and Tagge found Kinney at the Gopher 43 where Bill Light was called for face masking. After a 17-yard completion to Woody Cox and Kinney's 10-yard run, Kinney scored from the one. Sauger's kick made it 21-7.

In the third quarter, Rodgers broke three tackles after receiving a halfback option toss from Kinney at the Gopher 20 and went into the end zone. Later in the quarter, Tagge found Rodgers, this time for 37 yards and the fifth Nebraska touchdown. It was just the fourth play on a drive of 80 yards that was highlighted by a 25-yard screen pass to Rodgers. Sauger's PAT kick made the final score 35-7.

"I honestly felt we played with more spirit and were more together today than was the case against Indiana," Warmath said following the game. "However, penalties killed us and with such great talent as Tagge and Rodgers, you simply can't afford to do that. I'd like to play them again because I think we'd give them a much better game."

Warmath felt the third touchdown, the one with the face mask penalty on Light, killed the Gophers.

Light, the 1971 captain, said the Gophers would stop the run, but then give up the big pass play.

"Minnesota was tough against the run," Bob Devaney concurred, "so we thought we'd take advantage against their rather inexperienced secondary and we did."

The Gophers returned home to face Washington State.

The Gophers were clear favorites against the Cougars, who were winless in their last 11 games. At the start of the second quarter, it took just six plays for the Cougars to get the first score when they went 75 yards. The touchdown came when halfback

Bernard Jackson scampered 16 yards into the end zone. Don Sweet made the conversion.

George Honza took the kickoff to the Minnesota 42 and then caught a 53-yard throw from Curry. On the next play, Curry passed to Hamm for the touchdown and Clare evened the score with the extra point kick.

Washington State came back and scored twice before the half. First, it went 69 yards in five plays with quarterback Ty Paine passing 30 yards to Jackson for the touchdown. Then, following a Jim Henry fumble at the Washington State 34, Paine scored from the two. Sweet converted after both touchdowns.

Minnesota scored twice in the third quarter. Alderson returned a punt 28 yards to the WSU 30. Cook made one run of 13 to set up Curry's one-yard TD sneak. Clare made the PAT. A 61-yard Gopher scoring drive followed with Curry passing from the two to Marquesen in the end zone on the 11th play of the series. The Gophers decided to go for two, but Curry's pass to Cook was overthrown.

The Gophers let the game get away from them when with less than two minutes gone in the fourth quarter, Sweet made a 38-yard field goal. On the next series, Curry was intercepted by Tom Poe at the Gopher 26 and went the rest of the way for the touchdown. Suddenly, it was 31-20.

That's where the score stayed. The Gophers later drove to the Cougar seven but Chuck Hawthorne intercepted a Curry pass in the end zone.

The Gophers were stunned.

"They have very good speed," muttered Warmath. "That, and our mistakes, were the difference."

"I've never been hit so hard," moaned Curry.

Jim Sweeney, the Washington State coach, said his team made no major mistakes and hit short passes to the backs coming out of the backfield.

Earlier in the season, the Cougars lost to Kansas 34-0. Kansas was Minnesota's next opponent.

"Minnesota won because they intimidated Kansas."

That was one post-game observation on the 38-20 Gopher victory over the Jayhawks. It was offered by O.J. Simpson, who was in the Twin Cities for the Buffalo Bills game against the Minnesota Vikings the next day.

The Gophers did indeed dominate a good Kansas team. Minnesota scored early. First it was Cook from the three followed by Anderson's PAT. The Gophers had come 73 yards in six plays which featured a 19-yard quarterback sneak by Curry and an 18-yard pass reception by Marquesen. Later in the quarter, Curry hit Honza for a 29-yard scoring toss to cap a drive that started at the Minnesota 49. The PAT was good.

The Jayhawks came back and showed they could move the ball quickly. From their 25, they struck in just four plays, the clincher being Steve Conley's one-yard run. Dave Heck threw two big passes in the drive, a 15-yarder to Marvin Foster that saw another 15 yards tacked on for roughing, then a 40-yarder to Bob Brueggmo at the one. Bob Helmbacher made the point after.

In the second quarter, the Gophers expanded their lead when Paul Wright, the brother of Jeff Wright, took a punt to the Kansas 44. Cook's 24-yard run to the Kansas 12 was followed by a Marquesen catch at the four. Curry went around end for the touchdown and the PAT gave Minnesota a 21-7 halftime advantage.

In the third quarter, Minnesota showed it could sustain a long drive as the Maroon and Gold went 82 yards in 17 plays. Henry scored from the two and it was 28-7.

Conley came back with a 26-yard TD run up the middle set up by a Heck pass to John Schroll for 33 yards. The point after kick made it 28-14.

In the fourth quarter, Anderson made a 35-yard field goal for Minnesota. This was followed by a Kansas attempt to go for it on fourth down at the Minnesota 37. The attempt failed and the Gophers drove to the Kansas 17. On fourth down, Curry went around left end for the touchdown. The PAT was good. Kansas marched 75 yards for the final score with Conley going the final yard.

"We were determined to win," Light said in the Gopher locker room. "We knew Kansas was a good team and it would take a mistake-free game to win."

Kingsriter pointed out that Minnesota did not turn the ball over and added that "the score at the start of the third quarter really helped us."

Don Fambrough, the Jayhawk coach, said "the Gopher line just whipped us."

The Big Ten season picked up again in West Lafayette the next week and Minnesota left with its Big Ten record at 1-1.

Quarterback Gary Danielson's passed for more than 300 yards in Purdue's 28-13 victory.

Minnesota scored first in the opening quarter when a bad snap sailed over the punter's head and the Gophers got the ball at the opposition's 41. Curry found Kingsriter in the end zone for a seven-yard touchdown scoring pass. Three series later, Darryl Stingley scored on a run from the two to finish an 80-yard march.

In the second quarter, Purdue struck suddenly on a 76-yard pass from Danielson to Stingley, who got a break when the field judge, Dick Walterhouse, stepped in front of Gopher defender Paul Wright and blocked his path to Stingley. This brought howls of protest from Warmath and his staff, but to no avail. Purdue missed the PAT try.

Minnesota then went from its 32 in 14 plays to score as Curry went in from the two for the TD. The drive featured two pass receptions by sophomore tight end Keith Fahnhorst.

Anderson's point after kick was partially deflected and no good.

With just nine seconds left in the half, Danielson scored on a 19-yard scramble. Purdue began the drive from its 12.

In the second half, Minnesota never got untracked offensively and it was a third-quarter bomb of 66 yards from Danielson to Rick Sayers that sealed Minnesota's fate. The touchdown at the end of the first half clearly had hurt the Gophers' chances.

The Gophers were on the road again the next week in Iowa City. More than 51,500 watched Ernie Cook have a banner day against the Hawkeyes. The senior fullback rushed for 175 yards in 33 carries and scored two touchdowns in a 19-14 Minnesota victory.

The Hawkeyes scored first when Frank Sunderman threw a three-yard scoring pass to Don Osby on the 11th play of a 90-yard march in the second quarter. Osby had caught two other passes earlier for a total of 56 yards. Harry Kokolus kicked the extra point.

Mel Anderson then made two field goals before the quarter ended. The first, a 28-yarder, was set up on Cook's 27-yard run. Then with one second left in the half, Anderson made a 40-yard field goal. It capped a drive that started at the Gopher four. Passes from Curry to Hamm and Honza got the ball into field goal position.

In the third quarter, Perfetti put Iowa deep in a hole with a 60-yard punt. The Gophers got the ball back at the Hawkeye 42 and Cook scored his first touchdown on a short burst off tackle. Anderson's PAT made it 13-7 for the Gophers.

In the fourth quarter, the Gophers let Iowa off the hook. Following two sacks of Sunderman which forced Iowa into a third-and-26 from its 30, the Hawkeye quarterback passed to Jerry Reardon for 70 yards and a touchdown. The PAT gave the Hawkeyes a one point lead.

Iowa got the ball back, but Gopher defensive end Steve Neils nailed Sunderman and caused a fumble that tackle Scott Irwin recovered at the Iowa 28. Cook went for 10 and was aided by a piling-on call. From the seven, the Gopher fullback hit the line four times and scored. The PAT attempt was no good, but Minnesota led 19-14.

Iowa got as far as the Gopher 40 late in the game, but Sunderman fumbled while attempting to scramble on a fourth-down play and Minnesota recovered to end the game.

"Coach Warmath always tells us to take the fight to the other team," Cook said in a post-game interview. "We did just that."

Warmath cited not only Cook, but the defensive line play and Anderson and Perfetti's kicking as critical to the victory.

•    •    •

The Gophers faced four tough Big Ten opponents the next four weeks and the results were disheartening.

Michigan was Minnesota's homecoming opponent and the Wolverines were loaded and went on to win the Big Ten title. Once again it was Billy Taylor, the fine Wolverine halfback, who took it to the Gophers for the third straight year. More than 44,000 watched him lead his team to a 35-7 win.

In the first quarter, Taylor made a four-yard touchdown run to end a Michigan drive that started at its 26.

In the second quarter, trailing 7-0, Minnesota scored on a pass when Curry found Honza on a short post pattern behind the Michigan secondary. From the 27, Curry connected with Honza at the Minnesota 40 and the Gopher receiver outran his pursuers for the score. Anderson tied the game at 7-7.

Fritz Seyferth scored from the one to cap an 80-yard Michigan drive that stayed strictly on the ground. In 14 plays, Seyferth, Taylor, Glen Dougherty and Ed Shuttlesworth pounded the Gopher defense to take a 14-7 lead.

In the third quarter, Gopher Tom Waltower fumbled at the Minnesota 19. It took just three plays for the Wolverines to get into the end zone. All three plays featured runs by Taylor, who scored from the four. The kick was good by Dana Coin.

In the fourth quarter, Minnesota made a bid to get back in the game when Paul Wright intercepted Larry Cipa's pass at the Gopher 27 and took it to the Michigan nine. But the Wolverines pushed Minnesota back to the 18, then took over on downs.

Twelve plays later, Dougherty went the final 11 yards around right end for the touchdown. With 2:47 left in the game, Michigan scored one more time when a bad lateral fell into the Wolverines' hands at the 16. Cipa passed to Larry Gustafson from the five for the TD.

"Michigan is simply a better team than we are," Warmath said matter-of-factly. "They had the ball nearly twice as much as we did and that always kills you."

"This is sorta' a homecoming for me," said Taylor. "It was here two years ago that I got my first chance to really play." In three games against the Gophers, he had rushed for 151, 151 and 168 yards.

Ohio State was next on the Gopher schedule. Although, the 1971 version of the Buckeyes was not the caliber of the OSU teams of the previous three years (30-2, two Big Ten titles and one national championship), they still were a team with talent.

There was no scoring in the first quarter before a crowd of a little more than 36,000. In the second period, Minnesota recovered a fumbled punt at the Ohio State 31. Curry threw two incompletions and then, scrambling to avoid the Buckeyes' rush, found Kingsriter in the end zone for the score. Anderson was wide with the PAT attempt.

In the third quarter, Ohio State went from its 20 to the Gopher four where it faced fourth and goal. Quarterback Don Lamka hit Dick Wakefield for the touchdown and Fred Schram's extra point kick gave the Buckeyes a one-point lead.

Minnesota looked as if it had stopped a Buckeye drive in the fourth quarter when Farrell Sheridan intercepted a pass, but there was an interference call on Wright on the play so the ball stayed in Ohio State's hands. Rich Galbos scored from the four and Shram made the PAT and it was 14-6.

Then came the critical point in the game. There were less than four minutes left when Minnesota started at its 20. Curry passed to Anderson at the Ohio State 44. Cook ran to the 25. A pass to Kingsriter got to the 13 and a third-down pass for five yards to Cook went to the two. From there, Curry ran an option to the left and skirted the end for the score. It was 14-12 with time slipping away and there was obviously only one choice. The Gophers went for the tie.

Curry ran the same leftside option and appeared to some to just inch the ball over the goal line when hit by a couple of Ohio State defenders. There were no officials right on top of the play and as those nearest rushed up, they signaled that Curry had been stopped short. Minnesota protested the call, but the game ended with Ohio State the two-point victor.

Curry was in tears afterward. "I made it, I made it", he kept saying.

Kingsriter was also crying. "The officials were there too late. Craig was pushed back after getting over. They blew it."

Warmath avoided any comments on the call, instead citing the second Ohio State touchdown in the fourth quarter. "We let them drive 80 yards on us into the wind. If we would have held them early, we would have forced a kick into the wind."

Woody Hayes, meanwhile, praised the Gophers, especially the defense.

"I can't remember the last time we were held to only 135 yards rushing," the venerable Buckeye coach added.

A regional television audience and more than 31,000 at Dyche Stadium in Evanston, watched Northwestern beat Minnesota for the second year in a row.

Penalties and fumbles again stopped the Gophers. Al Robinson scored in the first quarter from the one to finish a 63-yard drive in 11 plays. Roger Planiskek made the PAT. In the second quarter, Terry McGann of Northwestern fumbled a punt snap at his one and Chandler recovered for the Gophers. Curry snuck for the TD and Anderson kicked the point after.

The Wildcats came right back, took the kickoff to their 34 and then moved the ball to the one where Marty Daigneau scored on a quarterback sneak. The kick was good.

Cook then lost a fumble at the Minnesota 42. The Gopher defense held the Wildcats to no yards in three tries, but a 22-yard pass to Barry Pearson was good for a first down. On the next play, Daigneau threw another pass to Pearson, this one for the score. Planiskek missed the point after attempt.

The Gophers marched 75 yards in eight plays as Curry connected with Kingsriter for 19 yards and Hamm for 28. In addition, the Wildcats' Jerry Brown twice was called for pass interference. Henry scored from the one, but the point after try was no good and Northwestern led 21-13.

Minnesota closed the gap in the third quarter when Chandler intercepted Daigneau at the Gopher 25 and returned it to Northwestern's 46. At the 33, Curry broke loose on an option play and streaked into the end zone. Anderson made the extra point to tie the game.

The rest of the game belonged to Northwestern. Later in the third quarter, Wright lost a fumble at the Gopher 18 and three plays later, Randy Anderson scored from the two. The kick made it 27-20.

The Wildcats scored two TDs in the fourth quarter— Robinson for six yards and Anderson again from short yardage as the Wildcats secured a resounding 40-21 victory.

"They converted their breaks and we didn't," a disheartened Chandler said in the Gopher locker room.

The outcome the next week in East Lansing was nearly identical as Duffy Daugherty finally got the "Minnesota monkey" off his back, thanks to a superb running back named Eric "The Flea" Allen.

Allen ran for 179 yards and four touchdowns and earned the praise of Warmath, who called him the "best back I've seen in 18 years in the Big Ten."

The little scatback scored three times in the third quarter to break open the game.

Michigan State scored in the first quarter when Mike Rasmussen connected with end Billy Joe DuPree on a 61-yard pass. Borys Schlapek made the extra point kick.

Minnesota answered in the second quarter when it came back with an 80-yard march in 12 plays. Curry passes of 17 yards to Kingsriter and 25 yards to Todd Randall helped set up sophomore fullback John King's one-yard TD plunge. Anderson kicked the PAT.

Late in the half, State started from its 19. Ten straight carries by Allen moved the ball to the Gopher 21 where Schlapek hit a 38-yard field goal with 2:10 left.

In the third quarter the floodgates opened. A screen pass to Allen got 33 yards and he eventually scored from the one. The score went to 24-7 shortly after that when Curry was intercepted at State's 32. Several plays later, Allen took a pitchout at the Gopher 37 and went all the way down the left sideline for the touchdown.

Brad Van Pelt returned a Gopher punt 30 yards to the Minnesota 32 and a few plays later Allen was in the end zone again, this time on a run of three yards.

Schlapek made a 54-yard field goal late in the quarter.

Minnesota scored on a one-yard plunge by Henry after Michigan State lost a fumble at its 25. Bobby Morgan tried a two-point pass play, but it was no good.

The Spartans added to their 34-13 lead when they went from their 11 to the Gopher 10 in eight plays. There, Allen burst into the end zone. The kick was no good.

Minnesota scored a meaningless TD with 1:27 left when Morgan hit Keith Fahnhorst with a short pass in the end zone. The Spartans were 40-25 victors.

Allen had scored 15 touchdowns in the last five Michigan State games of the 1971 season and had rushed for 1,032 yards.

# Thirty-Seven

 The week before the traditional season-ending game against Wisconsin, rumors began circulating that 1971 would be Warmath's last season as head football coach at the University of Minnesota. Since the 1967 season, the Gophers had been fighting a losing battle to attract crowds to Memorial Stadium. The Vikings were popular as Bud Grant had taken the local NFL team to the 1970 Super Bowl and had won three consecutive Central Division titles. The arrival of the Twins and the North Stars also meant Gopher sports, particularly football, had to fight for the entertainment dollar.

The world had turned over a few times since Warmath came to Minnesota in 1954.

The media speculated that Warmath probably would not return for the 1972 season. Throughout the week leading to the Wisconsin game, neither Warmath, his players nor the university administration said anything regarding his status. Team captain Bill Light said Warmath never discussed the situation with the team, adding that, "all of us have the highest respect for Coach Warmath and are behind him."

In the locker room before the Badger game, University of Minnesota President Dr. Malcom Moos spoke to the squad regarding how proud everyone was of them and the program, but made no mention of Warmath's future. He then left, Warmath spoke to the team, again said nothing about his situation, and took the field to coach his 172nd consecutive game at the University of Minnesota.

A crowd of less than 35,000 was on hand for the battle for Paul Bunyan's axe. In the first quarter, Minnesota went 70 yards in 16 plays. During the drive, Marquesen got 17 yards on a reception from Curry on a third-and-seven at the Gopher 47. Later on fourth-and-two at the Wisconsin eight, Cook bolted to the one. From there, Curry snuck for the touchdown, but Anderson missed the point after.

Wisconsin took the kickoff to its 44 and in 10 plays evened the score with Alan Thompson scoring from the two. Roger Jaeger kicked the extra point.

The score remained at 7-6 until the third quarter. From their 20, the Gophers drove for the only score of the quarter. The big play was a 42-yard pass completion from Curry to Anderson. From the two, Cook went in for the TD and Anderson added the extra point to put the Gophers ahead 13-7.

Late in the quarter, Wisconsin drove from its 35. On the first play of the fourth quarter, Thompson scored for Wisconsin and the extra point kick put the Badgers ahead 14-13.

Anderson kicked a 46-yard field goal with 10:30 left to put Minnesota back in front.

Wisconsin moved the ball from its 40 to score in five plays. The big play was a flat pass from Neil Graff to Gary Lund for 34 yards to the Minnesota four. On the next play, Rufus Ferguson ran for the score and Jaeger's kick made it 21-16 for Wisconsin.

Minnesota took the kickoff and moved to midfield. Curry, however, was dumped for a loss on a third down pass attempt and Warmath decided to punt with 2:46 left. Not everyone in the crowd agreed with the decision, but then they weren't schooled in the General Bob Neyland philosophy of ball position. Wisconsin got possession on its 31.

Following a holding call on the Badgers and then three incomplete passes by Graff (which helped because they stopped the clock), Wisconsin was forced to punt. John Krugman didn't help Minnesota's cause when he boomed one for 62 yards.

There were two minutes left and the ball was at the Gopher 20. Curry took to the air. He connected with Kingsriter for 17 yards and then Honza for 11. There was one minute left when he hit Kingsriter for nine to the Badger 43 on a second down pass. A sneak for the first down was short, so the Gophers took a time out.

Curry called on fellow-Floridian Ernie Cook and the Gopher fullback broke one for 14 yards to the 29. There were 52 seconds left when the play was blown dead. The Gophers used their last time out.

Curry missed the next two passes before connecting with Anderson for 17 yards to the 12. There were 35 seconds left. Two more incomplete passes ran the clock down to 14 seconds.

Curry called a pass play again to Anderson. The senior wide receiver lined up to the left. As the ball was snapped, he got bumped toward the middle by Wisconsin defender Greg Johnson. Anderson, however, stayed steady and cut to the outside and into the end zone corner, getting behind Johnson in the process. Curry had dropped straight back, got good protection and laid the pass into the left corner. Anderson let the ball float into his hands for the touchdown.

The stadium, albeit not nearly full, erupted and the Gopher bench and the 11 players on the field celebrated.

Anderson made the extra point for the 23-21 lead. The following kickoff ended the game.

•   •   •

Jon Roe of the Minneapolis Sunday Tribune captured the atmosphere and the historical significance of the moment with his report the next morning:

"They danced. They shouted. There were even tears mixed with the sweaty grins in the locker room. Sweet, sweet victory belonged to the Gophers.

"The biggest grin, so big it had turned his hat backwards, was worn by a 58-year-old man who walked among the Gophers, shaking hands, patting backs, hugging bodies. Sweet, sweet victory also belonged to Murray Warmath.

"I don't think I've ever been so happy," he said after the Gophers secured a 23-21 victory over Wisconsin Saturday at Memorial Stadium. "And I couldn't be happier for them."

As always, Warmath acknowledged his kids.

Meanwhile, the University of Minnesota administration decided changes were in order. Marsh Ryman, the athletic director who had succeeded Ike Armstrong a few years earlier, was replaced on Dec. 5, 1991. Paul Giel, then a 39-year-old sports director and broadcaster with WCCO-AM radio, the former Gopher All-American in football and baseball and runner-up in 1953 to Notre Dame's Johnny Lattner for the Heisman Trophy, was the new athletic director.

A week earlier, Moos met with Warmath and discussed his future with the university. On the day Giel was named the new athletic director, Warmath was on a pheasant hunting trip with friends in Iowa. He learned that he would be the assistant athletic director to Giel, but no longer the football coach. Giel made a point at the press conference that he was looking forward to working with Warmath, "a person I greatly admire as both a coach and a man."

Warmath, in his usual classy fashion, made no public comments about his new role. Instead, he set forth to do the best job possible as Giel's assistant.

The man who had the second-longest coaching stint at Minnesota, won a national championship, gone to two Rose Bowls, shared in two Big Ten titles and coached nine All-Americans, four Academic All-Americans, 23 All-Big Ten players, two Big Ten MVP's and two Outland winners, quietly stepped aside.

# Thirty-Eight

From late 1971 until the Spring of 1978, Murray Warmath remained at the University of Minnesota as the assistant athletic director. He also served as the color commentator for WCCO-AM radio's broadcast of Gopher football games from 1972 through the 1977 season during most of the time Cal Stoll was head coach.

"Murray was a delight to work with," recalled Giel. "As was the case when he coached, he did everything that was asked of him and he did it to the very best of his ability."

Giel said when the department wanted to get an in-depth look at graduation rates of athletes, the former coach rolled up his sleeves and provided a detailed, statistical report that Giel was able to take to the University administration and the public.

"There was simply no way you couldn't respect Murray, whether it was his work ethic, his integrity or his abilities," Giel added.

Ray Christensen, the voice of Gopher football and basketball on WCCO, recalled fondly the experience of working with Warmath.

"I had known Murray ever since he came to the University in 1954," Christensen recounted. "At the time, I was doing Gopher games for KUOM, the University's AM station. Later, I moved to WLOL and did games from 1955 through 1963 before coming to 'CCO. I remember when Murray was a coach, he gave me good, lengthy in-depth interviews. He always seemed to have time for you."

With Warmath available there was no question as to who Christensen and the WCCO people wanted as the color commentator.

"He was great to work with," Christensen added. "He was fully prepared as you would expect from Murray. His knowledge of football was so good he could have just shown up and done fine. However, he went way beyond that. He did a lot of in-depth research on the teams and the players before he arrived in the booth."

Christensen said Warmath's sense of timing was very good. He knew when to say something and when not to.

"Murray reflected on a particular game or situation, but never second-guessed another coach. He always was a true gentleman and, of course, everybody, including me, loved his unique style and use of Southern expressions and colloquialisms."

From late 1971 until the spring of 1978, Warmath stayed at the U of M as the assistant athletic director and the commentator for WCCO. But, there was no question he missed the game he loved.

On April 28, 1978, Murray Warmath, at age 65, returned to the coaching ranks. The Minnesota Vikings' Bud Grant named Warmath to be the new defensive line coach for the NFL team replacing Buddy Ryan who had left for the Chicago Bears.

"We are fortunate that Murray was available," said Grant at the press conference called to announce Warmath's appointment. "He was really the only candidate we considered."

"I enjoyed working with Paul and doing the radio broadcasts, but I missed the day-to-day activities of coaching and when the Vikings made the offer, I was delighted to accept," Warmath added.

For the next two season, 1978 and 1979, Warmath coached some of the legends of the Viking defensive line. They included his old charge from the U of M, Carl Eller, plus Jim Marshall, Doug Sutherland, James White and Alan Page.

In 1978, the Vikings were 8-7-1 in regular season play and got beat in the playoffs by the Los Angeles Rams 34-10.

The year 1979 was a transition year for what had been a premier franchise in the NFL for a decade. The Vikings were 7-9 and failed to make the playoffs. It also was the end of Warmath's coaching career. Suffering from "old football knees," he informed Grant that he simply wasn't able to physically keep up with the demands of coaching and resigned. However, Warmath's abilities and thorough knowledge of the game were such that the Vikings asked him to stay as a scout. Naturally, he accepted.

• • •

Today, Warmath serves as a part-time scout for the Vikings, confining his activities to looking at potential NFL players with the University of Minnesota and its opponents, as well as the Division I-AA, Division II and Division III schools in Minnesota, the Dakotas, Iowa and Illinois. As always, his work is detailed and his opinion on individual players and the game in general still is highly-regarded.

"Football is simply something I cannot get away from and I will continue to participate as long as I am physically able," Warmath said.

He looks back over the years, especially those at the University of Minnesota, with fondness.

"We had many fine players. Several like Roger Hagberg, John Williams, Charlie Sanders and Barry Mayer were the equal of our All-Americans."

Besides the players, coaches and others from the athletic department, he has kind words for many special friends who supported him and stood behind his program through the good times and the bad.

"There were several people from the media such as Dick Cullum, Rollie Johnson and John Croft, the Star Tribune photographer, with whom I was close. Cullum and Johnson came down to Mississippi State right after I was named Minnesota's head coach to interview me. Rollie turned out to be a longtime fishing and hunting buddy." Warmath recounted. "Otis Dypwick, the late sports information director at Minnesota, was also very supportive. The others were rabid football fans and boosters of Minnesota athletics such as Herman Lang, Fred Carlson, Bert Englebert, Don Knutson, Don McGlynn, Manny Pritchard, Ray King, Rudy Luther and Shelley Walsh. These people were extremely loyal friends of me and my family.

"Another person to whom I was grateful for his support was Carl Rowan. He did a lot in the late 1950s to show guys like Stephens, Munsey, Dickson, Eller and Bell that Minnesota was a good place to play football as well as receive a fine education."

Warmath's understanding of football continues to grow and solidify as time goes on. He is the consummate student of the game. As he approached his 80th birthday, he could not only recount in the sharpest detail those many, many games and the many, many players and coaches, but also could speak in great depth as to the basics of the game as well as to its history of shifting trends.

Shortly after retiring from the Vikings, he was interviewed extensively by Ralph Reeve of the St. Paul Pioneer Press.

Following are excerpts from that interview containing some of Warmath's personal observations on football.

"There have been several major changes in football since I first became involved in the game," he said looking back over 60 years. "When I came to Tennessee in 1930, we didn't have movies to scout other teams. We did by the time I got into coaching five years later and even developed films of our own practices. Movies, obviously, have made a huge impact on the ability to coach, prepare for an opponent and to study your own strengths and weaknesses."

He also has seen the development of the face mask, particularly the all-encompassing "bird-cage" masks worn by linemen and linebackers, as drastically altering the blocking and tackling techniques.

334

"They've thrown caution to the wind. Players hit with much more reckless abandon knowing the face mask will give them good protection from the hit.

"The game and even the football itself have been altered over the years to encourage a more wide-open, fan-oriented game. The ball has been streamlined and re-shaped to encourage far better passing and kicking. The hash marks have been brought in over the years to give the offense a larger playing field insofar as they can plan plays which can be effective to either side rather than to just one."

Warmath said rule changes, such as today's liberal use of hands in blocking, always are planned so as to aid the offense.

"What you always find is that defenses eventually wise-up to the new offensive schemes and eventually start shutting them down. Then, in an effort to open the game up, the rulemakers liberalize certain things that allow the offense to be more imaginative and have an advantage. After a while, the defense starts shutting them down, the rules get changed again and the whole thing starts all over."

Warmath sees the passing game as extremely sophisticated and highly-effective. He says the ability to rush the passer has been hampered by the broad use of hand blocking. The offenses continue to spread their formations and use up to five receivers at certain times on a given play.

"But despite that, defense still wins games," Warmath added. "I've always said you are in trouble in a football game if you always are receiving kickoffs. Once you control the other team's offense and cause them to breakdown, you will win the vast majority of the time."

There isn't anything terribly complicated about football or winning at it. Warmath said it comes down to talent.

"Damn few teams with lesser talent win a majority of their games. A mule never wins the Kentucky Derby and I don't recall Willie Shoemaker or Eddie Arcaro winning a horse race by carrying the horse on their backs around the track.

335

"Football is a unique American game because more than any other game, the fan gets involved. No game gets the fan more involved in the strategy. They all think they are quarterbacks and coaches." he chuckled.

Warmath never has placed a lot of concern on public opinion. Reflecting on his beleaguered times in the late 1950s, he recalled that he never had a moment of doubt as to his capabilities or those of his assistants.

"I never doubted what we were doing or that we weren't headed in the right direction. The profession by its very nature always has down times. I remember John Barnhill once telling me that the longer you stay in coaching the greater the risk you'll lose your job.

"The scoreboard is the best public relations tool. In the end, people don't care much about your style of coaching or the kind of football you play. They just want you to win."

For Murray Warmath, football has been nothing but a relationship of love. It's obvious to an impartial observer that he possesses the intellect, talent and hard work ethic to have made it in practically any profession he chose. Football, however, came at a time and place in his life that the fit was just right. All of the personal qualities he had fit football and from the time he reported for varsity ball as a freshmen in 1926 at Humboldt High School until today, there never was any question that he and the game were meant to be.

"I love football, it's as simple as that," he stated. "It's a wonderful game. It's been beneficial to our society, our schools and in the end, has been a great game for America."

Be there no doubt, Murray Warmath has been great for American football.

# Epilogue

If Murray Warmath has left any kind of legacy, its the impact he has made on those who have played or coached for him. Obviously, they number in the hundreds and thus, it is impossible to give the thoughts of all of them. However, here are some reflections on Coach Warmath by a cross-section of players, former assistant coaches and others. Their comments have to do with his coaching abilities, his upstanding character, his style, or anecdotal situations from seasons past.

## Warmath as a Coach:

"Murray always was very competitive and very organized. Yet, he let you coach. I was only two years out of college when I joined his staff at Mississippi State and he basically turned me loose to do my thing. He had a great personality and always was upbeat. He is respected as a sound football man. His place as a coach is assured."

—*Darrell Royal, former assistant to Warmath and later the legendary head coach at the University of Texas.*

"At any coaches' clinic around the country, if Murray was giving a lecture it was standing room only. That's how highly regarded he was among his peers."

—*Billy Jack Murphy, former player and assistant coach, later head football coach and athletic director at Memphis State.*

"Murray was a coach for whom I had profound respect. His teams always were very sound in the fundamentals and rarely beat themselves. They were very hard hitting, but clean. We had a lot of great games against Minnesota which usually seemed to come down to the wire."

*—Ara Parseghian, famed head coach at Northwestern and Notre Dame.*

"Bud Grant once told me that Murray was among a handful of coaches who, if he was speaking, every other coach stopped and listened because they knew his concepts were solid."
*—Mike Wright, 1959 Gopher captain.*

"When I think of Murray, I think of his intensity, energy, stubbornness of principles and his dedication to the work ethic. These are things I have tried to apply to my own life."
*—Dick Larson, former U of M player and assistant coach.*

"He was one of the great influences on the game. His ability to command and to communicate were flawless. With Murray, there never were any shortcuts or easy ways out. It was all direction and hard work. I wouldn't trade the experiences I had with him for anything I have done in the profession before or since."
*—Mike McGee, former assistant coach and present athletic director at the University of Southern California.*

"By my senior year, I was impressed by his willingness to look at change and to grow as a coach to make us better."
*—Frank Brixius, former U of M player.*

"I never saw anything like pep pills or uppers which I knew existed at a lot of places. We didn't need them. Murray was a master psychologist who got you ready to play and got the best out of each player. He was straightforward and very fair."
*—Dr. John Williams, former U of M player.*

"You can't say enough goods things about him. He was advanced in everything he did. He always was making small, but

338

critically important, changes to his plans, changes that in the long run worked. He was very fair in the way he treated everyone."

—*Joe Salem, former player, assistant coach and later head coach at the University of Minnesota.*

"He taught me a lot about the game. When I played for the Bears in the NFL, I was ready because of Coach Warmath."

—*Joe Fortunato, former Mississippi State player.*

"Murray was a sound coach fundamentally and commanded respect around the country. I was sick when he left us."

—*Bob Hartley, long-time sports information director at Mississippi State.*

"He was the most organized coach I ever knew. He always was prepared and we knew our game plans inside and out."

—*John Hankinson, former U of M player.*

"He was the best coach I ever had, including Neyland. He would get on you when you deserved it, but he had a policy of never, ever berating a player in public."

—*Denver Crawford, former player at Tennessee and an assistant coach to Warmath.*

## Warmath as a Person:

"If he had any spite for the way he was treated in the late 1950s, he never showed it. He taught me how to survive adversity with courage and dignity."

—*Bob Frisbee, former U of M player.*

"I went to him toward the end of the 1961 season and said I was getting married. He talked to me about the responsibilities of marriage and asked me to make sure I wanted to do it at that

point in my life. When I said I did, he wished me the very best and he and Mary Louise were at our wedding."
—*Dave Mulholland, former U of M player.*

"He taught me how to work in a disciplined environment and how to be structured and prepared. That has served me well all of my life."
—*Dana Marshall, former team student manager.*

"Over the years, there were kids like myself who didn't have fathers and he was our father. He always was honest and fair, had a great work ethic and the highest moral standards."
—*Bobby Cox, former U of M player.*

"Murray was tough and a hard worker. I always will remember how he stood above the things that were being done to him our senior year and simply went about his job."
—*Mike Svendsen, 1958 Gopher captain.*

"I remember the feeling of being honored when he came into my home to recruit me. I had met a lot of big-time college coaches and nobody impressed me with their integrity and character like Coach Warmath. I love the man."
*Doug Kingsriter, former U of M player.*

"Along with my father, I hold him in the highest esteem like no other man I have known. He exemplified the very best and I always was taken by his willingness to do things for other people, not just his players."
—*Sandy Stephens, former U of M player.*

"He was a fundamentally sound person, not just as a coach. He never backed down and stood by his principles and I've tried to apply that to my own life."
—*Julian Hook, former U of M player.*

"I always will have a relationship with, and special place for, Coach Warmath simply because he is such a fine person."
—*Bob McNamara, 1954 Gopher captain.*

"Murray stood for the right things. He had great integrity as a coach, was completely knowledgeable and showed respect and compassion to all his assistants and players. I am proud to call him my friend."
—*Butch Nash, long-time U of M assistant coach.*

## On Race and Cultural Diversity:

"He made all the black athletes feel welcome and took a strong interest in us as people. Once when I was very upset at a racial remark made by someone at practice, he took me aside and said the key to life isn't how one gets along with the big shots, but rather that you are judged by how you don't let the petty, little people of the world get the best of you and make you lose your sense of integrity. I have never forgotten that."
—*Judge Dickson, former U of M player.*

"I was told by black players who were ahead of me, that Coach Warmath was very fair. I learned quickly that was indeed true. He treated all of us—black and white—honestly and as individuals."
—*McKinley Boston, former U of M player and current athletic director.*

"My junior year I approached Warmath about the fact it was Yom Kipper (the Day of Atonement) the Saturday we were to play Illinois. Being that it was the most holy of Jewish holidays, I felt I needed to observe it and not suit up for the game. He was perfectly fine with that and quickly gave me permission to miss the game. There was no pressure at all to play. When I think about him and his relationship with his players, it's not coincidental at all to me that so many of the guys who played for him have gone on to do well in later life given the example he set."

—*Bob Stein, former U of M player and current president of the Minnesota Timberwolves.*

"In 1969, during the height of the black movement, there was talk of some supposed dissension on the team by some black players. Whatever incidents there were, they were minor. One night after a team meal, I rode back to Cooke Hall with Warmath and he talked at some length about his approach to all of his players regardless of their race, color, or creed. I was struck by how impartial and fair he was and that he only judged people on their character and performance."

—*Jim Carter, 1969 Gopher captain.*

## On Preparation for Pro Football:

"The training I got from Warmath and his assistants really prepared me for my career with the Vikings. I had the greatest respect for him insofar as teaching us about football and getting us ready to play."

—*Milt Sunde, 1963 Gopher captain.*

"He saw my future as being best served in Minnesota. He was close to Norm Van Brocklin and convinced the Vikings to draft me if I was available. He helped me in terms of knowing what to do when I went to negotiate a contract."

—*Carl Eller, former U of M player.*

"I could always talk to him about things on my mind. He really was a major factor in preparing me for pro football and had me mentally prepared to play. His influence on me has lasted all of my life."

—*Bobby Bell, former U of M player.*

342

## Personal Discipline and Behavior:

"Murray was demanding in that we were all expected to act like gentlemen and not embarrass ourselves or the team. Once in my sophomore year, I got pulled from a game against Purdue and in front of nearly 60,000 people, threw the cape down in anger as it was handed to me coming off the field. He quietly called me over, put his arm around my waist and grabbed one of my 'lovehandles' on my side. He was incredibly strong. He had me paralyzed. He then whispered in the ear hole of my helmet if I ever acted in such a manner again, I'd be in real trouble. Believe me, I never did."

*—Tom King, former U of M player.*

## Academics:

"One of the reasons I came to Minnesota was because of the outstanding medical school. Coach Warmath spent a lot of time with me over the years discussing my academic work and making certain I was staying focused on my dream to become a physician. He also was very kind and warm to my parents and expressed interest in them."

*—Dr. Ernie Cook, former U of M player.*

## On Loyalty to his Players:

"I never had a coach in high school, college or the pros who was as loyal to his players and would go out of his way to help them, even years after they were through playing, as he was."

*—Keith Fahnhorst, former U of M player.*

"I was seeking an appointment to the bench in Ramsey County and when I asked him to write a letter of recommendation, he did it right away and with a great deal of enthusiasm."

*—Walt Bowser, former U of M player.*

## On Taking Personal Responsibility for The Program:

"I never once saw him make an excuse or point a finger at a ballplayer or one of his assistants for a loss or something going wrong, although invariably it was our screw up, not his, that lost games. He took full responsibility and never, never singled out anyone in public. There were never any politics in the program, unfairness or inconsistencies in the way he treated people."
—*Tom Moe, former U of M player.*

## A Perspective on Murray Warmath Years Later:

"You don't really appreciate him to his fullest until some time has passed. It's the things he taught you that apply in business or personal relationships. It's his sense of the fundamentals, the basics. They apply in every aspect of life."
—*Jeff Wright, 1970 Gopher captain.*

## Final Thoughts:

Perhaps it is fitting to end this book by taking a look at the comments of three newspaper columnists who knew Warmath when he coached as well as in the years afterward. Their opinions are from articles they wrote toward the end of the 1971 season.

"When you stop to analyze Murray Warmath's 18-year coaching record at Minnesota, you have to conclude he did a fantastic job considering the conditions under which he was hired. At the time of his appointment, Bud Wilkinson was riding high at Oklahoma. The Minnesota fans wanted Wilkinson to be the football coach—that is everybody but athletic director Ike Armstrong, who never officially offered Wilkinson the job.

"When Warmath was hired, there was a lot of animosity toward the University. The new Gopher coach was a virtual unknown and the majority of fans wanted a Minnesota man as a coach. Warmath found it hard to recruit in the state because he didn't have a lot of support. But he overcame these problems with hard work."

—*Sid Hartman, Minneapolis Tribune.*

"He is a man, a person of decency, courtliness in public, toughness on the coaching lines. I think we have been honored to have him in our midst."

—*Jim Klobuchar, Minneapolis Star*

"While the subject is still alive, I'd like to say something about my friend Murray Warmath.

"The manner in which he has conducted himself in these trying times has been so much that of a gentleman that it must shame those who attacked him with malice and with disregard of the underlying facts.

"I do not hesitate to say I do not know a man, in any field of endeavor, who has greater character. Who can have greater character than a man who has it all? Through these many years I have never known him to do a small, malicious, or harmful thing.

"Someone said he has shown a lot of courage.

"Yes, I suppose that is so, but I don't think he has ever had to draw on courage. Instead, his flawless character caused him to do the right thing without ever having to back it up with courage. There has never been, for him, more than one course of action, more than one decision to be made.

"His character dictated that act or decision. He never considered a second choice and his choice was right because there was a lucid mind behind his character.

"In particular, I must say that, measuring these qualities, he so distinctly outclasses those who have attacked him with malice that he makes these people hard to tolerate.

"Let them show any part of the same character and competence, or pause for a while for self examination."

—*Dick Cullum, Minneapolis Tribune.*

# PHOTO CREDITS

**Murray Warmath as a varsity player at the University of Tennessee in the early 1930s.**

**The legendary Robert R. Neyland, head football coach at Tennessee for 21 years.**

**Allyn McKeen**

**Bobby Dodd**

**Herman Hickman**

**Jackie Parker**

**Bob McNamara**

**Bobby Cox**

**Carl Eller**

**Aaron Brown**

**Bob Stein**

**Billy Jack Murphy**

**Denver Crawford**

**Bob Suffridge**

**Beattie Feathers**

**Earl "Red" Blaik**

**Bob Hobert**

**Roger Hagberg**

**Sandy Stephens**

**Barry Mayer**

**Jim Carter**

**Doug Kingsriter**

**Dick Larson**

**Butch Nash**

Warmath's two Outland Trophy Winners, Tom Brown (1960), above left, and Bobby Bell (1962), above right.

Three players who helped turn around Warmath teams. Joe Fortunato, above left, was a stellar fullback and linebacker at Mississippi State in 1952. John Williams and Charlie Sanders were switched to tackle and end respectively prior to the 1967 season. Williams, left, and Sanders went on to illustrious NFL careers.

Warmath greets his incoming assistants (right) as they arrive in the Twin Cities in the winter of 1954. Left to right, Bill Hildebrand, Denver Crawford, Billy Murphy and Jim Camp.

Warmath is carried off the field by members of his 1960 team (below) after the big 10-0 victory over Michigan in Ann Arbor.

Following the controversial loss to Wisconsin (left) in 1962, a dejected Bob Bossons, left, and Butch Nash, two long-time Warmath assistant coaches, sit silently in the Gopher locker room.

In front of Northrup Auditorium (below) at the University of Minnesota, Warmath addresses a huge pep rally before the big game against No. 1 ranked Iowa in 1960.

. . . MUNSEY MAKES LEAPING CATCH

END ZONE

BOTH FEET INSIDE LINE

Gopher halfback Bill
Munsey snares a
touchdown pass from
Sandy Stephens
(above) in the 13-0
victory over top-
ranked Michigan State
in 1961. Munsey
scored both Gopher
TDs that afternoon.

Minnesota halfback
Tom King (right) is
about to be brought
down by a Purdue
defender in the 1961
game against the
Boilermakers in
Minneapolis. Minne-
sota won a brutally-
fought 10-7 game.

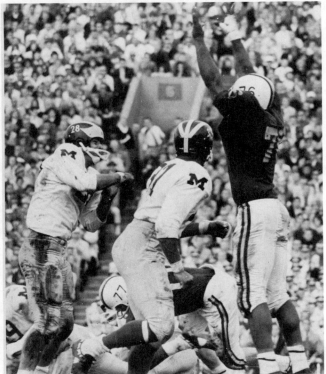

Gopher quarterback
Craig Curry (above)
pitches out at the last
second in the
Gophers' 49-7 win in
1970 over Ohio
University.

All-America tackle
Carl Eller leaps (left)
to try and block a
pass by Michigan's
Bob Timberlake in
the Minnesota 6-0
victory in 1963.

Famed comedian Jack Benny (above) chats with Gopher players prior to the 1962 Rose Bowl game. Left to right are Jerry Jones, Sandy Stephens, Jerry Pelletier, Benny, Judge Dickson, Bobby Bell and Bill Munsey.

Warmath conferring with his quarterback, John Hankinson (right), during the 20-20 tie with USC in Los Angeles in 1965.

An avid outdoorsman, Warmath displays a stringer of smallmouth bass (right) taken with his close friend, the late Norm Van Brocklin, the former Minnesota Vikings coach. The two were on a 1966 fishing trip on the Winnipeg River in Manitoba

Warmath never hesitated to let an official know what he thought of a "bad" call against his Gophers (upper right). This is during the 1971 Nebraska game. Craig Curry looks on. At the same time, he has always had a great sense of humor and an engaging laugh and smile. He reacts to a quip made by the famed Ohio State coach, Woody Hayes, at a Warmath Appreciation Banquet in 1985.

The Warmath family quickly became avid Gopher fans upon their arrival at Minnesota. Mary Louise Warmath, (near right) and the oldest Warmath child, Murray, Jr., are shown during a happy moment at a home game in 1955.

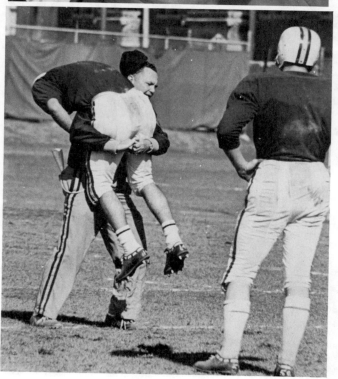

An intense and detailed practice coach, Warmath never hesitated to show his players how it should be done. Here he demonstrated the proper tackling technique at fall practice in 1963.

# The Warmath Coaching Record

## Mississippi State
### 1952

| MSU | | Opp |
|---|---|---|
| 7 | Tennessee | 14 |
| 41 | Arkansas State | 14 |
| 14 | North Texas State | 0 |
| 27 | Kentucky | 14 |
| 19 | Alabama | 42 |
| 49 | Auburn | 34 |
| 21 | Tulane | 34 |
| 33 | L.S.U. | 14 |
| 14 | Mississippi | 20 |
| 225 | | 186 |

Won 5, Lost 4, Tied 0
SEC: W-3, L-3, T-0

### 1953

| MSU | | Opp |
|---|---|---|
| 34 | Memphis State | 6 |
| 26 | Tennessee | 0 |
| 21 | North Texas State | 6 |
| 21 | Auburn | 21 |
| 13 | Kentucky | 32 |
| 7 | Alabama | 7 |
| 20 | Texas Tech | 27 |
| 21 | Tulane | 0 |
| 26 | L.S.U. | 13 |
| 7 | Mississippi | 7 |
| 196 | | 119 |

Won 5, Lost 2, Tied 2
SEC: W-2, L-2, T-2

## Minnesota
### 1954

| UM | | Opp |
|---|---|---|
| 19 | Nebraska | 7 |
| 46 | Pittsburgh | 7 |
| 26 | Northwestern | 7 |
| 19 | Illinois | 6 |
| 0 | Michigan | 34 |
| 19 | Michigan State | 13 |
| 44 | Oregon State | 6 |
| 22 | Iowa | 20 |
| 0 | Wisconsin | 27 |
| 195 | | 127 |

Won 7, Lost 2, Tied 0
Big 10: W-4, L-2, T-0

### 1955

| UM | | Opp |
|---|---|---|
| 0 | Washington | 30 |
| 6 | Purdue | 7 |
| 18 | Northwestern | 7 |
| 13 | Illinois | 21 |
| 13 | Michigan | 14 |
| 25 | USC | 19 |
| 0 | Iowa | 26 |
| 14 | Michigan State | 42 |
| 21 | Wisconsin | 6 |
| 110 | | 172 |

Won 3, Lost 6. Tied 0
Big 10: W-2, L-5, T-0

### 1956

| UM | | Opp |
|---|---|---|
| 34 | Washington | 14 |
| 21 | Purdue | 14 |
| 0 | Northwestern | 0 |
| 16 | Illinois | 13 |
| 20 | Michigan | 7 |
| 9 | Pittsburgh | 6 |
| 0 | Iowa | 7 |
| 14 | Michigan State | 13 |
| 13 | Wisconsin | 13 |
| 127 | | 87 |

Won 6, Lost 1, Tied 2
Big 10: W-4, L-1, T-2

### 1957

| UM | | Opp |
|---|---|---|
| 46 | Washington | 7 |
| 21 | Purdue | 17 |
| 41 | Northwestern | 6 |
| 13 | Illinois | 34 |
| 7 | Michigan | 24 |
| 34 | Indiana | 0 |
| 20 | Iowa | 44 |
| 13 | Michigan State | 42 |
| 6 | Wisconsin | 14 |
| 201 | | 188 |

Won 4, Lost 5, Tied 0
Big 10: W-3, L-5, T-0

## 1958

| UM | | Opp |
|---|---|---|
| 21 | Washington | 24 |
| 7 | Pittsburgh | 13 |
| 3 | Northwestern | 7 |
| 8 | Illinois | 20 |
| 19 | Michigan | 20 |
| 0 | Indiana | 6 |
| 6 | Iowa | 28 |
| 39 | Michigan State | 12 |
| 12 | Wisconsin | 27 |
| 115 | | 157 |

Won 1, Lost 8, Tied 0
Big 10: W-1, L-6, T-0

## 1959

| UM | | Opp |
|---|---|---|
| 12 | Nebraska | 32 |
| 24 | Indiana | 14 |
| 0 | Northwestern | 6 |
| 6 | Illinois | 14 |
| 6 | Michigan | 14 |
| 20 | Vanderbilt | 6 |
| 0 | Iowa | 33 |
| 23 | Purdue | 29 |
| 7 | Wisconsin | 11 |
| 98 | | 159 |

Won 2, Lost 7, Tied 0
Big 10: W-1, L-6, T-0

## 1960

| UM | | Opp |
|---|---|---|
| 26 | Nebraska | 14 |
| 42 | Indiana | 0 |
| 7 | Northwestern | 0 |
| 21 | Illinois | 10 |
| 10 | Michigan | 0 |
| 48 | Kansas State | 7 |
| 27 | Iowa | 10 |
| 14 | Purdue | 23 |
| 26 | Wisconsin | 7 |

Won 8, Lost 1, Tied 0
Big 10: W-6, L-1, T-0

| 7 | Washington | 17 |
|---|---|---|
| 228 | (1961 Rose Bowl) | 88 |

## 1961

| UM | | Opp |
|---|---|---|
| 0 | Missouri | 6 |
| 14 | Oregon | 7 |
| 10 | Northwestern | 3 |
| 33 | Illinois | 0 |
| 23 | Michigan | 20 |
| 13 | Michigan State | 0 |
| 16 | Iowa | 9 |
| 10 | Purdue | 7 |
| 21 | Wisconsin | 23 |

Won 7, Lost 2, Tied 0
Big 10: W-6, L-1, T-0

| 21 | UCLA | 3 |
|---|---|---|
| 161 | (1962 Rose Bowl) | 78 |

## 1962

| UM | | Opp |
|---|---|---|
| 0 | Missouri | 0 |
| 21 | Navy | 0 |
| 22 | Northwestern | 34 |
| 17 | Illinois | 0 |
| 17 | Michigan | 0 |
| 28 | Michigan State | 7 |
| 10 | Iowa | 0 |
| 7 | Purdue | 6 |
| 9 | Wisconsin | 14 |
| 131 | | 61 |

Won 6, Lost 2, Tied 1
Big 10: W-5, L-2, T-0

## 1963

| UM | | Opp |
|---|---|---|
| 7 | Nebraska | 14 |
| 24 | Army | 8 |
| 8 | Northwestern | 15 |
| 6 | Illinois | 16 |
| 6 | Michigan | 0 |
| 6 | Indiana | 24 |
| 13 | Iowa | 27 |
| 11 | Purdue | 13 |
| 14 | Wisconsin | 0 |
| 95 | | 117 |

Won 3, Lost 6, Tied 0
Big 10: W-2, L-5, T-0

## 1964

| UM | | Opp |
|---|---|---|
| 21 | Nebraska | 26 |
| 26 | California | 20 |
| 21 | Northwestern | 18 |
| 0 | Illinois | 14 |
| 12 | Michigan | 19 |
| 21 | Indiana | 0 |
| 14 | Iowa | 13 |
| 14 | Purdue | 7 |
| 7 | Wisconsin | 14 |
| 136 | | 131 |

Won 5, Lost 4, Tied 0
Big 10: W-4, L-3, T-0

## 1965

| UM | | Opp |
|---|---|---|
| 20 | USC | 20 |
| 13 | Washington State | 14 |
| 6 | Missouri | 17 |
| 42 | Indiana | 18 |
| 14 | Iowa | 3 |
| 14 | Michigan | 13 |
| 10 | Ohio State | 11 |
| 27 | Northwestern | 22 |
| 0 | Purdue | 35 |
| 42 | Wisconsin | 7 |
| 188 | | 160 |

Won 5, Lost 4, Tied 1
Big 10: W-5, L-2, T-0

## 1966

| UM | | Opp |
|---|---|---|
| 0 | Missouri | 24 |
| 35 | Stanford | 21 |
| 14 | Kansas | 16 |
| 7 | Indiana | 7 |
| 17 | Iowa | 0 |
| 0 | Michigan | 49 |
| 17 | Ohio State | 7 |
| 28 | Northwestern | 13 |
| 0 | Purdue | 16 |
| 6 | Wisconsin | 7 |
| 124 | | 160 |

Won 4, Lost 5, Tied 1
Big 10: W-3, L-3, T-1

## 1967

| UM | | Opp |
|---|---|---|
| 13 | Utah | 12 |
| 0 | Nebraska | 7 |
| 23 | SMU | 3 |
| 10 | Illinois | 7 |
| 21 | Michigan State | 0 |
| 20 | Michigan | 15 |
| 10 | Iowa | 0 |
| 12 | Purdue | 41 |
| 33 | Indiana | 7 |
| 21 | Wisconsin | 14 |
| 163 | | 106 |

Won 8, Lost 2, Tied 0
Big 10: W-6, L-1, T-0

## 1968

| UM | | Opp |
|---|---|---|
| 20 | USC | 29 |
| 14 | Nebraska | 17 |
| 24 | Wake Forest | 19 |
| 17 | Illinois | 10 |
| 14 | Michigan State | 13 |
| 20 | Michigan | 33 |
| 28 | Iowa | 35 |
| 28 | Purdue | 14 |
| 20 | Indiana | 6 |
| 23 | Wisconsin | 15 |
| 208 | | 191 |

Won 6, Lost 4, Tied 0
Big 10: W-5, L-2, T-0

## 1969

| UM | | Opp |
|---|---|---|
| 26 | Arizona State | 48 |
| 35 | Ohio University | 35 |
| 14 | Nebraska | 42 |
| 7 | Indiana | 17 |
| 7 | Ohio State | 34 |
| 9 | Michigan | 35 |
| 35 | Iowa | 7 |
| 28 | Northwestern | 21 |
| 14 | Michigan State | 10 |
| 35 | Wisconsin | 10 |
| 210 | | 259 |

Won 4, Lost 5, Tied 1
Big 10: W-4, L-3, T-0

## 1970

| UM | | Opp |
|---|---|---|
| 12 | Missouri | 34 |
| 49 | Ohio University | 7 |
| 10 | Nebraska | 35 |
| 23 | Indiana | 0 |
| 8 | Ohio State | 28 |
| 13 | Michigan | 39 |
| 14 | Iowa | 14 |
| 14 | Northwestern | 28 |
| 23 | Michigan State | 13 |
| 14 | Wisconsin | 39 |
| 180 | | 237 |

Won 3, Lost 6, Tied 1
Big 10: W-2, L-4, T-1

## 1971

| UM | | Opp |
|---|---|---|
| 28 | Indiana | 0 |
| 7 | Nebraska | 35 |
| 20 | Washington State | 31 |
| 38 | Kansas | 20 |
| 13 | Purdue | 27 |
| 19 | Iowa | 14 |
| 7 | Michigan | 35 |
| 12 | Ohio State | 14 |
| 20 | Northwestern | 41 |
| 25 | Michigan State | 40 |
| 23 | Wisconsin | 21 |
| 212 | | 278 |

Won 4, Lost 7, Tied 0
Big 10: W-3, L-5, T-0

# Honors and Recognitions

**Murray Warmath**

> National Coach of the Year as named by the American
> Football Coaches Association and the Football
> Writers Association of America – 1960
> President of the American Football Coaches
> Association – 1968
> Recipient of General Robert Neyland Trophy – 1990

**Warmath Players**

### All-Americans

Mississippi State
  Jackie Parker – 1953
Minnesota
  Bob McNamara – 1954
  Bob Hobert – 1956
  Tom Brown – 1960
  Sandy Stephens – 1961
  Bobby Bell – 1961 & 62
  Carl Eller – 1963
  Aaron Brown – 1965
  Bob Stein – 1967
  Doug Kingsriter – 1971

## All-Conference

Mississippi State All-SEC
    Jackie Parker – 1952 & 53
    Joe Fortunato – 1952
    Hal Easterwood – 1952

Minnesota All-Big Ten
    Bob McNamara – 1954
    Bob Hobert – 1956
    Mike Svendsen – 1958
    Tom Brown – 1960
    Greg Larson – 1960
    Bobby Bell – 1961 & 62
    Tom Hall – 1961
    Sandy Stephens – 1961
    John Campbell – 1962
    Julian Hook – 1962
    Carl Eller – 1963
    Aaron Brown – 1964 & 65
    Kraig Lofquist – 1964
    McKinley Boston – 1967
    Tom Sakal – 1967
    Bob Stein – 1967 & 68
    John Williams – 1967
    Dick Enderle – 1968
    Noel Jenke – 1968
    Ray Parson – 1969
    Bill Light – 1970 & 71
    Jeff Wright – 1970
    Doug Kingsriter – 1971

**Outland Trophy Winners**

Tom Brown – 1960
Bobby Bell – 1962

**National Football Foundation College Hall of Fame**

Bobby Bell – 1991

**Southeastern Conference M.V.P.**

Jackie Parker – 1952 & 53

**Big Ten M.V.P.**

Tom Brown – 1960
Sandy Stephens – 1961

**Academic All-Americans**

Bob Hobert – 1956
Frank Brixius – 1960
Bob Stein – 1968
Barry Mayer – 1970

# Assistant Coaches

Darrell Royal ............................(1952)
Charley Shira ......................(1952-53)
Mac Cara ...........................(1952-53)
Bill Hildebrand ...................(1952-55)
Jim Pittman .........................(1952-53)
Jim Camp .........................(1953-1960)
Denver Crawford .............(1952-1971)
Billy Jack Murphy ...........(1952-1957)
Butch Nash .........................(1954-71)
Wally Johnson .....................(1954-69)
Bob Blaik ...............................(1956)
Ray Malavasi ......................(1956-57)
Dave Skrien ........................(1957-58)
Bob Bossons .......................(1958-66)
Dick Larson .......................(1958-64)
Jim Reese ................................(1959)
Dick Borstad ......................(1959-60)
Don Grammer .....................(1961-71)
Joe Salem............................(1961-65)
Jerry Annis..........................(1961-70)
Bob Delaney..........................(1965)
Mike Reid ...........................(1966-70)
Bob Gongola.......................(1966-71)
Mike McGee ......................(1967-70)
Roger French ......................(1970-71)
Maurice Forte .....................(1970-71)
Chip Litten ..............................(1971)
Lauri Niskanen....................(1971)

# Warmath's Lettermen

(The following lettermen are listed in alphabetical order by school. Each year that they lettered is also listed. Please note that many received additional letters at their respective school either under the coach prior to Warmath's arrival or under the coach who followed him.)

## Mississippi State

| | |
|---|---|
| Jim Barron | 1953-54-55 |
| Tom Boisture | 1952-54 |
| Grady Bolton | 1953-54 |
| Art Broome | 1950-51-52 |
| Charles Caven | 1952-53-54 |
| Joe Cimini | 1951-52 |
| Steve Clark | 1950-51-52 |
| Bobby Collins | 1951-52-53-54 |
| Art Davis | 1952-53-54-55 |
| Ken DeLoe | 1951-52 |
| Norman Duplain | 1950-51-52 |
| Hal Easterwood | 1952-53-54 |
| Charles Evans | 1953-54 |
| Ollie Fairchild | 1951-52 |
| Joe Fortunato | 1950-51-52 |
| Tom Fulton | 1951-52-53 |
| Bill Glasgow | 1952-53-54 |
| Levaine Hollingshead | 1953-54-55 |
| Donald "Bucket" Joseph | 1951-53 |
| John Katusa | 1951-52-53 |
| J.E. Logan | 1952-56-57-58 |
| John McKee | 1952-53 |
| Don Morris | 1952-53-54 |
| Tom Morris | 1952-53 |
| Al Munsch | 1953 |
| Frank Newsome | 1952-53 |
| Jackie Parker | 1952-53* |
| Bo Reid | 1950-51-52* |
| Murphy Roberson | 1951-52-53 |
| Joe Robertson | 1952 |
| John Santillo | 1952-53 |
| Billy Shepherd | 1951-52-54 |
| Bill Stanton | 1953-54-55 |
| Vic Stuver | 1952 |
| Scott Suber | 1953-54-55 |
| George Suda | 1953-54 |
| Lou Venier | 1953-54-55 |
| Gil Verderver | 1951-52 |
| Max Williams | 1953-54-55 |
| Zerk Wilson | 1951-52-53 |
| Ron Yarnick | 1952-53 |
| Bill Zimmerman | 1952-53-54 |

## Minnesota

| | |
|---|---|
| Dan Adams | 1971-72-73 |
| Terry Addison | 1968-69 |
| Tim Alderson | 1970-71-72 |
| Chet Anderson | 1964-65-66 |
| Mel Anderson | 1970-71 |
| Norm Anderson | 1956 |
| Ron Anderson | 1969-70 |
| Clint Andrus | 1952-53-54 |
| Jerry Annis | 1959-60 |
| John Babcock | 1969-71 |
| Frank Bachman | 1954 |
| Bob Bailey | 1969-71-72 |
| Dave Baldridge | 1966-67 |

Jim Barle ........................... 1965-66
Paul Barrington................. 1956-57
Mike Barron ......................... 1971
Dick Bassett ....................... 1963
John Baudler ........................ 1966
John Baumgartner .. 1951-52-53-54
Bob Bedney ...................... 1966-67
Bobby Bell ................. 1960-61-62
Neil Bengtson ........................ 1959
Paul Benson................. 1960-61-62
John Bergstrom ...................... 1967
Bill Bevan, Jr. ............. 1963-64-65
Jerry Bevan ........................... 1966
Tom Bienemann .............. 1969-70
Dick Blakely .......................... 1955
Bob Blakely ...................... 1956-57
Duane Blaska.................... 1961-62
Ken Bombardier .......... 1955-56-57
Arlie Bomstad .................. 1958-59
Jim Boren............................... 1966
Dick Borst............................. 1963
Dick Borstad ............... 1955-56-57
McKinley Boston ........ 1965-66-67
Walt Bowser................ 1968-69-70
Frank Brixius............... 1958-59-60
Bob Brothen........................... 1967
Aaron Brown............... 1963-64-65
Andy Brown ................. 1966-67-68
Terry Brown .......................... 1963
Tom Brown ................. 1958-59-60
Tim Browne...................... 1970-71
Bob Bruggers .............. 1963-64-65
Jim Brunzell ..................... 1969-70
Ken Brustad ........................... 1964
Jim Bruton ............................ 1966
Hubie Bryant .............. 1965-66-67
Ed Buckingham ...................... 1956
Bart Buetow ................. 1969-70-71
Darrel Bunge ............... 1971-72-73

Ted Burke ............................. 1969
Dave Burkholder ......... 1955-56-57
Jim Cairns ..................... 1961-62
Brian Callahan ................. 1964-65
John Campbell ................. 1961-62
Geno Cappelletti ......... 1952-53-54
Carleton Carlson ................... 1957
Larry Carlson.................... 1966-67
Jim Carter ................. 1967-68-69 *
Tim Cashman ......................... 1962
Tom Chandler ............. 1969-70-71
Bob Charon .......................... 1958
Bill Chorske ............... 1956-57-58
Ed Christian .......................... 1967
Bill Christison ....................... 1969
Louis Clare ...................... 1970-71
Darrell "Shorty" Cochran ..... 1950-
    54-55
Gary Colberg ........................ 1962
Dave Colburn ........................ 1965
Gordon Condo ............. 1965-66-67
Ernie Cook ................. 1969-70-71
Dennis Cornell ...................... 1966
Bob Cornell........................... 1969
Willie Costanza ........... 1962-63-64
Bobby Cox......................... 1956-57
John Cranston ................. 1969-70
Rich Crawford............. 1968-69-70
Bill Crockett ..................... 1962-64
Craig Curry ................. 1969-70-71
Mike Curtis ................. 1967-68-69
Elden Dahl ............................ 1954
Jim Dahn ............................... 1957
Bill Dallman ..................... 1963-65
Paul Danahy ........................... 1965
John Darkenwald ............. 1967-68
Bob Deegan.................... 1959-60-61
Judge Dickson ............. 1959-60-61
Harold Drescher.................... 1954

356

Dan Drexler ........................... 1963
Jim Dropp ............................. 1966
Ed Duren ......................... 1966-67
Douglas Dykes ...................... 1963
Bob Eastlund .............. 1968-69-70
Bob Edelman ........................ 1958
Walt Edelman ....................... 1954
Carl Eller ..................... 1961-62-63
Burnham "Rocky" Elton ...... 1952-
    53-54
Rodney Elton ........................ 1964
Dick Enderle .............. 1966-67-68
Dick Enga ................ 1960-61-62 *
Keith Fahnhorst .......... 1971-72-73
Dick Fairchild ...................... 1956
Mike Falls ................ 1953-54-55 *
Fred Farthing .................... 1963-64
Paul Faust ................ 1963-64-65 *
Tom Fink ..................... 1966-67-68
Al Fischer .......................... 1961-62
Ken Fischman ....................... 1955
Merlin Flugum ..................... 1962
John Force ........................... 1968
Maurice "Mo" Forte .... 1966-67-68
Jerry Friend ................. 1957-58-59
Bob Frisbee ...................... 1960-61
Casey Fron ........................... 1962
Vern Frye ............................. 1954
Jim Fulgham ..................... 1964-65
Bill Garner ....................... 1954-55
Perry Gehring ............. 1956-57-58
Ken George ...................... 1969-70
Ev Gerths .................... 1956-57-58
Gale Gillingham .............. 1964-65
Archie Givens ....................... 1965
Mike Goldberg ................. 1969-70
Ralph Goode .................... 1952-54
Paul Gorgos ......................... 1960
Jeff Gunderson ........... 1971-72-73

Bob Haake ........................... 1957
Roger Hagberg ............ 1958-59-60
Bob Hagemeister ......... 1952-53-54
Phil Hagen .................. 1967-68-69
Andrew Haines ...................... 1964
Dennis Hale ................. 1966-67-68
Tom Hall ..................... 1959-60-61
Dale Halvorson ..................... 1960
Kevin Hamm .............. 1969-70-71
Jonathan Hammer .................. 1967
Bruce Hammond .............. 1957-58
John Hankinson ................. 1964-65
Paul Hanson ......................... 1959
Dick Harren ......................... 1963
Al Harris ............................. 1963
Larry Hartse ..................... 1962-63
Gerald Hassett ...................... 1955
Gene Hatfield ....................... 1966
Don Haugo ....................... 1968-69
Alvin Hawes ............... 1968-69-70
Dale Hegland .................... 1971-72
James Heid ........................... 1959
Melvin Henderson ................. 1965
Jim Henry ........................ 1971-72
Dave Herbold .............. 1955-56-57
Jim Herman ...................... 1971-72
Jerry Hermann ...................... 1966
Bob Hobert .................. 1954-55-56
Dennis Hoglin ....................... 1968
Gary Hohman ........................ 1969
Joe Holmberg .................... 1965-66
Dick Holmstrom .................... 1968
Gordon Holz ......... 1951-52-53-54
George Honza ............. 1970-71-72
Julian Hook ................. 1960-61-62
Dick Humleker ................. 1969-70
Scott Irwin.................... 1971-72-73
Ken Jacobson ........................ 1964
Jon Jacoby ........................... 1958

Jon Jelacic ................. 1955-56-57 *
Steve Jelacic ........................... 1960
Noel Jenke ................. 1966-67-68 *
Del Jessen ..................... 1966-67-68
Larry Johnson .............. 1958-59-60
Dick Johnson ..................... 1958-59
Ezell Jones ................... 1966-67-68
Jerry Jones .................. 1960-61-62
Tom Juhl ...................... 1954-55-56
Bill Jukich .................... 1955-56-57
Ron Kamzelski ............ 1966-67-68
Bill Kauth .................... 1958-59-60
Anthony Kehl ......................... 1962
George Kemp .............. 1967-68-69
Steve Kereakos ...................... 1961
Chuck Killian ........... 1964-65-66 *
John King .................... 1971-72-73
Ron King .................... 1969-70-71
Tom King .................... 1959-60-61
Wayne King .......................1967-68
Doug Kingsriter ......... 1970-71-72
Kelvin Kleber .............. 1955-56-57
Ron Klick .......................... 1966-67
Franz Koeneke ................ 1954-55
Kent Kramer ...................... 1964-65
Jim Krause ....................... 1963-65
Jim Krohn ............................. 1964
John Krol ........................ 1971-73
Chuck Kubes .............. 1950-53-54
Dick Kubes ....................... 1954-55
Don Kuether .......................... 1955
Bill Laakso .................. 1966-67-68
Greg Larson .............. 1958-59-60 *
Richard A. Larson ....... 1955-56-57
Richard C. Larson............. 1959-60
Ken Last ..................... 1964-65-66
Tom Lavaty ...................... 1969-70
Bobby Lee ............................. 1967
Jim Leslie ............................. 1964

Bill Light ................. 1969-70-71 *
Dave Lindblom ................. 1956-57
John Lindquist ....................... 1956
Charles "Chip" Litten.. 1966-67-68
Tom Loechler ................... 1960-61
Kraig Lofquist ................. 1963-64
Jim Long ............................... 1966
Dave Lothner ..................... 1960-62
Steve Lundeen ................. 1967-68
Dean Maas ................. 1954-55-56 *
Tom MacLeod ...................1971-72
Dennis Maloney .......... 1970-71-72
Stew Maples ........................... 1965
Frank Marchlewski ..... 1962-63-64
John Marquesen .......... 1969-70-71
Dana X. Marshall ................... 1960
Bill Martin ............................1957
Barry Mayer ............... 1968-69-70
Curtis Mayfield ........... 1969-70-71
Phil McElroy ............... 1952-53-54
Tim McGovern ...................... 1967
Mike McMahon ..................... 1954
Bill McMillan ....................... 1962
Richard "Pinky" McNamara 1954-
    55-56
Bob McNamara.... 1951-52-53-54*
Bob McNeil ...................... 1960-61
George Meissner ..................... 1959
Gary Melchert ....................... 1958
Roger Michalski ..................... 1966
Don Miller .......................... 1962
Monte Miller ......................... 1957
Dick Miller .......................... 1960
Tom Moe ..................... 1957-58-59
Bob Morgan ................. 1970-71-72
Lonnie Morgan ...................... 1965
Ken Mourer........................... 1969
Rolland Mudd ....................... 1961
Dave Mulholland ........ 1959-60-61

358

| | |
|---|---|
| Scott Mullen ...................... 1968-70 | Randy Rajala .......................... 1967 |
| Tom Mullin ............................. 1971 | Deryl Ramey .......................... 1965 |
| John Mulvena ............ 1959-60-61* | Paul Ramseth ..................... 1962-63 |
| Bill Munsey ................. 1960-61-62 | Todd Randall ............... 1971-72-73 |
| Dave Myers....................... 1956 | Lee Rankin ......................... 1969-71 |
| Steve Neils .................. 1971-72-73 | Bob Rasmussen .......... 1955-56-57 |
| Curtis Nelson ......................... 1969 | Jerry Rau ..................... 1952-53-54 |
| Jerry Newsom .............. 1964-65-66 | Matt Rauh ............................. 1968 |
| Dave Nixon ...................... 1967-69 | Jim Reese....................... 1957-58 |
| Fred Nord ..................... 1962-63-64 | Mike Reid ......................... 1963-64 |
| Jeff Nygren ...................... 1968-69 | Gary Reierson ............. 1964-65-66 |
| Jim O'Brien ....................... 1969-70 | Doug Roalstad ...................... 1968 |
| Dean Odegard ............. 1958-59-60 | Tom Robbins............... 1958-59-60 |
| Charles Olson ...................... 1961 | Jim Rogers ................. 1958-59-60 |
| Mike Orman...................... 1964 | Myron Rognlie ................. 1962-63 |
| Arnold Osmundson ..... 1957-58-59 | Don Rosen.................... 1963-64-65 |
| Anthony Pahula ........... 1967-68-69 | Joseph Rosenfield .................. 1970 |
| Francis Paquette .................... 1968 | Ed Rossman ...................... 1955 |
| Jack Park ......................... 1960-61 | Dale Rucker ......................... 1965 |
| Ray Parson......................... 1968-69 | Ted Rude ......................... 1960-61 |
| Jerry Pelletier .............. 1961-62-63 | Bob Sadek ............................ 1963 |
| Jim Perault ............................ 1961 | Tom Sakal ................ 1965-66-67* |
| Mike Perfetti ...................... 1970-71 | Joe Salem ..................... 1958-59-60 |
| Jack Perkovich.................. 1961-62 | Charlie Sanders............... 1966-67 |
| Larry Peterson ................... 1963-64 | Bill Sausen ............................ 1964 |
| Dick Peterson .............. 1965-66-67 | Clayt Scheuer .............. 1970-71-72 |
| Russ Peterson ........................ 1962 | Bob Schmidt............... 1955-56-57 |
| Jim Phillipe ......................... 1957 | Ken Schultz .................. 1956-57-58 |
| Steve Politano ................... 1971-72 | Bob Schultz ................. 1955-56-57 |
| Dan Powers ...................... 1960 | Jan Schwantz ........................ 1963 |
| Bob Prawdzik .............. 1960-61-62 | Dick Seitz ......................... 1965-66 |
| Tom Pribyl ............................ 1971 | Jay Sharp ......................... 1962-63 |
| Walt Pribyl ...................... 1968-69 | Farrell Sheridan ............... 1971-72 |
| Joe Pung .................... 1962-63-64* | Jerry Shetler ............. 1957-58-59 |
| John Purmort........................ 1954 | Tom Simon ......................... 1969 |
| Ken Quinn............................ 1971 | Norm Sixta .................. 1955-56-57 |
| Dale Quist ................... 1952-53-54 | Lyle Skandel .......................... 1960 |
| Gene Rabel ......................... 1963 | Stan Skjei....................... 1963-64 |
| John Rajala .................. 1963-64-65 | Ron Smith ........................ 1953-54 |

Tom Smrekar ......................... 1963
Jim Soltau ..................... 1952-53-54
Bob Soltis .................... 1956-57-58
Jon Staebler .......................... 1964
Chuck Stamschor ........ 1952-53-54
Randy Staten .................... 1964-65
Mike Steidl ................... 1971-72-73
Bob Stein ...................... 1966-67-68
Ray Stephens .................... 1967-68
Sandy Stephens ........... 1959-60-61
Larry Stevenson ..................... 1969
Len Stream ............................ 1964
Milt Sunde ................. 1961-62-63*
Bruce Suneson ........................ 1966
Mike Svendsen .......... 1956-57-58*
Don Swanson ......... 1951-52-54-55
Henry Tasche .................... 1968-69
Tom Teigen ...................... 1961-62
Robin Tellor ................ 1959-60-61
John Thompson ................ 1969-70
Steve Thompson .......... 1968-69-70
Paul Tollefson ................. 1970-71
Leon Trawick .............. 1967-68-69
Rhody Tuszka ............. 1955-56-57
Richard Tyree ........................ 1970
Erle Ukkelberg ................. 1954-55
Bruce Van De Walker ...... 1964-65
Bob Veldman .............. 1970-71-72
Collin Versich ........................ 1962
Tom Wagner .......................... 1959
Jerry Wallin ..................... 1957-58
John J. Walsh ........................ 1969
John W. Walsh ...................... 1969
Tom Walthower ................ 1971-72
Jim Wheeler ...................... 1960-61
Tim Wheeler ............... 1964-65-66
Mike White ................. 1969-70-72
Ray Whitlow ................ 1964-65-66
John Williams ............. 1965-66-67
Curtis Wilson .............. 1965-66-67

Vern Winfield ............. 1969-70-71
John Wintermute ......... 1966-67-68
Glen Wirtanen ....................... 1964
Jeff Wright ................ 1968-69-70*
Mike Wright .............. 1957-58-59*
Paul Wright ............................ 1970
Jim Wrobel ...................... 1968-69
Ken Yackel ...................... 1954-55
Dick Yates ............................. 1957
Frank Youso ................ 1955-56-57
Jim Zak ................................. 1962
Ray Zitzloff ............................ 1962

**\* team captain their senior year**

# The Murray Warmath Book Committee

The following individuals offered their time and talent to organize the effort to publish the book on coach Murray Warmath:

Frank Brixius
Walter Bowser
Jim Carter
Bobby Cox
Carl Eller
Keith Fahnhorst
Paul Giel
John Hankinson

Dick Larson
Bob McNamara
"Pinky" McNamara
Dana Marshall
Tom Moe
Bob Stein
Sandy Stephens
Mike Wright

# Major Donors

The following individuals, companies and organizations each made major contributions to the funding of *The Autumn Warrior: Murray Warmath's 65 Years in American Football*:

Frank Bachman
Billy Bye
Jerry Burns
Curt Carlson
Jim Carter
Bobby Cox
John Hankinson
Tom King
Dick Larson
Rudy Luther
"Pinky" McNamara
Tom Moe
Carl Pohlad
Dan Powers
Mike Svendsen
Jack Thesenga
W.T. "Tom" Teigen
Rod Wallace
Shelley Walsh
Mike Wright
Gary Eikass-Wintz Companies
Gopher Touchdown Club
Geo. A. Hormel, Inc.
Lutheran Brotherhood
The Minnesota Vikings
The University of Minnesota M Club

# About the Author

Mike Wilkinson is a public relations and marketing consultant and a freelance writer. A graduate of the University of Minnesota School of Journalism, he is a life-long Golden Gopher fan. He resides in Hopkins, Minn. with his wife and children. *The Autumn Warrior* is his first book.